THE GERMAN PHOENIX

WILLIAM HENRY CHAMBERLIN

THE
GERMAN
PHOENIX

DUELL, SLOAN & PEARCE
New York

First Edition

Affiliate of
MEREDITH PRESS
Des Moines & New York

Library of Congress Catalogue Card Number: 63-16817
MANUFACTURED IN THE UNITED STATES OF AMERICA FOR MEREDITH PRESS
VAN REES PRESS   •   NEW YORK

Contents

	Introduction	vii
I	Germany's Historical Inheritance	3
II	Germany in the Depths	30
III	The Political Upward Climb	49
IV	The Economic Miracle—and Afterward	68
V	The Old Architect of the New Germany	93
VI	Adenauer's Political Heirs	109
VII	Germany Divided	128
VIII	Divided Berlin	156
IX	The Face of the New Germany	179
X	The Spirit of the New Germany	200
XI	Germany Rearmed	220
XII	Is Nazism Outlived?	241
XIII	"Bonn Is Not Weimar"	260
XIV	America and Germany: Allies for Peace	274
	Bibliography	290
	Index	303

Introduction

GERMANY'S phoenix-like economic rise from rags to riches and its less spectacular but equally significant return to free institutions and the rule of law after Hitlerite tyranny are two of the most heartening developments in the history of Europe since World War II. (This applies, of course, only to the Federal Republic, the larger and more populous part of Germany, the part that has remained free.)

The German revival has marched hand in hand with the general movement in Europe to reach and surpass by far prewar standards of output; the two are closely interdependent. The emergence of a new Germany as a free, prosperous, and anti-Communist national community is also a conspicuous victory for United States foreign policy. The United States' share in the buildup of a new Germany has been considerable, through Marshall Plan economic aid, through military assistance, and through the mutually fruitful cultural exchange which has brought Americans and Germans closer together in thought and understanding.

The constructive accomplishments of Germany under the leadership of Konrad Adenauer have been obscured by one-sided emphasis in popular books and films on the atrocities of the Nazi period. There have also been some profoundly distorted attempts to represent modern Germany as seething with neo-Nazi spirit.

This book is an attempt to describe the new Germany and to analyze its moving forces. I was familiar with Germany at the time of the Weimar Republic, and also during the first phase of Nazi dictatorship. Since the war I have made ten trips to Germany as a journalist, the earliest in 1946, the latest in 1962. During these visits I have tried to look beyond immediate details and follow the broad lines of the country's development, talking with as many knowledgeable Germans of all points of view and of various occupations and backgrounds as possible, visiting universities and schools, factories, and military establishments. At various times I have been able to meet and talk with most of the prominent political personalities of the Federal Republic.

This book is largely based on notes which I took during these trips, supplemented by what seemed to be the most reliable reference sources, in English and in German. It is designed as an over-all survey, not a detailed examination of any one aspect of German development. Several of the separate chapters could easily have been expanded to book length, but I have tried to neglect no significant trend—in politics, economics, foreign relations, or everyday life.

My thanks are due to many Germans, to some personal friends, and to many more casual acquaintances who have given generously of their time and patience in answering the innumerable questions of an inquiring reporter who has taken a whole nation as his field of study.

Acknowledgment is due to the *Wall Street Journal* and the *Freeman* for permission to incorporate in this book some material which I have previously contributed to these publications.

WILLIAM HENRY CHAMBERLIN

THE GERMAN PHOENIX

AN EPITAPH TO GERMAN HISTORY

"Himmelhoch jauchzend, zum Tode betruebt."
"Rejoicing to Heaven, depressed to the depths."

Goethe, *Egmont*

CHAPTER I

Germany's Historical Inheritance

FEW peoples have experienced so many and such sharp alternations of fortune as have been apparent in German history. The Prussia of Frederick the Great, which held at bay the combined military power of Austria, Russia, and France, fifty years later collapsed ingloriously before the onslaught of Napoleon. Deserted by its Russian ally, Prussia was reduced by the Peace of Tilsit to the status of one of Napoleon's vassal states.

The merger of Germany's separate states, large and small, into a united empire, after the successful war with France in 1870–71, made Germany the strongest military and economic power in continental Europe. But the fruits of Bismarck's bold and adroit statesmanship were thrown away by his inept successors. Unable to choose between western and eastern orientations in foreign policy, Germany in World War I found itself, with weak allies, involved in a conflict with a coalition of nations. No one member of the coalition matched German military power on land, but together, and with the ultimate decisive intervention of the United States, this coalition proved superior in manpower, in resources, and in command of the sea.

After seeing their armies everywhere on foreign soil, the Germans, of whom some had dreamed of imposing a conqueror's peace, experienced the traumatic shock of finding the victories of their soldiers turned to dust and ashes and their country subjected to all the consequences of a lost war. These included losses of territory in the West and in the East, a reparations tribute of undetermined size and duration, and various restrictions on sovereignty.

Defeat was followed by a raging inflation, constituting the first occasion when the currency of a modern industrial and commercial nation became completely worthless. This had the grave political consequence of transforming a considerable part of the middle class, normally a solid and moderate element, into impoverished, embittered fanatics. And it became all too easy for nationalist and Nazi agitators to identify the republic that had been set up after the abdication and flight of the Kaiser with both the loss of the war and the misery caused by inflation.

After a striking but basically unsound economic recovery in the years 1925–28, Germany was again plunged into the depths of despair by the long economic crisis that began in 1929, hitting Germany especially hard because of her previous impoverishment. The economic crisis, more than any other factor, tipped the scales in favor of Adolf Hitler, whose following had been negligible while Germany was fairly prosperous. The figures of the Nazi vote and the number of unemployed rose in parallel columns.

Hitler's measures relieved unemployment (partly through rearmament), and then came the second plunge into war, in 1939, with disastrous results for Europe and for Germany.

By 1945, after a short-lived orgy of military conquest that extended the boundaries of Hitler's Third Reich from the Pyrenees to the Volga, Germany had sunk to a level of national humiliation and physical misery comparable to the situation at the end of the Thirty Years War, three centuries earlier. Millions of Germans had been killed; millions more were in foreign prison camps and forced labor; great numbers had been harried from their homes. The frontiers of Germany were far narrower than those prescribed at Versailles, and the remaining territory was divided between the occupation regimes of the four victorious powers. But then came a fantastically rapid political and economic recovery, an upward climb from pariah status to that of an ally of its former Western enemies, a swift return from ruin, desolation, and hunger to a full share in the prosperity of a reviving Europe. This transition from rags to riches, like the downfall of Hitler's empire, came with dizzy, breathtaking speed.

These swift alternations of fortune have been a conspicuous element in Germany's historical experience. Another is the wide range between reach and grasp, a sense of unfulfilled aspiration, which, in turn, may be traced to three characteristics of Germany's development from the Middle Ages down to modern times. One of these was the involvement in Italy, arising because the ruler of Germany was automatically the head of that rather mystical entity, the Holy Roman Empire. Second, Germany's frontiers were more changeable than those of other European powers such as Great Britain and France. The German trend was to expand to the east, through conquest and settlement, while receding in the west. Finally, while Germany took only a late and minor part in overseas colonization, Germans in considerable numbers settled in such countries of southeastern Europe as Hungary, Romania, and Yugoslavia, even in Russia, creating enclaves of German language and customs in alien populations.

When Pope Leo III crowned Charlemagne as emperor on Christmas Day, in the year 800, he introduced a concept, the Holy Roman Empire, that was to flutter like a fantastic vision through the pages of German medieval history and to exert a profound—and on balance, negative—influence on the buildup of a German national state. Charlemagne ruled over a realm whose territory comprised substantially that of France and the German Federal Republic today, also including portions of Spain and Italy.

After a period of confusion and strife among the unworthy and feeble descendants of this great sovereign, whose reign is one of the few rays of light in the Dark Ages, embryonic French and German states began to emerge. Germany consolidated more rapidly than France, and it became accepted practice that the ruler of Germany, elected by four temporal and three ecclesiastical princes, was entitled to be crowned in Rome by the pope.

Apart from this coronation ceremony, the emperor exercised little authority in the turbulent city of Rome; riotous brawls between the natives of Rome and the German knights and retainers who attended the emperor occurred frequently during the imperial visit. But from the tenth to thirteenth centuries the possession of the imperial title tended to divert the attention of Germany's rulers, among whom were some strong and able personalities, away from

German affairs. Here was the root of the deep-seated fragmentation of power in Germany that reached its climax after the fall of the Hohenstaufen dynasty in the middle of the thirteenth century.

The three Ottos of the Saxon dynasty in the tenth century were constantly engaged in Italian expeditions, either supporting friendly and opposing hostile claimants to the office of pope, which was then often a matter of bloody dispute, or trying to assert their authority against invading Saracens, city-states in northern Italy, or the remnants of the Byzantine Empire in southern Italy and Sicily. The brilliant young Otto III, who, with his former tutor Gerbert (pope under the name of Sylvester II), was one of the most learned men of his time (about 1000), dreamed of making Rome again the center of a universal empire. He called himself Consul of the Roman Senate and People and issued a seal with the inscription "Restoration of the Roman Empire." Otto perhaps owed his obsession with the memories of departed Roman grandeur to the influence of his mother Theophano, a Byzantine princess. His death at the age of twenty-two marked the end of dreams that could not have been realized in any case.

The lure of the South, the snare of extra-German adventures in sovereignty and diplomacy was even more fatal to the brilliant Swabian dynasty of the Hohenstaufen, which ruled Germany, with one brief interlude, from 1138 until 1254. Frederick Barbarossa, who left the legendary memory of a German kaiser sleeping in a mountain, to emerge in the hour of his country's greatest need, was one of the ablest, most gifted, and most serious of twelfth-century monarchs, admired and respected abroad as well as at home.

But despite his prestige, Barbarossa's Italian policy was a failure. His hold on northern Italy was broken when the forces of the combined Italian city-states inflicted a defeat on him at Legnano in 1176. His difficulties of administration were aggravated by a long feud with the Papacy. He lost his life, symbolically enough, leading the Third Crusade in Asia Minor. Before his death Frederick did have some reason to believe that he had achieved compensation for his reverses in Italy: His son Henry (who succeeded him as Henry VI) married Constance, heiress of the Norman kingdom of Sicily and Naples, and the rebellious Lombard cities and the States of the Church seemed to be caught in an encircling vise.

But events did not work out as Frederick had anticipated. Henry VI, whose soaring ambition included designs against the Byzantine Empire, died in his early thirties leaving a son, later Emperor Frederick II, too young to rule. Sicily fell into administrative confusion, and Germany lapsed into civil war. When a new non-Hohenstaufen emperor, Otto IV, turned against the Papacy, Pope Innocent III encouraged the young Frederick to go to Germany and claim his ancestral title of emperor. Frederick's venture succeeded; until his death in 1250 he held combined sovereignty over Germany and over Sicily and Naples.

Frederick II was probably the most remarkable personality among medieval rulers—an enlightened despot of the eighteenth century set down in the thirteenth. He made out of his southern kingdom, which he always preferred to Germany as a seat of residence and administration, a modern type of state, with appointed royal officials replacing the power of feudal nobles. Taxation was scientifically adjusted; commerce, learning, and the arts were encouraged. Frederick's court was a center of learning, with some features of Oriental pomp, where poets, scholars, and scientists were welcomed. Frederick himself was a gifted linguist, fluent in Arabic as well as in European languages and very tolerant in his attitude toward Moslems. Some of his most reliable soldiers were Saracens, who were permitted the free exercise of their religion.

But most of the energies and resources of this gifted emperor were absorbed in his struggle with two hostile popes, Gregory IX and Innocent IV, who found allies in the Lombard city-states and among disaffected elements in Frederick's kingdoms. Germany received only perfunctory attention from this Mediterranean-minded monarch. The authority of the central government north of the Alps, always severely limited by the feudal system, diminished still further under the rule of an emperor who spent most of his time in southern Italy, absorbed in extra-German enterprises.

Following the death of Frederick II and of his son Konrad IV (1254), a long interregnum set in until Rudolf of Habsburg became emperor in 1273. The end of the Hohenstaufen was dramatic and tragic. The last heir of this house, Konradin, son of Konrad IV, grew up in his native Swabia and undertook to reclaim his grandfather's kingdom of Naples and Sicily, which had been seized by Charles of Anjou, a French military adventurer whom the pope had encouraged to overthrow the rule of Manfred, the talented illegitimate son of Frederick II. Captured after being defeated in battle, Konradin was executed in Naples in 1268. In the nineteenth century the memory of the Hohenstaufen, of their brilliant qualities and final complete eclipse, was revived by German nationalists, and it is commemorated in tapestries preserved in Hohenschwangau, one of the picturesque mountain castles of the "mad king" of Bavaria, Ludwig II, himself an excessive and unbalanced romantic.

With the passing of the Hohenstaufen there was no longer the semblance of a unified German state. The imperial title became more or less hereditary in the Habsburg family, but these Austrian emperors exercised no real authority over such principalities as Bavaria, Saxony, and Brandenburg, the last the core of the later kingdom of Prussia. By a combination of methods—voluntary association, dynastic marriage, and conquest, mostly at the expense of the declining Turkish Empire—the Habsburgs built up Austria into a big cosmopolitan Danubian realm with a polyglot population of Czechs, Slovaks, Poles, Ruthenians, Hungarians, Croats, Slovenes, and Italians, in which the Germans, although prominent in the administration, were numerically in a minority. The rest of Germany for six centuries was an aggregation of sovereignties, ranging from medium-sized kingdoms to tiny specks of land, including a small town and a few villages ruled by a "Serene Highness." At the end of the eighteenth century there were 1,789 such sovereignties in Germany, most of which had been consolidated and absorbed into larger states by the end of the Napoleonic wars.[1] So the influences in German history include both the vague supranational conception of the Holy Roman Empire and the parochial outlook of the free city or the little dukedom.

Germany was a full participant in the culture and civilization of medieval Europe, still symbolized in the soaring Gothic cathedrals of Cologne and Freiburg, Vienna and Ulm, in the Marienkirche of Lübeck, the Frauenkirche of Munich, and many other monuments of the Middle Ages, some religious, some secular. Economically and politically there were many disadvantages in the fragmentation of Germany into small states and independent towns. But this process stimulated the self-expression of many small communities. No European country surpasses Germany in the wealth of its memorials of the past, its old town halls, churches, monasteries and castles—some fully preserved, others in a state of picturesque ruin, still others, like the ancestral castle of the Hohenstaufen in Northern Württemberg, so completely destroyed that only a few stones remain. The influence of a German style of achitecture may also be found outside the frontiers of present-day Germany, in the Strasbourg Cathedral, in Colmar and other Alsatian towns, in Danzig and Toruń and Riga and Prague. Germany also had its medieval saints and scholars, its chroniclers, like Otto of Freising, its Meistersinger and Minnesinger, whose song contests are depicted in *Tannhäuser* and *Die Meistersinger*.

It was not altogether an accident that the Protestant Reformation began in Germany. There had been a good deal of sympathy with the resistance of the Hohenstaufen and other medieval emperors to the claims of the Papacy, and there was resentment against the draining away of German contributions for the support of a distant ecclesiastical authority in Rome. Luther's teachings fell on prepared soil.

In England, Scotland, and Scandinavia the Reformation prevailed, while Catholicism remained the dominant faith in France, Spain, and Poland. Germany was split in twain by the new faith. The parts of Germany that had been settled earlier, Bavaria and the Rhineland, remained predominantly Catholic. The North and East, notably the rising state of Prussia, embraced the teachings of Luther.

At first the innovation in faith seemed to carry seeds of social radicalism. Anabaptists and other extreme sects preached community of goods. One of Germany's few movements of social revolt, the Peasant Rebellion, flaring up in 1524–25, was stimulated to some extent by the challenge to the established authority of the Church. Some of the more radical reforming ministers gave sympathy and support to this movement. But Luther, after some hesitation, came out clearly on the side of established authority and published a fiercely worded appeal against "the thieving and murderous peasant bands."

There is a striking dualism in Luther's thought that influenced considerably the subsequent politically conservative attitude of German Lutheranism. Although he was an optimist about the ability of the individual believer, without priestly mediation, to find his way to God with the aid of the Bible and the gift of faith, he was too pessimistic about human nature to be a liberal democrat. He believed that the Christian, free in his religious faith, should pay implicit obedience to the secular authorities in matters of this world.

And these secular authorities, the princes large and small, were the political and economic beneficiaries of the partial success of the Reformation in Germany. Their authority was no longer checked by that of the Church, and, like the aristocracy and well-to-do classes in England, they benefited from the seizure of the lands that had belonged to the Church.

A disastrous aftermath of the Reformation in Germany was the Thirty Years' War (1618–48). Starting as a religious war, with the emperor of Austria leading the Catholic forces and Sweden's warrior king, Gustavus Adolphus, intervening on the side of the hard-pressed Protestants, this protracted and devastating struggle later took on nationalist overtones. Cardinal Richelieu, who then directed the policy of France, supported the Protestant side because he believed this was the best means of advancing French national interests and pushing the French frontier farther to the east. And the Swedes gave up their larger role as crusaders for Protestantism and became concerned mainly with rounding out their Baltic empire by the annexation of Germany's Baltic province of Pomerania.

Politically the consequence of the long war and the Treaty of Westphalia which marked its termination was to confirm the independence of the separate German states, large, medium, and small, and the principle was established that the subjects should conform to the religion of the ruler. But, with more humanity than has been observed in some modern expulsions of population on national grounds, arrangements were made for the peaceful migration of nonconformists, with compensation for property. The state of Prussia, which began its rise under the able administration of the so-called Great Elector, finally pushed the Swedes out of Pomerania. But French encroachment on Germany's western border continued under Louis XIV and the Rhineland suffered from many campaigns and invasions, notably from the deliberate devastation of the area around Mainz and Heidelberg known as the Palatinate.

Culturally, economically, and socially Germany was thrown back many decades by the endless ravaging and pillaging of the mercenary armies that fought over the country for three decades. Towns were sacked; rich farming areas were stripped bare of foodstuffs; famine conditions, even to the point of cannibalism, prevailed in some districts. Although statistics of the time are not reliable, some estimates are that the population of Germany was reduced by one third during this savage and increasingly senseless conflict. Little more than a geographical expression, the country tended to sink into the background of European development as England, France, and the Netherlands forged ahead. A factor of considerable influence on German development and psychology was the failure of the impoverished, partially landlocked, fragmented country to take any part in enterprises of overseas exploration and colonization. Germans migrated as individuals and in groups, especially to the United States. But there was no German colonial empire, as there was little German maritime development.

After the end of the war, as has already been mentioned, a new powerful Protestant state, Prussia, emerged under the rulers of the house of Hohenzollern. Prussia, like most of the rest of the country, lay in ruins, but a gifted, energetic ruler, the Great Elector Friedrich Wilhelm, achieved an impressive work of reconstruction. In the words of an English historian,[2] "he successfully rebuilt his state, aided and witnessed its restoration from the losses of the war, united its several parts, fostered its economic development, equipped it with the best, if not the largest army in Germany and made it the undisputed master in Northern Germany, the successor to Saxony as leader of the Protestant forces in the Empire, a serious rival to Austria and a power to be reckoned with in Europe."

The work of the Great Elector was carried on by his successors, among whom Frederick I assumed the title of king. Out of the old feudal system a new type of state emerged, with a well drilled and well trained army, a bureaucracy with a strong sense of rank and duty, and a spare, frugal type of administration. The king, in this system, was the first servant of the state, self-willed and overbearing but hardworking and conscientious. He found military and civilian executives for his policies in the members of the landed nobility, some of them descended from the medieval order of Knights of the Cross, an organization which conquered and colonized much eastern territory for Germany until its power was broken by Poland in the Battle of Grünewald in 1410.

Serfdom persisted in Prussia until the reforms of Stein and Hardenberg in the early nineteenth century. And even after serfdom was abolished there was a marked difference in social and economic atmosphere between Prussia, dominated by its Junkers, as the nobility were called, and the southern and western parts of Germany, where liberal ideas found a hearing from a more developed middle class and a small landowning peasantry.

The careful military build-up of Prussia yielded fruits when a soldier of genius, Frederick the Great, came to the throne (1740–86). In the Seven Years War (1756–63) Frederick, with some very minor military assistance and financial subsidies from England, fought to a standstill the military forces of Austria, Russia, and France, retaining the original cause of the war, the province of Silesia, which he had earlier seized from Austria. Frederick also extended Prussia's borders considerably to the east when he shared with Russia and Austria in the spoils of the first partition of Poland.

Ironically enough Prussia, long considered the embodiment of extreme German nationalism, took its name from a forgotten heathen Slav tribe, and until the end of World War I, always included within its frontiers a considerable number of subjects of Polish and mixed Polish-German extraction. And Frederick the Great, one of the heroes in the pantheon of German nationalism, esteemed French culture far above German, prided himself on his French literary compositions, and cultivated the friendship of Voltaire. Frederick was a tolerant skeptic in religion, willing, as he put it, to let his subjects go to heaven in their own way; he was a pessimist in his view of human nature, and in tastes and ideas a typical product of the eighteenth-century Enlightenment.

Although "Prussianism" has had a bad reputation in America since World War I, although its former ruling class may be fairly criticized for arrogance, for an antiquated political and social outlook, for excessive reliance on armed force, its considerable influence on German character has not been entirely bad. It was a school of old Spartan virtues, patriotism, fortitude, courage in adversity. Its record in religious tolerance was good; French Huguenots were given asylum when they were driven out of France by Louis XIV and many rose high in its service. The incorruptibility of its meagerly paid officials was proverbial. The struggle with a hard, none too fertile soil may have given to the Prussians an energy and determination not always found in Rhinelanders and South Germans. Much of this energy went into creative scholarly research, and the University of Berlin attracted some of the leading historians, philosophers, and scientists to its chairs.

I sensed the positive side of Prussia during my last meeting with the late Herbert von Dirksen, whom I had known as German ambassador in Moscow and in Tokyo. This meeting took place in a Bavarian farmhouse, which furnished rough shelter to von Dirksen and a number of other refugees from the East. (The former ambassador was a native of Prussia.) By all material standards von Dirksen was a ruined man. His large fortune, located in the Soviet Zone, had been confiscated. His wife had recently died. His refugee quarters were a striking contrast to the luxurious appointments of the German embassies over which he formerly presided. But in his manner there was not a trace of dejection or self pity or hysterical despair. He discussed the future of Germany and international affairs as calmly and objectively as if he had been giving a briefing from the vantage point of an embassy. Here was the admirable, stoic side of the old traditional Prussia.

Prussia was almost swept out of existence by the Napoleonic storm, but it survived to become a member of the coalition that finally achieved the downfall of France's great military adventurer. It ranked with Great Britain, Austria, Russia, and France as one of the five great European powers at the Congress of Vienna. Its territorial possessions expanded until it became by far the largest and most populous German state, stretching across northern Germany from the Rhine to the Vistula.

The period from the French Revolution to the fall of Napoleon was for Germany a time of turmoil and trouble, of French invasions and foreign occupation. But this period also marked the climax of an intellectual renaissance, characterized by such names as Goethe, Schiller, Herder, and Lessing in literature, Kant and Fichte in philosophy, Beethoven in music. The towering figure of Johann Wolfgang Goethe, Germany's greatest glory in the realm of the spirit, was apolitical and supranational. He was not caught up in the wave of German nationalism which accompanied the "War of Liberation," after Napoleon's power had been sapped by his disastrous invasion of Russia in 1812. Goethe's fatherland was rather to be found in the classical age of Greece, which furnished inspiration for some of his finest dramas and poems. In striking contrast to the mystical worship of the *Volk* that was to develop in the nineteenth century, reaching a final pitch of apocalyptic insanity under the Nazis, Goethe preferred the Germans as individuals to the Germans as a nation.[3]

"The German nation is nothing," Goethe told his friend Friedrich von Müller on December 14, 1808, "but the individual German is something. Yet they imagine the reverse to be true. The Germans should be dispersed throughout the world, like the Jews, in order fully to develop all the good that is in them for the benefit of mankind." [4]

Schiller also stood for universal, humanistic, rather than nationalist ideals. It is perhaps significant that these two creative geniuses, whose personal friendship is touching and exceptional, were not citizens of the one strong German state of their time, Prussia. Goethe was born in the old free city of Frankfurt-on-the-Main, later becoming a citizen and for a time a government minister in the little state of Saxe-Weimar. Schiller, after escaping from the petty tyranny of the Duke of Württemberg, found asylum and opportunities for publication in several small states, finally dying in Weimar, then widely known as the German Athens. Wieland, Herder, and other men of letters were attracted to its cultivated little court; it was Weimar that won for the Germans the reputation of being a people of poets and thinkers. In this calm atmosphere national exaltation, revenge, conquest, glory seemed very alien ideals. Schiller believed that the division of Germany into a multitude of principalities, mostly small, was an aid to liberty, because what was forbidden in one state could be practiced in another.

However, this liberal cosmopolitanism gave way in time to other ideals and influences. The romantic movement which swept Europe after the Napoleonic Wars inspired in Germany a revival of interest in the Middle Ages and in the old sagas of the remote German past, such as the Nibelungenlied. German nationalism, at a low ebb during the eighteenth century, surged up in the nineteenth in the wake of the war that drove the French out of Germany. Typical of the new spirit was the poet-publicist Ernst Moritz Arndt, whose *Was ist der Deutschen Vaterland* ("What is the German's Fatherland?") became the battle hymn of the new nationalism. Answering his own question, Arndt responded that the Fatherland was wherever the German language was spoken. Arndt and other exponents of nationalism were generally anticosmopolitan, often anti-Semitic, filled with mystical enthusiasm for the destiny of the Germanic race.

For a generation after the fall of Napoleon, Germany was calm under the status quo system imposed by the powerful conservative Austrian chancellor, Prince Metternich. But 1848 was a year of upheaval, spreading eastward from Paris, where the "bourgeois king," Louis Philippe, was driven from his throne, to give way first to a republic, then to the empire of Napoleon III. In Germany the movement of revolt revealed a mixture of nationalist aspirations and political liberalism. The movement was strongest in the South and Southwest. A parliament composed of representatives of some of the state assemblies met at Frankfurt with the dual objective of creating a unified German state and providing this state with a liberal constitution. But a heavy preponderance in this parliament of professors and lawyers, combined with a German weakness for longwinded discussion of fine legal points, paralyzed its capacity for action. Austria withdrew its representatives from the Frankfurt parliament and the doom of the whole movement was sounded when King Frederick William IV of Prussia refused to head the projected new German state, preferring to remain king of Prussia with its comfortably conservative constitution. The liberal movement petered out in unsuccessful demonstrations and local revolts; the old order remained basically unshaken. Again, as in the case of the Peasant Rebellion three centuries earlier, revolution from below had failed.

When long deferred German unity was achieved, it was from above, by the clever machinations of the master statesman Bismarck, not by a group of earnest, liberal professors and politicians trying to work out a constitution in the historic St. Paul's Church of Frankfurt. It was in the moment of Germany's swift triumph in the Franco-Prussian War (1870–71) that the sovereigns of the German states proclaimed King William I of Prussia emperor of a new German Reich, organized along federal lines with certain autonomous privileges for the individual states. This development had long been favored both by economic considerations and by the strong pull of emotional nationalism.

Old-fashioned liberals regretted the quieter atmosphere and more sober ideals, preferring the time when free cities and small principalities added variety and color to the pattern of German life.[5] But the majority of the German people were well satisfied with the new order, especially as the growth of industry and overseas trade increased national wealth and prosperity. The "Vons," who predominated among army officers and high civilian officials, the professors in the universities, and the state-subsidized Lutheran pastors became, with few exceptions, loyal supporters of the new empire.

The Social Democratic Party developed into a numerically strong opposition, which won the political allegiance of the majority of the industrial workers. But although there was theoretical lip service to the teachings of Marx and Engels, few of the Social Democrats were revolutionaries at heart. This was proved by German solidarity during World War I. What the typical Social Democrat wanted was social reform, more popular control over the national government, and more educational and other opportunities for the poorer classes.

Germany on the eve of World War I was governed with efficiency and integrity. Its municipal administration was a model. It was a *Rechtsstaat,* in the sense that the courts were independent and guaranties of freedom of speech and press were rather well maintained. Effective executive power, to be sure, was in the hands of the kaiser and the confidential advisers who helped to shape his decisions, for the chancellor (as the German prime minister was called) was appointed by the sovereign and could not be ousted by a parliamentary vote of nonconfidence. And although the lower house of the national parliament, the Reichstag, was elected by universal male suffrage, the Prussian state assembly, or Landtag, was chosen on the basis of the so-called three-class franchise.

Under this system the voters who paid the top third of the taxes, however few, were entitled to choose one third of the deputies to the Landtag. Those who paid the second third elected the second third, and the large majority of nontaxpayers or small taxpayers elected the final third. This insured a predominance of conservative strength in the Prussian parliament, and it affected the chancellor, who was also prime minister of Prussia, in his dealings with the Reichstag.

Another of the many conservative brakes in the German Constitution was the right of the Bundesrat, or federal council, to pass in advance on legislation submitted to the Reichstag. The Bundesrat was composed of representatives of the various states and free cities and was also biased in a conservative direction.

However, these limitations on democracy did not cause much visible discontent. So long as the Germans were well governed they were not much concerned about being self-governed. Bismarck had been a pioneer in social legislation. And national pride and patriotism were not limited to the upper classes.

The fall of the German Empire in November, 1918, was not the result of any well organized republican movement. It was a consequence of the lost war, of the flight of the Kaiser for asylum to the Netherlands, of the chaotic situation which prevailed for a time after the end of the fighting. The republic was proclaimed almost casually by a conservative Social Democrat, Philipp Scheidemann, at a time when there was considerable pressure from street crowds led by radicals. Some of these, such as the left wing Social Democrats Karl Liebknecht and Rosa Luxemburg, hoped to establish in Germany a Soviet Republic, more or less on the Russian model.

But all the voting indicated that these left wingers were a fairly small minority, even of the Social Democrats, to say nothing of the German people as a whole. After a few months of turbulent uncertainty, in which hunger, the result of the wartime blockade, was a considerable stimulus to disturbances in the larger cities and industrial districts, order was restored by a combination of moderate Social Democrats in office and old-line troops who had remained as disciplined units.

The so-called Weimar Republic was launched on the basis of a constitution prepared by a national assembly in the quiet atmosphere of the town of Goethe and Schiller and Liszt, far away from then turbulent Berlin. This first experiment in German republicanism started under heavy handicaps. It was identified in the public mind with defeat, national humiliation, hunger, and inflation, even though these were the consequences of a war for which German liberals and leftists certainly bore no responsibility.

Both on the right and on the left, considerable segments of the German public were never reconciled to the new republic. Conservative nationalists took every opportunity to ridicule and defame the Republic and its leaders. Murder bands of young extremists assassinated, among others, such prominent political figures as Matthias Erzberger, leader of the Catholic Center Party, and the Jewish industrialist Walter Rathenau, who as foreign minister had concluded the spectacular Treaty of Rapallo with the Soviet government, keeping open Germany's window to the east. At the other extreme, the more left wing elements in the Social Democratic Party broke away and formed the Communist Party of Germany, with a German Soviet form of government as its goal.

Principal support for the Republic came from the middle-of-the-road political groups, the Democrats, the Social Democrats and the Catholic Center, which, as its name implied, occupied a position between extreme nationalist conservatism and Marxian socialism. A coalition of these three parties maintained for many years a stable administration in Prussia, where the three-class system of voting had been abolished, along with the monarchy.

The first years of the new regime were bleak and bitter. The poorer classes in the cities were hungry. Inflation ruined and embittered the middle class. On top of what was resented as the humiliation of the Versailles Treaty, with what the Germans called its "war guilt lie," came the French extension of military occupation to the Ruhr industrial area in 1923 as a reprisal against a minor default in reparations payments.

From the very beginning of the Republic, normally orderly Germany sputtered with riots and armed clashes. Both on the right and on the left there were more or less serious attempts to seize power by violence. Berlin was a center of disorder. The two outstanding Communist leaders, Karl Liebknecht and Rosa Luxemburg, were killed after a revolt against a moderate Social Democratic government in January, 1919. There was further fighting in Berlin in March of the same year, and a short-lived Soviet Republic was set up in Munich in the spring of 1919.

There was also much subversive activity on the part of the extreme nationalists. An adventurer named Kapp, with the aid of the Ehrhardt Brigade, one of many paramilitary groups which furnished training for future Nazis, took over Berlin for a few days in March, 1920. This movement quickly collapsed; the trade-unions called a general strike and the conspirators, a band of politically naïve reactionaries, had no idea of how to organize an administration.

Tension in Germany heightened after the French occupation of the Ruhr and the gradual breakdown of the German policy of passive resistance and nonco-operation. There was a Communist uprising in Hamburg in the autumn of 1923, and in November of that year the name of Adolf Hitler came prominently into the news for the first time as the leader of an abortive *coup d'état* in Munich. While Bavaria was a hotbed of reaction, left wing extremists won a temporary victory in industrial Saxony, where a coalition government of Social Democrats and Communists was set up, to be thrown out of office by the intervention of the Reichswehr, the armed force of the central government.

But the Weimar Republic weathered these early storms. When economic conditions began to improve after the French withdrawal from the Ruhr and the provisional settlement of the reparations question by means of the Dawes and Young Plans, the natural German conservatism and love of order reasserted themselves. The election of Paul von Hindenburg as president of the Reich in 1926 showed that nationalist sentiment was still strong. But during his first term of office, before his mental and physical powers began to fail, Hindenburg played a correct, dignified role and remained faithfully within the limits of the constitution.

Between 1925 and 1929 there was a marked economic revival, assisted by a rather reckless flow of American capital into German municipal and industrial bonds.[6] At that time, with internal conditions improving while Gustav Stresemann conducted a shrewd and moderate foreign policy, aimed at abatement of friction with the West while also keeping open a line of communication to Moscow, it might have seemed that the German Republic had achieved a stable position within the European community. At that time Adolf Hitler, to most Germans and to most foreign observers in Germany, was written off as a crank, discredited by an unsuccessful revolt that started in a Munich beer hall. That this former unemployed Austrian house painter, who had served in the war with no more and no less distinction than millions of other gray-uniformed soldiers, would acquire despotic power over a people so well educated, so conscious of rank and class as the Germans would then have seemed a fantastic nightmare.

But Hitler, who had first acquired a following in the early stormy postwar years, got his second chance when Germany was prostrated by the long economic crisis that began in 1929. His Nazi (National Socialist) Party, which had only a dozen deputies in the Reichstag of 1928, had over 100 in the election of 1930.

And this party, steadily swelling in numbers and votes as years passed in the deepening shadow of mass unemployment, was a big emotional revivalist movement, rather than a political group pursuing normal objectives. Of the three men who were the true victors of World War I, with its aftermath of revolutions—Vladimir Ilyitch Lenin, Benito Mussolini, and Adolf Hitler—the last was the least known. Lenin and Mussolini had some reputation as revolutionary agitators. Hitler was the absolutely unknown ex-soldier. Yet his rise to power, given the crisis-ridden atmosphere of postwar Germany, was not a miracle and not an accident. He possessed qualities that were well calculated to attract a mass following in a time of despair, when people were looking for some extraordinary deliverer.

Hitler was impressive as an orator, rapt, passionate, almost hypnotic. He professed unbounded self-confidence at a time when the German people felt helplessly uprooted from old moorings, political, economic, and moral. His speeches were suffused with a cloudy mysticism, with a tragic emphasis on self which might have seemed banal or ridiculous to more skeptical people, but which appealed to the sentimental Germans.

Hitler's popular appeal was enhanced because he was a man of the people, not a member of the sharply defined German upper class. When he extolled national pride and the German soldierly spirit he won more applause because he had fought through the war as a private soldier, not as an officer. To many in the audiences which he aroused he seemed a figure out of another world, a savior in Germany's hour of need, a Lohengrin or a Parsifal. This impression was strengthened by the simplicity of his personal life, by his abstinence from women, alcohol, tobacco, and meat.

Hitler possessed other attributes of the mass leader. As his testament *Mein Kampf* shows, he was no mean psychologist. He was a master showman, keenly conscious of the value of constantly iterated propaganda. As he cynically observes, people will more readily believe a big lie, just because it is big, than a small one.

Perhaps the basic secret of his success against the bleak background of year after year of closed factories, ships tied up at wharves, masses of unemployed on a subsistence diet, was his ability to voice the subconscious feelings of many of his countrymen. National prestige, unity, order, to many Germans, ranked ahead of individual liberty in their scale of values. Hitler promised a Third Reich, more glorious than the first, the Holy Roman Empire, and the second, the empire of the Hohenzollerns.

The average German felt frustrated and bitter, in a mood to look for scapegoats, as a consequence of defeat in the last war and the sequence of misfortunes that followed. Hitler expressed this frustration and bitterness in passionate diatribes against the "November criminals" who established the republic, against the alleged traitors at home who stabbed the army in the back. He rejected all pacifist and humanitarian ideas and exalted power politics in its crudest and most cynical forms—again reflecting the mood of an embittered people.

Anti-Semitism was rampant in Germany for various reasons. The Jews were a natural scapegoat for a people that had always been susceptible to racist theories of history. Some Jews were active in the Communist and Social Democratic movements; others were prominent and successful as bankers, merchants, and professional men. Although these two groups had nothing in common, both furnished targets for the propaganda of hatred and envy that adds up to anti-Semitism. Jews were also prominent in some of the modernistic experiments in music, art, and the theater, against which the Nazi upsurge was to some extent a "plain man's" hostile reaction. There was a considerable influx of Jewish immigrants from eastern Europe, because of postwar upheavals there, and some of these were engaged in various speculative enterprises. While most political figures remained silent on the subject, Hitler screamed his hatred for the Jews—perhaps imbibed during his years of poverty and social degradation in cosmopolitan Vienna—from the housetops, in such frenzied outbursts as the following passage in *Mein Kampf*:

"If, with the help of the Marxist creed, the Jew conquers the nations of the world, his crown will become the funeral wreath of humanity, and once again this planet, empty of mankind, will move through the ether as it did thousands of years ago."

The German shopkeeper, artisan, small businessman, white collar employee, and peasant (and these groups were most responsive to Nazi agitation) hated socialism and communism, while at the same time cherishing a feeling of antagonism to big bankers and big businessmen. With considerable adroitness Hitler pitched his propaganda in the key of "national socialism" (a vaguely defined concept which meant just about what Hitler wanted it to mean). The idea was that the bad sides of capitalism (identified with the Jews) would disappear, while private property would be preserved and the traditional German virtues would be cultivated.

Hitler possessed in rare degree the unscrupulous politician's gift of being all things to all men. From the beginning he appealed to old officers and other nationalists with his promise to free Germany from the shackles of disarmament. And yet at the same time he played the role of a "peacemonger." Both before and after he came into power, he often dwelt on his personal knowledge of the horrors of war and his desire to reach an honorable settlement with Germany's former enemies.

Early in 1932 he obtained a much needed boost for the straitened finances of his movement by addressing a group of leading businessmen in Düsseldorf and depicting national socialism as a sovereign antidote to communism, an assurance of industrial peace.[7] At the same time some of his lieutenants, notably Paul Joseph Goebbels and Gregor Strasser, were beating the anticapitalist drum in working class districts. It would have been easy for a reasonable public opinion to recognize this and other inconsistencies of Nazi propaganda; but German public opinion in those crisis-haunted years was not reasonable.

The Nazis gained a big success in the national election of July 31, 1932, polling 37 per cent of the votes cast and emerging as by far the strongest single party in the new Reichstag. A significant result of this election was that the two parties which rejected democracy and individual liberty on principle, the Nazis and the Communists, received between them more than half of the votes cast. The majority of the German people had voted for one or the other form of dictatorship.

Hitler had learned caution from the failure of his attempted coup at Munich. Even with more than a third of the people apparently behind him he did not propose again to come into conflict with the armed forces of the state. Perhaps he knew enough German history to realize that big changes have been accomplished from the top, not from below. So his plan was to infiltrate and capture the state and the army as the indispensable prerequisites to instituting his personal rule. After some uncertainties and one political setback, when the Nazi vote declined in an election, he realized this goal when the aged Hindenburg, who had outlived his faculties, became easily susceptible to the intrigues of Nationalists like Franz von Papen, who cherished the illusion that they could manipulate Hitler for their own purposes.

Once Hitler had been legally appointed head of the government, his road to despotic personal power was short and easy. An election on March 5, held under considerable pressure by the Nazi storm troopers and the Nazi-controlled police, but still honest as regards the counting of the votes, gave Hitler's party about 44 per cent of the votes. With the Nationalists, with whom they were in a rather uneasy and precarious alliance, this gave them a bare majority in the new Reichstag, the fate of which was symbolized by a mysterious fire which had destroyed the Reichstag building.

The Communist Party was promptly outlawed, and a system of extralegal terror, murders, and beatings by Nazi strong-arm squads, and imprisonment of political suspects in concentration camps quickly snuffed out any open opposition. The new Reichstag, for all practical purposes, voted itself out of existence by accepting, with the votes of all parties except the Social Democrats, an enabling act with the demagogically attractive title, Law for Removing the Distress of the People and the Reich. This gave the new government the right to enact legislation by decree, without consulting the Reichstag. The National Socialist Party was declared the only legal political organization in Germany. From this time constitutional government in Germany ceased to exist. The Nazis proceeded to rule by means of a formula first introduced in Russia: unlimited terror plus unlimited propaganda.

As sometimes happens with dictatorships, the first phase of Hitler's rule was fairly successful—except, of course, for the Jews, who were quickly subjected to a variety of discriminatory laws (the grim period of genocidal extermination came later, after the outbreak of the war), and for the political victims of his terror, Social Democrats, Communists, some liberals, and a few dissidents who at first had been in Hitler's camp, but who later became disillusioned.

Unemployment declined substantially as youth camps and public works projects took many younger people off the relief rolls. Finance Minister Hjalmar Schacht performed various feats of financial wizardry with the mark, which had become inconvertible because of the depletion of Germany's gold reserve, and he made possible extensive barter deals with foreign countries. The rearmament of Germany was a further blow to unemployment.

And the Nazis were quick to put into practice the old principle: *Panem et circenses,* bread and circuses. The old trade unions were dissolved and replaced by a Nazi labor organization, the Arbeitsfront. A special organization with the sentimental name of Kraft durch Freude ("Strength Through Joy") took charge of holiday trips and other recreation for the workers. The annual monster rallies of the Nazi Party were turned into gigantic spectacles, with banners, floats, parades, and orchestras playing such works as Wagner's *Entrance of the Gods into Valhalla.*

A remarkable series of bloodless victories in foreign policy helped to tighten Hitler's grip on the German people. Great Britain and France weakly gave up to Hitler's forceful unilateral actions far more than they were willing to concede to the reasoned representations of the peaceful Weimar Republic. The first victory was the overwhelming vote of the people of the Saar Territory, which had been placed under League of Nations administration for fifteen years, in favor of reunion with Germany. Then came rearmament, passively accepted by Paris and London.

The final green light for Hitler's career of conquest was flashed when Hitler moved troops into the demilitarized area of the Rhineland in March, 1936. This was a violation not only of the Treaty of Versailles, but of the four-power Treaty of Locarno, in which Great Britain and Italy were made guarantors of the territorial integrity of Germany against France and of France against Germany, the demilitarization of the Rhineland being part of this freely negotiated agreement. At that time the British-French margin of military superiority was sufficient, in all probability, to have stopped Hitler without hostilities. It was subsequently reported that the Reichswehr units had received orders to withdraw without opposition in the event of French or British military action.

But the will to act was lacking in Paris and London. And successive acts of aggressive expansion followed at a quickening tempo: the unopposed march into Austria in March, 1938; the acquisition, under threat of war, of the German-speaking Sudetenland area of Czechoslovakia, ratified at the Munich conference in

September, 1938; the seizure of the whole of Czechoslovakia in March, 1939; finally, the fateful plunge into World War II with the invasion of Poland on September 1, 1939.

Then followed kaleidoscopic alternations of victory and defeat, conquests greater than Napoleon's, and finally a total military collapse that brought Germany far lower than France was after the downfall of Napoleon. For Hitler, the Pied Piper who lured the German people to destruction after bringing terrible suffering to almost all Europe, the end came when he committed suicide with his companion Eva Braun in the bunker under the Chancellery, as the avenging guns of Russian troops entering Berlin boomed louder and louder.

A new era of German history began as the larger and more populous part of the country, which remained free, began to rise like the phoenix from the ashes and rubble of defeat—at first slowly and painfully, later at dizzy speed.

It is evident, even from this brief and imperfect sketch of the historical background, that the German experience has not been uniform, that Nazism was not the predestined fate of the German people. One is indeed impressed by the multiplicity of influences that helped to shape the German national personality: the vision of the Holy Roman Empire and the quiet life of the small German state, the cosmopolitanism of Goethe and the nationalism of Arndt; the impulse to migrate that brought Germans as visitors or settlers to almost every country of Europe and America and the deep-rooted attachment to German soil; the coexistence of external order and daring freedom of creative thought and artistic experimentation.

One can think of many developments that might have precluded the tragic aberration of Nazism. If Brüning, the last constitutional chancellor, had displayed more economic imagination and flexibility in dealing with the crisis ... if Hitler had perished with some of his followers in the Munich Putsch ... if he had been deported to his native Austria after serving his sentence of imprisonment ... if more German conservatives had realized that Nazism was not a shot in the arm for nationalism, but a revolution of nihilism that would fatally destroy many old German values ... if so many German workers had not split the forces of democracy by pursuing the *ignis fatuus* of communism . . . if. . . . One could multiply the possibilities indefinitely.

Now a new phase of German historical development has commenced, and for reasons which will be set forth in later chapters, there are now better prospects for the permanent survival of free institutions than the unfortunate Weimar Republic ever possessed.

NOTES TO CHAPTER I

1 Cf. Golo Mann, *Deutsche Geschichte des neunzehnten und zwanzigsten Jahrhunderts* ("German History of the 19th and 20th Centuries") (Frankfurt: S. Fischer, 1958), p. 23.

2 Ralph Flenley, *Modern German History* (New York: E. P. Dutton & Co., Inc., 1959), p. 36.

3 This observation might apply also to other peoples. Many Russians and Spaniards as individuals are much more attractive than the forms of government under which Russia and Spain have lived.

4 Cited in Hans Kohn, *The Mind of Germany* (New York: Charles Scribner's Sons, 1960), p. 35.

5 This mood of nostalgic regret is well depicted in the latter part of Thomas Mann's *Buddenbrooks,* which depicts life in the novelist's birthplace, the old Baltic town of Lübeck.

6 Payment on these bonds, first suspended because of the crisis of convertibility and the suspension prolonged under the Hitler regime, was resumed as soon as Germany again possessed a sound convertible currency in the fifties.

7 Cf. Alan Bullock, *Hitler: A Study in Tyranny* (New York: Harper & Row, Publishers, 1952), pp. 177–179.

CHAPTER II

Germany in the Depths

THE treatment meted out to Germany after the total defeat and collapse of the Nazi regime was far more ruthless than what France suffered in the aftermath of the wars unleashed by Napoleon. France's cities in 1815 were untouched; no authentically French territory was annexed by the victors; there were no limitations on France's armed forces or on its industrial output. Through a very able diplomatic representative, Talleyrand, France had a voice at the Congress of Vienna, which was drawing the new political map of Europe. The price exacted for the Napoleonic Wars was a limited occupation of brief duration and a modest indemnity.

Hitler's ruthlessness had far exceeded Napoleon's and the German expiation was correspondingly heavier. The large cities of Germany already lay in ruins, as a result of air bombardment, supplemented in some cases by artillery action. Every square inch of German territory was under foreign military occupation. At the Potsdam Conference, which established Germany's provisional boundaries, there was no German representative. Some forty thousand square miles of territory which had been ethnically German for centuries, the lands east of a line marked by the rivers Oder and Neisse, between a quarter and a fifth of Germany's prewar territory, were annexed by Poland and the Soviet Union. Almost all the Germans who lived in this area and survived the Soviet invasion were driven from their homes and dumped as destitute refugees in the shrunken area of occupied Germany.

Among the early measures of the occupation powers were the confiscation of all German property in foreign countries, and of all

German patents; also plans for the dismantling of a large part of German industry (carried through in full rigor only in the Soviet Zone) and extremely severe limitations on Germany's future industrial development. Some industries, such as aircraft and shipbuilding, were forbidden altogether, and the British blew up the big Blohm and Voss shipyard in Hamburg.

An agreement on the permitted level of industry in Germany, concluded in March, 1946, limited Germany to an annual steel output of 5.8 million tons a year. (Actual production in the early sixties exceeded 30 million tons.) This plan, which imposed still more drastic cuts in the machine tool industry, was designed to reduce German industrial output to about half the figure of 1938.

American occupation policy in Germany during the first postwar years was governed by four statements of policy: the so-called Morgenthau Plan; Occupation Directive 1067, of April 26, 1945; the joint Potsdam Declaration of the occupation powers in August, 1945; and the level of industry agreement of March, 1946.

The essence of the Morgenthau Plan,[1] drawn up by Roosevelt's secretary of the treasury, Henry Morgenthau, Jr., with the co-operation of Harry Dexter White (later designated as a Communist agent by the FBI) and others was accepted as American-British state policy in a communiqué issued by Roosevelt and Churchill on September 15, 1944, after their second Quebec Conference. This communiqué called for the closing down of the industries in the German industrial heartland, the Ruhr, and in the subsidiary industrial region of the Saar, and for "converting Germany into a country largely agricultural and pastoral in character."

The full Morgenthau Plan spelled out the details of destroying a large part of the industry which furnished, directly or indirectly, the livelihood of the majority of the German people, and it contained a suggestion which would certainly have been welcome to the Kremlin and would have facilitated a Soviet takeover of all Western Europe if it had ever been put into practice: [2]

"The primary responsibility for the policing of Germany and for civil administration in Germany should be assumed by Germany's continental neighbors. Specifically these should include Russian,

French, Polish, Czech, Greek, Yugoslav, Norwegian, Dutch, and Belgian soldiers.

"Under this program United States troops could be withdrawn within a relatively short time."

Acceptance of the basic principles of the Morgenthau Plan at Quebec shocked and angered two leading members of Roosevelt's cabinet, Secretary of War Henry L. Stimson and Secretary of State Cordell Hull. Stimson pressed the issue at a luncheon with the President, who at first declared that he had no intention of turning Germany into an agricultural and pastoral state. When Stimson confronted Roosevelt with the words of the communiqué, the President's reaction was one of dumbfounded amazement: [3]

"He was frankly staggered by this and said he had no idea how he could have initialled this . . . that he had evidently done it without much thought."

The Morgenthau Plan was never literally put into operation. But much of its spirit of economic destructionism was mandatory for American policy during the first phases of the occupation. This is clear from the following excerpts from Occupation Directive 1067: [4]

"Germany will not be occupied for the purpose of liberation but as a defeated enemy nation. . . . You will strongly discourage fraternization with the German officials and population.

"No action will be taken, in execution of the reparations program or otherwise, which would tend to support basic living conditions in Germany or in your Zone at a higher level than that existing in any of the neighboring United Nations." [5]

"You will take no steps (a) looking toward the economic rehabilitation of Germany or (b) designed to maintain or strengthen the German economy."

The Potsdam Declaration was published after the meeting of the American, Soviet, and British heads of government in July–August, 1945. The gist of its economic decisions was as follows: [6]

"In order to eliminate Germany's war potential, the production of arms, ammunition and implements of war, as well as all types of aircraft and seagoing ships, shall be prohibited and prevented. Production of metals, chemicals, machinery and other items that are directly necessary to a war economy shall be rigidly controlled and restricted to Germany's approved postwar peacetime needs. . . . Productive capacity not needed for permitted production shall be removed in accordance with the reparations plans recommended by the Allied commission on reparations and approved by the governments concerned or, if not removed, shall be destroyed."

The Potsdam Declaration also provided for minute Allied control, for strictly negative purposes, over all German public or private scientific bodies, research and experimental institutions, laboratories and economic and financial transactions. In short, Germany, never self-sufficient in food, was first to be deprived of much of its best arable land, located in the regions transferred to Poland, and was also to be placed under a multitude of restrictions extremely prejudicial to its industry and foreign trade.

The crimes of the Nazis had been terrible and they made the impulse to inflict revenge understandable. But many of these early occupation decisions, happily long rescinded, make strange reading fifteen or twenty years afterward. Certainly no one responsible for making these decisions deserves much credit for foresight and enlightened statesmanship.

A trip to Germany in the summer of 1946 revealed the results, in human terms, of the lost war, followed by an occupation policy which stressed vengeance rather than constructive rebuilding of free institutions. When I got out of the airport bus in Frankfurt a crowd of barefooted boys clamored for a chance to carry my bags to the hotel, where they expected recompense not in paper marks, virtually worthless at the time, but in the universal substitute currency, cigarettes. The scene suggested some poverty-stricken Asiatic country, not Western Europe.

Like all the large German cities at that time, Frankfurt was a mass of ruins. One sensed hunger everywhere, in the strained look of children begging outside the American commissary stores, in the green and sallow faces of most individuals, in the widespread prostitution, a consequence both of lack of food and lack of men. Berlin presented the same picture of desolation, on a vastly bigger scale because of the size and expanse of the former capital. Where rows of apartment houses, offices, and shops had once stood there were now skeleton outlines of buildings and huge piles of rubble. The

Tiergarten, one of Berlin's principal parks, was a wasteland. The heavy, inartistic statues in the Sieges-Allee looked curiously naked without the background of trees.

What was striking, in one city after another, was the complete absence of traffic movement, except for the cars and trucks of the occupation forces. One also noticed the small number of young men. Some three million Germans had perished in the war; also an unknown but considerable number had fled or been driven from their homes. And at that time more than four million German war prisoners were still held for forced labor, most of them in Russia, but hundreds of thousands in Great Britain and France.

There was no mass starvation, at least in the Western Zones. Prompt action by the military authorities had restored water supply, where this had been disrupted, and averted the outbreak of widespread epidemics. But there was an abnormally high death rate among the most vulnerable age groups, the very old and the very young. There was an excess of deaths over births in the three states of the American Zone in the first months of 1946. And the American Zone was the least hungry of the four. A high official of the American Military Government told me that infant mortality had been as high as 50 per cent in Berlin in the first months of occupation and had ranged around 20–25 per cent in the larger cities of the American Zone.

Hamburg impressed me as the hungriest city I visited—and this impression was all the more vivid because I remembered Hamburg as Germany's biggest and busiest port, its shop windows stocked with comforts and luxuries from all parts of the world. The population had been living for months on a basic ration of 1,000 or 1,100 calories a day, barely half the minimum figure for health and efficiency.

People were collapsing at work in factories and offices. About a thousand cases of hunger edema, the swelling of the stomach that comes with an advanced state of malnutrition, had been admitted to hospitals. A British official (Hamburg was in the British Zone) described the local rations: The principal items were about half a pound of bread and a pound of potatoes a day. Other allotments were negligible, four ounces of jam, half an ounce of cheese, and a little over a pint of skimmed milk a week; less than half a pound of fats a month. There was some eking out of this starvation dole through the black market and through individual garden plots. But no fruit was on sale in the stores, and it was possible to buy only a few pounds of vegetables a month.

Hunger in Germany in 1946 must be seen in the perspective of general want and suffering in Europe at that time. Warsaw was more completely destroyed than any German city. So were many towns that changed hands during the German invasion of Russia. The Netherlands suffered near starvation in the last months of the war. England was still on a severe regime of austerity. Those in France and Italy who had little or no access to the flourishing black markets were living through lean times. But what gave a peculiarly hopeless aspect to the misery in Germany was the revengeful occupation policy that sought to obstruct, not to help along the natural process of recovery.

Amid the general want and desolation there were a few oases of plenty: the self-sufficient communities in which the occupation officers and officials were installed. There were plenty of undamaged houses to be requisitioned in German residential suburbs; food, liquor, tobacco, and other goods were available at low prices in canteens and "PXs," or commissary stores; and there was no servant problem in a situation where employment in a foreign household offered the best insurance against hunger.

Nor was there any lack of opportunities for self-enrichment for persons with quick imaginations and few scruples. The German mark had collapsed so completely that cigarettes were far preferable in payment for services. At the time of the German military collapse in 1945 the amount of currency in circulation was 60 billion marks, as against 6 billion before the war. The occupation powers then put many more billions into circulation, the Russians being especially industrious in this respect. The United States Treasury, in which Harry Dexter White was a prominent official, had obligingly furnished the Russians with plates for printing American occupation marks, redeemable at the rate of ten to the dollar. It is estimated that this particular demonstration of friendship for the Soviet Union cost the American taxpayer $250 million.[7]

Opportunities for self-enrichment by American military and civilian personnel were numerous and were not overlooked. The Allied powers, so zealous in extirpating other real or imagined traces of Nazism, continued to apply Hitler's system of tight wage and price controls. Wages had been held at a low level, from 200 to 400 marks a month. Prices of rationed goods, what little was available, were also kept low; but on the free market the sky was the limit. I found the following prices prevailing in Berlin in the summer of 1946: a pound of coffee, 600 marks; a pound of butter, 300 marks; a pair of women's shoes, 600 marks; a package of American cigarettes, 150 marks; a cake of soap, 50 marks.

It was easy in the beginning for Americans to buy coffee and cigarettes at low prices in the PXs, to sell these goods at astronomical paper mark prices, and to complete the transaction by converting these marks into dollars at the ten-to-one rate. Meissen china and other German valuables could also be acquired in exchange for cigarettes and coffee. Various checks were devised for this currency racket. But it could be entirely eliminated only after a new solid German currency was issued in 1948. Semismuggling deals in coffee and cigarettes, sold in American service stores without paying normal duty, plagued American-German relations for some years.

Apart from profitable transactions made possible by the shortage of consumer goods and the disordered state of the German currency, there was considerable outright looting in the first phase of the occupation, when the Germans were regarded as having few, if any, rights. On this point Harold Zink, chief historian of the Office of the United States High Commissioner for Germany, offers the following observations: [8]

"It would not be fair to conclude that looting was all prevailing among the American forces in Germany. But there was a good deal of it. One of the truly sensational cases involved the theft of the crown jewels of the Prince of Hesse from Kronberg castle. One commanding general of a division went so far as to justify looting on the part of his troops by stating that many of his men had lost their lives or been wounded by the Germans and now that victory had come it was quite proper that they should take what they wanted of German chattels. Certainly it could not be said that a majority of American senior officers endorsed such a point of view. Looting always remained a serious offense on the books. Nevertheless it must be admitted that looting was all too frequent and that the efforts to punish such conduct during the early period of the occupation were not as vigorous as they might have been."

Nothing happened in the United States Zone comparable to the wild orgies of pillage, drunkenness, murder and wholesale rape that occurred in Berlin and other cities captured by the Russians. And living conditions in the American area were somewhat better than in the other zones because the Americans, alone among the occupation powers, had surplus food and other commodities, and some crumbs fell to the Germans.

The ruling against fraternization was enthusiastically and generally disregarded by the American soldiers in their relations with German women. Dependents were not admitted to Germany at this time, and it was a rare GI who did not have his *Fräulein*. There were some cases of rape; but in general milder methods were effective. In the prevalent atmosphere of hunger and privation, social and moral breakdown, many young women were to be had for cigarettes, chocolate, and nylon stockings. And because of the tremendous shortage of German males in the younger age groups, many girls probably enjoyed the companionship and protection of association with an occupation soldier. Some officers seem to have carried sexual exuberance to extremes; at least the candid Zink remarks: [9]

"The sexual antics of some colonels and a larger number of lower officers who belonged to the age group over 40 certainly must have served to reduce the respect of some Germans for the American Military Government personnel almost to the point of ridicule. This had a serious effect on the operations of military government. But, as far as the conduct of the rank-and-file of GIs went, it seems probable that it was regarded by the majority of the German people as more or less to be expected."

Justice Minister Fritz Neumayer in 1956 stated in the Bundestag that the Allied troops had left behind almost 68,000 illegitimate children, of whom over half, about 37,000, were of American parentage. (The American troops considerably outnumbered the British and French.) A substantial number of these were of Negro parentage, indicating that the hungry and sex-starved girls of this period were not much affected by Nazi racist propaganda.

One of the principal objectives of the occupation was denazification—the punishment, elimination from public life and sometimes from all profitable employment of former Nazis. American Military Government Law No. 8, effective in September, 1945, contained this sweeping proscription: [10]

"However slight the apparent extent of Nazi party participation, a member's continued employment, except in ordinary labor, is unlawful."

In the beginning the Americans, of all the four powers, displayed the greatest zeal for carrying denazification to extremes. All Nazis of any prominence, many merely suspected of Nazi sympathies, were arrested and held in concentration camps. Of those arrested for "Nazi or militarist activity" the British, up to January 1, 1947, tried 2,296; the French 17,353; the Russians 18,328; and the Americans 169,282.[11]

One unique feature of the American denazification procedure was the circulation to the entire adult population of the United States Zone (some 12 million persons) of a *Fragebogen,* or questionnaire, containing a list of 131 questions, which had to be answered on pain of criminal penalties. This move excited much severe criticism among Germans, even among those with unimpeachable non-Nazi records.

Recipients of the questionnaire were required to denounce any relatives who "held office, rank or post of authority" in any one of over fifty suspect organizations. Question No. 18 called for a list of titles of nobility which the individual, his wife, his parents, or any of his four grandparents had held. There was also interrogation on points that had nothing to do with Nazi affiliation, such as how much money the person earned, how much land he owned, whether he belonged to a university fraternity. The aristocrats who were prominent in the attempt to overthrow Hitler in July, 1944 would have been incriminated by this kind of test. Whoever was responsible for the *Fragebogen* seems to have held the Communist dogmatic view that Nazism was a movement of the aristocracy and the propertied classes. Actually, while Germans of all social groups could be found in the Nazi ranks, the predominant element could be described as lower middle class.

The *Fragebogen* [12] was not the only evidence of pro-Communist influence in the first phase of American Military Government. This was largely eliminated as the cold war heated up, but not without leaving some perceptible effects. Newspapers in Germany at that time were permitted only by license from the Military Government and such licenses were freely granted to Communists. The radio and other means of communication were also infiltrated.

Certainly very few American officers were conscious Communist sympathizers. But in many cases they were politically inexperienced and naïve, and hence more susceptible to pressures from Washington that served the communist cause. [13] Reference has already been made to the service which Harry Dexter White rendered to the Soviet occupation authorities by procuring for them copies of the plates on which occupation marks were printed. General Eisenhower's financial adviser, supplied by the Treasury, was a Col. Bernard Bernstein, who was quoted in the American Communist newspaper, the *Daily Worker* of February 21, 1946, as saying: "Only the Russians have shown that they mean to exterminate fascism and nazism and have already taken decisive steps in that direction." Bernstein was active in "decartelization," arbitrary breaking up of German industrial corporations and financial institutions into smaller units. Most of this was repealed as Germany acquired more self-government; but not before a good deal of confusion and economic injury had been caused.

The OWI in Washington during the war set up no effective bars against Communist infiltration. So Gerhart Eisler, who later turned up as chief of propaganda for the Communist administration of the Soviet Zone, was for a time chief of the broadcasting station of the OWI, which was sending propaganda to Germany. One George Shaw Wheeler, head of the denazification branch of Military Government, sought "political asylum" in Communist-ruled Czechoslovakia in 1947.

Bernstein, Eisler, and Wheeler occupied high influential positions, and during my trip in Germany in 1946 I got the impression that there were a good many officials of lower rank, especially in the division of press and publications, who held similar views. It was not the number of conscious Communist sympathizers that made them a factor of some importance in the first phase of the occupation. It was rather the fact that they knew exactly what they wanted to accomplish, whereas Military Government at this time had no clear, coherent or constructive policy, apart from the enforcement of a multitude of repressive and negative regulations, political and economic.

Indeed, in some of the actions of that period it is hard to determine with certainty whether the underlying motivation was pro-Communist sympathy or desire for indiscriminate revenge on the German people as a whole. These motivations led logically to the same course of action. It was obvious Communist policy to create in West Germany as much misery and economic chaos as possible, with a view to softening up the Germans for an ultimate Red take-over of the entire country.

A few excesses of this early phase of fanatical denazification may be mentioned. An American general barred Wilhelm Furtwängler, one of the greatest living orchestra conductors, from directing a concert in West Berlin. Furtwängler was later cleared by a German denazification tribunal and there was testimony that he had done what he could to help members of the Berlin Philharmonic Orchestra who were of Jewish or partly Jewish origin. (The Russians here scored a minor propaganda victory by inviting Furtwängler to conduct in East Berlin.)

A prominent surgeon, Willy Sauerbruch, was dismissed from the public health administration just when the need for medical experience was most acute. In the winter of 1945–46, during a severe transportation crisis, hundreds of railway workers were dismissed as former Nazi Party members, although the chances are that the great majority had taken party cards mainly to protect their jobs.

What was lacking in the early American approach to denazification (both the British and the French followed more reasonable policies) was any sense of the terrific pressure for conformity under Nazism, as under communism or any other totalitarian regime.

This made it difficult, if not impossible, to lead an active life in almost any occupation or profession without joining, if not the Nazi Party, at least some Nazi-controlled organization. In the end the kind of wholesale purge envisaged by the distribution of the *Fragebogen* broke down because of the sheer physical impossibility of processing millions of such exhaustive questionnaires.

The number of those liable to punishment was cut by an amnesty for those born after January 1, 1919, for the disabled, and for individuals with low incomes. (Again this curious Marxist approach!) Finally, under a law that went into effect on June 1, 1946, German tribunals were made responsible for denazification, persons charged being divided into four categories:

(1) Major offenders, who might be sentenced to imprisonment up to ten years and excluded from public office, with confiscation of property.

(2) Offenders, who could be imprisoned, fined, and/or excluded from public office, but were admitted to probation.

(3) Lesser offenders, liable to fine.

(4) Followers, exempt from penalty.

These German tribunals were intensely unpopular, first, because differentiation was often very difficult, and second, because of alleged cases of corruption. The whole procedure was wound up after 1,549 people had been sentenced as major offenders and 21,000 as offenders. There can be little doubt that the net, immediately after the occupation, was thrown much too widely, with the result that some big Nazis escaped and many "little people," guilty mainly of lack of moral courage, were unnecessarily persecuted. The whole German people had been caught in the Nazi totalitarian machine, actively supported by a minority, overtly resisted by a smaller minority. To determine the individual guilt of the majority who conformed without personally taking part in acts of inhumanity was a thankless and probably hopeless undertaking.

Apart from mass purges, there were special trials of outstanding Nazis and of diplomats and industrialists, also of German soldiers and concentration camp guards, charged with exceptional brutality and with such specific offenses as the murder of American aviators who had parachuted to earth after air raids and with the killing of war prisoners near Malmédy, in Belgium, during the last German offensive on the Western Front.

The most spectacular of these trials, which was held in Nürnberg from November, 1945, until October, 1946, was before an international court with judges and prosecutors from the four occupation powers. Death sentences by hanging were pronounced on Goering (who committed suicide), Ribbentrop, and nine other defendants. Seven received long prison terms; three were acquitted. No reasonable person could feel sentimental pity for these men, who had brought on Europe and on their own country incalculable suffering by an aggressive war and were identified with a regime that perpetrated monstrous genocidal crimes. Yet the Nürnberg trials did not embody the ideal of impartial justice. It could hardly be otherwise, since it was a case of victors passing judgment on the vanquished. The defense attorneys made the most of acts of ruthlessness on the part of the Allies, such as unlimited submarine warfare and the saturation bombing of such cities as Hamburg and Dresden, which caused hundreds of thousands of casualties among civilian noncombatants.

One cloud on the proceedings at Nürnberg was the charge in the original indictment that the Germans had murdered some four or five thousand Polish officers, whose bodies were found buried in a forest near Smolensk during the war. While there were apparently no survivors of this massacre, circumstantial evidence is overwhelming that these Poles, and some ten thousand others, whose bodies were never found, were slaughtered by the Soviet political police in the spring of 1940, more than a year before the German invasion of Russia. So weak was the evidence of German responsibility for this particular atrocity that the Nürnberg Tribunal rather shamefacedly let the whole matter drop rather than risk a convincing revelation that the Soviet Union, with its judges sitting in judgment, had itself been guilty of an abominable war crime.

Some of the sentences passed in the United States Zone, especially those on diplomats and industrialists, were disallowed when a calmer atmosphere prevailed in Washington. Alfried Krupp, heir of one of the biggest and most famous of German firms, who had been condemned to imprisonment with confiscation of property, was released with restoration of the ownership of his factories and other enterprises. Altogether 1,538 persons were convicted in the American Zone special trials, 444 received death sentences, and 250 were executed.[14]

The methods employed to extort confessions from German soldiers accused of killing war prisoners in the so-called Malmédy case came under sharp criticism from an Army commission of investigation. General Clay felt obliged to cancel the death penalties, "unless there were evidence other than that of witnesses claiming that their confessions were extorted under force and duress." [15]

There was an interesting contrast between Soviet and American approaches to the occupation of a defeated Germany. For years before the end of the war the Soviet Government had made all possible propaganda use of disaffected German officers captured in Russia. They were given preferential treatment, permitted to broadcast even nationalist propaganda to Germany, so long as it was anti-Hitler. Stalin reckoned quite correctly that messages from such officers would appeal to groups which would be impervious to stock Communist agitation slogans.

At the same time a group of German Communist *émigrés*—including Walter Ulbricht, for many years dictator of the Soviet Zone, Wilhelm Pieck, president of the "German Democratic Republic" and others—was carefully groomed as the future government of the Soviet Zone of Occupation. There is a firsthand account [16] of how Ulbricht and the first group of future Communist rulers were sent by air to Germany on April 30, 1945, fully equipped, down to such details as an allowance of occupation marks for their expenses. Everything was planned; nothing was left to chance.

There was no comparable American effort to promote the political fortunes of German non-Communist democratic individuals and groups. Allen W. Dulles, as representative of the OSS, was in contact with Hans Bernd Gisevius, Eugen Gerstenmeier, and other representatives of the German underground opposition groups which brought about the revolt of July 20, 1944.[17] But he was never allowed to give these men who were fighting for Germany's freedom and honor at enormous risk to their own lives (thousands were slaughtered after the failure of the plot) the encouragement of hoping that, if they did succeed in ridding their country of the Nazi horror, Germany would get a fair application of the principles of the Atlantic Charter in the peace settlement. Any serious attempt at American political warfare, designed to encourage the rebirth of free institutions in Germany after the end of the war, was inhibited by the commitment to Unconditional Surrender and the prevalence of the Morgenthau Plan spirit in influential circles in Washington.

Germans who were driven from their country by Nazi persecution, but who were anti-Communist as well as anti-Nazi, received little consideration in United States planning for postwar occupation. The sweeping nonfraternization order under which Military Government operated for a time would have applied to Konrad Adenauer, to Eugen Gerstenmeier, to other anti-Nazi Germans, whether conservatives or Social Democrats, as much as to individuals compromised by association with the Hitler tyranny.

Whereas the Russians from the beginning (apart from the wild, uncontrolled excesses of the Red Army) gave favored treatment to Germans who were sympathetic to communism, a corresponding process for Germans who believed in freedom came about much more grudgingly and slowly in the Western zones. For a long time rules were maintained that Germans must be treated as social pariahs and not entertained on a basis of social equality. One well-known Social Democrat who passed over to the East Zone and occupied a high post in the Soviet puppet administration, Otto Grotewohl, may have been influenced in this decision by rough handling he received from overzealous MP's in Berlin, to whom he was just another "Kraut."

Although Russia had suffered much more than the United States or Great Britain at the hands of the Germans, the Soviet representatives in Germany displayed from the beginning a flexible sense of propaganda values that was lacking in the Western zones. The case of Furtwängler has already been mentioned. The United States bombing of Dresden in the spring of 1945, one of the biggest holocausts in the war, was undertaken at the request of the advancing Soviet forces, but this did not prevent Soviet and German

Communist propaganda from recalling this bombing again and again as a sign of American barbarism.

Yet, despite all the superior finesse displayed on the Soviet side, it is America and the West that won and Moscow that lost in the competition for the minds of the German people. The government of the Federal Republic is freely elected and fully representative; the government of the Soviet Zone is an alien-dominated dictatorship. Germany's alliance with the West is free and unforced. The link between the Soviet Zone and Moscow would not last long if the twenty-two divisions of the Red Army were removed.

One reason for this important political victory of the West is the constructive change which occurred in American and Western occupation policy and which prepared a happy ending for an occupation policy that began under very unfavorable auspices. Another reason was that the Russians, although in straight political warfare with the United States they sometimes showed the superior skill of professionals against amateurs, were torn and frustrated by conflicting impulses and diverging aims.

The Asiatic savagery of the Red Army advance, the massacres of civilians, the outrages against women,[18] the wholesale looting, burning, and destruction excited in the Germans an ineradicable feeling of loathing and horror. The flight of Germans in the last months of the war was always to the West, never to the East before the advancing American, British, and French troops. And after the first extreme excesses were over and the Soviet troops had been brought under normal discipline, the wholesale spoliation of everything from factory and railway equipment to pianos and feather beds frustrated the best efforts of the Soviet professional propagandists. It seems that one branch of Soviet Military Government, anxious to create a popular base for a Communist-type regime, could not control or restrain another branch, which had instructions to seize all the machinery and equipment it could lay its hands on. Dismantling in the Soviet Zone went much further than in the West and was accompanied and followed by heavy exactions of payment in goods. So the Communist administration could be maintained only by military force and police terror.

Historically, the United States occupation of its zone of Germany, in the first years, reveals some points of similarity to the military rule that persisted for a decade after the end of the Civil War in the Southern states. There was the same queer mixture of revengefulness, corruption, and uninformed idealism. While many of the measures of military control were bound to arouse strong repulsion, there was in both occupations a sense of missionary obligation to reform and "re-educate" the conquered. Accordingly, some starry-eyed idealists in the education department of the cumbersome American Military Government set out to turn the German educational system upside down, to abolish religious teaching in the schools, to implant something like the United States comprehensive high school in place of the German (and European) system of separating children, according to aptitude and capacity, between the Gymnasium, which prepares for the university, and the Volksschule, which emphasizes vocational subjects. This was all part of a vague, grandiose scheme to "re-educate" the Germans out of their evil ways—as if this could be done by foreign bureaucratic formulas, enforced at the point of the bayonet. The outspoken chronicler of the occupation, Professor Zink, offers the following comment on these early educational experiments: [19]

"Actually most of the plans, probably fortunately for both Germans and Americans, remained on paper and were never executed. ... There was a great deal of fuzziness of reasoning and too much rather pompous talk."

In its first years military occupation was not a re-educational inspiration of any kind, but rather an evil to be borne—more philosophically by those Germans fair-minded enough to realize that they were paying the price for Hitler's mad schemes of conquest and that German armies of occupation had also lived off the fat of the land in foreign lands and otherwise misbehaved. As hostile occupation evolved into friendly alliance and co-operation, the influence of American contacts became much stronger and more favorable.

Germans came in large numbers to the "America Houses" which were set up in many German cities, with libraries, reference services, lectures, and entertainments. The massive exchange programs that brought many American scholars and students to Germany and sent thousands of German professors, students, scientists, political figures, businessmen, trade-unionists to the United States made a big contribution to mutual understanding. Some Germans have told me of being impressed by such aspects of American living as the simpler, less formal relations between chiefs and subordinates in American offices, by the easier discipline in American homes. German educationists, long cut off from the outside world, were glad to be brought abreast of modern developments in pedagogy, once it became clear that there was no intention of turning the excellent German school system upside down. Businessmen were eager for information about new methods in production and marketing. Most Germans, especially of the younger generation, were more than normally susceptible to new trends in foreign living, because they had lived so long in isolation and because the whole Hitlerite scale of values had crumbled in the dust and rubble of total defeat. But the full effect of this psychology had to wait until the barriers against social contact were removed and the improvement in Germany's trade and financial position made possible widespread travel abroad.

Military Government in its first phase may be credited with restoring essential services and averting epidemics and mass starvation. Otherwise it is more memorable for its blunders, political and psychological, than for constructive achievements. Perhaps these blunders were unavoidable, in view of the spirit of the time, the harsh directions that emanated from Washington, and the inexperience of many officers and officials in dealing with German affairs.

At any rate, it was a proof of the rugged vitality of the German people, and their phoenix-like will to live and recover, that they overcame and outlived in time both the terrific human and material losses of the war and the consequences of the early negative and repressive occupation measures.

NOTES TO CHAPTER II

1 For the full text of the Morgenthau Plan and the arguments for its acceptance see Henry Morgenthau, Jr., *Germany Is Our Problem*, (New York: Harper & Row, Publishers, 1945).

2 Morgenthau, *op. cit.*, p. 4.

3 Henry L. Stimson and McGeorge Bundy, *On Active Service* (New York: Harper & Row, Publishers, 1948), p. 581.

4 Published in Department of State *Bulletin,* Vol. XIII (1945), pp. 596–607.

5 All the United Nations in eastern Europe, the Soviet Union, Poland, Czechoslovakia, and Yugoslavia, historically had a much lower living standard than Germany.

6 The full text of the Potsdam Declaration may be found in Morgenthau, *op. cit.,* pp. 213–229.

7 Eugene Davidson, *The Death and Life of Germany* (New York: Alfred A. Knopf, Inc., 1959), p. 84.

8 Harold Zink, *The United States in Germany, 1944–1955* (New York: D. Van Nostrand Co., Inc., 1957), p. 136.

9 Zink, *op. cit.,* p. 138.

10 Weekly Information Bulletin of HICOG (Office of the High Commissioner for Germany), October 13, 1945, p. 5, cited by Davidson, *op. cit.,* p. 130.

11 Zink, *op. cit.,* p. 165, citing W. Friedman, *The Allied Military Government of Germany.* The figure for the Soviet Zone seems unduly low.

12 Perhaps the most constructive result of this inquisition was a book by a German conservative non-Nazi, Ernst von Salomon, who used the questions in the *Fragebogen* as a take-off point for a book with the same title, a vivid sketch of his life and ideas.

13 For a fuller treatment of Communist influence, see Davidson, *op. cit.,* pp. 37–39.

14 Zink, *op. cit.,* pp. 147, 148.

15 Lucius D. Clay, *Decision in Germany* (Garden City, N.Y.: Doubleday & Company, Inc., 1950), p. 253.

16 See Wolfgang Leonhard, *Child of the Revolution* (Chicago: Henry Regnery Co., 1958), pp. 284 ff.

17 For a full account of Mr. Dulles's contacts with the German underground and the limitations under which he worked see *The German Underground,* by Allen W. Dulles (New York: The Macmillan Co., 1947).

18 The most detailed account in English of the havoc during the Soviet advance may be found in Jürgen Thorward's *Flight in the Winter* (New York: Pantheon Books, Inc., 1951).

19 Zink, *op. cit.,* pp. 203, 207.

CHAPTER III

The Political Upward Climb

TEN years passed between the surrender of Germany in May, 1945 and the recognition of full sovereignty for the German Federal Republic, composed of the American, British, and French zones of occupation, in 1955. The transition in Germany's status from a conquered pariah enemy to a respected NATO ally was gradual and uneven. It was delayed and complicated by differences among the three powers and by conflicting tendencies among the occupation officials. The economic destructionist psychology was not outlived overnight. As late as 1949 one could find occupation officials more interested in waging a quixotic crusade against the bogey of German cartels than in promoting the German economic revival which was to prove of such benefit to all Europe.

Bureaucratic vested interests were involved in the maintenance of such control organizations as the Coal Authority and the Steel Authority in the Ruhr, and JEIA, the initials standing for Joint Export and Import Agency, which for a time directed all German foreign trade operations. The head of this agency assured me with every sign of conviction in 1949 that American and British officials could handle Germany's foreign trade much better than German businessmen. Few Germans agreed. A standard joke was that the initials stood for *Jeder Export und Import ausgeschlossen* ("Any export and import excluded"). As soon as JEIA was liquidated, German exports and imports boomed. German foreign trade, $2,-849,000,000 in 1949, reached the figure of $18,182,000,000 in 1959. And this was typical of the general effect of turning back control of their own affairs to the Germans.

The general political trend, after the early "hard" period of occupation, was in the direction of more self-government for the Germans and a friendlier, more co-operative attitude on the part of the occupation authorities. The United States usually took the lead in pressing for the removal of oppressive restrictions, the French fought a last-ditch battle against concessions, and the British usually took an intermediate position.

One of the first constructive steps toward improving the desperate condition of the West German economy was the economic fusion of the American and British zones in the summer of 1946. The French for a time held out against merging their smaller zone, in line with their general opposition at this time toward any move that suggested a more centralized German administration.

All attempts to reach a workable understanding with the Soviet authorities for a common economic administration of Germany, as contemplated in the Potsdam Declaration, had failed. The Soviet Government followed the policy of keeping its zone—composed of the part of Germany lying east of a line of demarcation running from the Baltic Sea just east of Lübeck in a generally north-south direction, turning east along the northern frontier of Bavaria— politically and economically isolated from the rest of Germany, milking it to the limit of reparations. At the same time the Soviets demanded reparations deliveries from the Western zones. Some dismantled equipment from the Ruhr was sent to Russia. But this practice ceased as the United States and British governments realized that they were, in effect, being asked to pay reparations to the Soviet Union, since no exchange deliveries of food or other products from the Soviet Zone were permitted.

An important shift of emphasis in the American attitude was announced with pomp and ceremony when the then Secretary of State James F. Byrnes delivered a speech at Stuttgart on September 6, 1946 before an audience of occupation officials and German representatives of the state administrations which had been created in the United States Zone. Byrnes was stern and uncompromising on such issues as demilitarization and denazification and supported the French claim to the solidly German Saar Territory.[1] However, he made clear that the Saar would be the only territorial cession required of Germany in the West; there would be no detachment of the Rhineland or the Ruhr.

Thus for the first time a high United States official offered the Germans the hand of friendship and a prospect of peaceful economic recovery. Byrnes also offered a categorical assurance that American military power would remain in Europe: "As long as an occupation force is required in Germany, the Army of the United States will be part of that force."

Byrnes had hesitated about this sentence, but retained it at the urging of Gen. Lucius D. Clay,[2] then deputy military governor of the American Zone, later commandant of American forces in Berlin in the critical period of the blockade. Clay was the most forceful and in the last years of his mission, the most constructive figure in Military Government.

Byrnes held out a hope that artificial obstacles to German economic recovery would be ended: "Germany is a part of Europe, and recovery in Europe will be slow indeed if Germany with her resources of iron and coal is turned into a poorhouse."

Also he struck a note long eagerly awaited by Germans who wished to rebuild their government on the basis of free institutions: "The American people want to return the government of Germany to the German people. The American people want to help the German people to win their way back to an honorable place among the free and peaceloving peoples of the world."

There were tears in the eyes of some of the 150 Germans present who rose to applaud. A little light was visible to them at the end of a long dark tunnel. A new military order, JCS 1779, superseding the bleakly negative JCS 1067 in 1947, pointed in the same direction, with the following intimation of a modified economic policy: "An orderly and prosperous Europe requires the economic contributions of a stable and productive Germany as well as the necessary restraints to insure that Germany is not allowed to revive its destructive militarism."

The last German war prisoners in American hands were released in 1947; the French and British released the last of theirs in the following year. An important factor in arousing the American conscience to the existence of avoidable hunger in Germany was the publication of a report by ex-President Herbert Hoover, who visited Germany early in 1947. Hoover found widespread want and malnutrition, 10,000 cases of hunger edema in Hamburg alone. Food output in West Germany was 65 per cent of the prewar figure, with 9 million more mouths to be fed because of the vast influx of expellees and refugees. Germany, according to Hoover, had been reduced to a level not known in Europe for a hundred years.

In addition to recommending supplementary feeding, especially for children, the Hoover Report made the point that this hunger was avoidable. There were stocks of surplus food available—fish in Norway, for instance—if the Germans were only allowed to pay for these foodstuffs by being able to manufacture export goods freely.

Two important milestones in Germany's upward climb to a cooperative relation with the United States occurred in 1948. A currency reform went into effect. It was drastic medicine, perhaps more drastic than an independent German government would have felt able to prescribe. For the second time in a generation the Germans saw almost all the face value of their paper money nullified; the rate of exchange was about sixteen old marks for one new mark.

But the old marks had long been worthless, for practical purposes, and the new money could purchase goods which were now freely offered in the shops. The effect in reviving trade, industry, and the will to work was almost magical.

Three years passed between my first postwar visit to Germany, in 1946, and my second. The country had become almost unrecognizable. In 1946 the whole atmosphere was apathetic, listless, hopeless. In 1949, although many ruins and much poverty remained, the signs of a drive toward recovery were impressive: stores that were beginning to offer luxuries and comforts as well as staple goods, printing offices starting up in the cellars of bombed buildings, everywhere a concerted effort to clear away ruins and start repairing damaged houses and building new ones. The only tip that had been appreciated in 1946 was cigarettes or some article of value; now the new money was distinctly preferred.

There were signs of a changed atmosphere in politics also. In

1946 the Munich newspaper *Süddeutsche Zeitung* was severely reprimanded and almost suppressed because it published an editorial article on the cruelties and indignities inflicted on the Sudeten Germans when they were driven out of Czechoslovakia after the war. The article, entitled "They Reaped the Hate," was written by an unimpeachable anti-Nazi of part Jewish origin, who carefully stressed the point that Hitler's actions had started the chain of events that ended in tragedy for the Sudeten Germans. But its publication nearly cost the newspaper its right to publish. In 1949, on the other hand, a German newspaper was denouncing Czech outrages against the Germans in the strongest terms—and without any suggestion of reprisals by the Military Government. Of course, in the meantime Czechoslovakia had been drawn into the enemy camp by the Communist seizure of power in 1948.

The other event in 1948 was the Soviet blockade of West Berlin. All ground movement into the city by rail, road, and canal barge was halted on transparently frivolous pretexts by the Soviet military authorities. This was designed as a reprisal for the setting up of the Federal Republic in the West. The Soviet calculation was that the Western powers would not dare to resort to military force and would be forced out of Berlin, with immense loss of prestige. There were some fainthearts in Paris and London, even in Washington, who would have given up West Berlin or sacrificed the plan for an independent West German state under this pressure.

But General Clay rendered an incalculable service to the United States, to Germany, and to the whole free world by insisting that there be no retreat. He put the issue briefly, eloquently, and vigorously in a communication to the Department of the Army on April 10, 1948: [3] "We have lost Czechoslovakia. Norway is threatened. We retreat from Berlin. When Berlin falls Western Germany will be next. If we mean to hold Europe against communism we must not budge."

Clay had favored meeting the Soviet challenge by sending an armored convoy over the blocked highway. But a compromise solution was found, a gigantic and unprecedented airlift. Food, coal, medicines were flown into Berlin by huge fleets of transport planes, and the operation gained steadily in volume and efficiency. In the spring of 1949, when the Soviet Government called off its blockade without achieving its blackmailing objective, daily air deliveries had reached the figure of 8,000 tons, as much as Berlin had previously received by all other means of transportation. About 1.5 million tons of supplies were airlifted into the city.

Forty-five airmen, most of them Americans, a few British, lost their lives in accidents during this vast "air bridge" operation. The effect on German psychology, especially in Berlin, was very strong. Tempelhof Platz, in front of the air terminal, was promptly renamed Luftbrücke Platz (Air Bridge Place). One of the principal streets in the western section of Berlin, the street on which American headquarters was located, was renamed Clayallee. In the beginning General Clay had been a harsh proconsul, implementing the most severe decisions about denazification and limitation of industrial output. But all this was forgotten after his stand for Berlin, where his name today carries more prestige than that of any other American.

From the time when the big transport planes began to boom in on a high frequency schedule there has been a special warmth of feeling toward Americans in West Berlin. This is one European city that has never seen signs: "Yankee, Go Home." Indeed, even in the time when American occupation methods were harshest and most negative, Germans who criticized these methods were usually quick to reply *"Nein"* when asked whether they would like to see the Americans pull out of Germany altogether and leave the country to the Russians. Evidently there was a sense of distinction between greater and lesser evils.

Military government came to an end in West Germany in May, 1949, following protracted discussions among the Western powers and with the German political leaders about the details of a new "Basic Law" or "Provisional Constitution" for the establishment of a federal republic in the portion of Germany outside the Soviet Zone. Various conferences with the Soviet Union, looking to agreement on a united Germany, had ended in futile deadlock. However, the West Germans emphasized the point that the new constitutional arrangement could be regarded only as temporary—until Germany was reunited.

The new constitution was strongly federalistic in character; the official title of the new state was Federal Republic (Bundesrepublik). Especially among the Americans and the French, for differing reasons, there was strong, perhaps excessive distrust of any centralized German authority. Although the constitution has worked fairly well, experience has shown that the financial powers of the central government were unduly limited. The creation of a military establishment, not envisaged when the constitution was drawn up, has imposed heavy new expenditures upon the federal budget.

The constitution affirms basic civil and personal liberties, freedom of speech, press, and assembly, freedom of the ballot and trade-union organization, independence of the courts, safeguarding of the legal rights of individuals. It provides for a two-chamber legislature. One house, the Bundestag, elected every four years on the basis of universal suffrage and a modified proportional representation system, is the principal legislative body. The Bundestag elects the chancellor on the nomination of the president of the republic. The president is elected for a five-year term by the federal convention, a body composed of the members of the Bundestag, plus an equal number elected by the parliaments of the twelve *Länder,* or states.

The other house, the Bundesrat, is composed of representatives of the state governments, each state having no less than 3, no more than 5 delegates, depending on population. As of 1962 there were 41 members of the Bundesrat, besides 4 from West Berlin who could speak but not vote. With this same limitation, there are also representatives from West Berlin in the Bundestag. The allied governments, for fear of aggravating complications with Moscow, have refused to permit the incorporation of West Berlin into the Federal Republic. At the time when the Republic was founded such a step would have undermined the Western position that the city of Berlin, West and East, should be considered a single community under four-power authority and responsibility. This position had some value for a time as a means of making possible free movement between the two sectors of Berlin. But it was destroyed, for all practical purposes, when the separating wall was put up in August, 1961.

Political parties which seek, by their aims or by the behavior of their members, to impair the free and democratic basic order or to jeopardize the existence of the Republic are forbidden to exist. The highest judicial tribunal, the Federal Constitutional Court, elected half by the Bundestag, half by the Bundesrat, has ruled that both the Communist Party and the neo-Nazi Socialist Reich Party are unconstitutional and hence ineligible to conduct propaganda and take part in elections. There is an exception only for West Berlin, where the Communists, because of the special status of the city, are permitted to vote.

Simultaneously with the promulgation of the new constitution, military government of the Western zones of Germany came to an end. An administration of three high commissioners, American, British and French, was substituted, its headquarters located in the picturesquely situated Petersberg Hotel on a high hill across the Rhine from Bonn. The first American high commissioner was John J. McCloy, and his tact and understanding and close personal relationship with Chancellor Adenauer contributed much to the evolutionary transformation of the Federal Republic into a friendly ally.

Mainly because of French insistence, the Occupation Statute, which governed relations between the allied powers and Germany after the termination of Military Government, contained a formidably long list of external controls and restrictions. Germany was forbidden to maintain diplomatic or consular relations with foreign countries or to join international organizations. The occupation powers retained the right to supervise German domestic affairs and administration and to veto German legislation. Restrictive controls over German industry, including the fixing of annual steel production at the extremely low figure of 5.8 million tons, were retained. And dismantling, not only of war industries but of so-called surplus productive capacity, was to continue.

It was under this heavy burden of handicaps, prohibitions, and restrictions that the first freely elected German government since the fall of the Weimar Republic began to function under the leadership of Konrad Adenauer. Political parties had gradually revived in Germany under the occupation. The Social Democrats and Communists still had cores of leadership and membership that had escaped Hitler's persecution or had emerged from concentration camps or returned from exile abroad. A new party, the Christian Democratic Union, CDU, first sprang up in several regional centers, in West Berlin, Munich, Frankfurt, and Cologne. It represented a combination of former adherents of the Catholic Center Party, with a substantial contingent of Protestant voters. It was soon to become the dominant element in the federal government and also in a number of state governments, especially in the more Catholic parts of the country. Closely affiliated with it was the Bavarian Christian Social Union, which, however, in line with Bavarian particularism, retained a certain political autonomy.

At first, especially in Hesse, the CDU displayed some hospitality to such left-wing ideas as nationalization of basic industries and extensive planning of economic life. But as German economic life recovered with amazing speed under the impetus of Economics Minister Erhard's policy of rejecting controls, the more conservative trend in the party—with which Adenauer had always sympathized —took the upper hand. The CDU in 1949 went to the voters with a program that included many social welfare measures (this was inevitable in a country with Germany's high proportion of destitute refugees, widows, orphans, and war cripples), but with a firm commitment to the private enterprise system and the rights of private property.

The CDU emerged from the election as the strongest single party, with 7,590,000 votes and 141 seats. It was closely followed by the Social Democrats (SDP), with 6,900,000 votes and 130 seats. The remaining seats were divided among the Free Democrats (FDP), with 52, the German Party, with 17, and the Communists with 15. The FDP was a middle-class liberal party, suspicious of clerical influences in the CDU and opposed to Marxism. The German Party was the most conservative of the competing groups. The showing of the Communists was markedly weak, compared with their strength in the last years of the Weimar Republic.

Both the German Party and the Communist Party have disappeared from the political scene, the former for lack of followers, the latter because the constitutional court ruled it a subversive organization. It is highly probable that the Communist Party in later elections would have failed to poll the 5 per cent of the total vote necessary to qualify for representation in the Bundestag. A substitute left-wing pacifist party, the Deutsche Friedens Union [4] ("German Peace Union"), although praised in the Soviet Zone, has never won any significant vote.

The new Bundestag elected Konrad Adenauer chancellor by 202 votes out of 402. This was just enough for a majority and gave rise to the story that he gained office the first time by voting for himself. The stern old statesman has often indicated that he does consider himself the best man for the job. But his choice was not by such a narrow margin. There were 44 blank ballots, some of which would almost certainly have gone to Adenauer on a later vote. At a conference of CDU leaders at his villa in Rhöndorf, across the Rhine and upstream from the university town of Bonn, which had been selected as the capital of the Federal Republic, Adenauer made clear his intention to exclude the Social Democrats from his cabinet.[5] He had the votes to support a moderate conservative coalition of CDU, FDP, and the German Party, and it was on this basis that he organized his first administration.

For the next few years Adenauer carried on a two-front political struggle, against the Social Democrats in the Bundestag and against the high commissioners to speed the full restoration of German sovereignty. He won both contests clearly and decisively.

Leader of the Social Democrats until he was replaced after his death by the milder, rather colorless Erich Ollenhauer, and still later by Willy Brandt, was Kurt Schumacher, a brilliant, passionate, bitter man, who had suffered more than his share in Germany's turbulent era of wars abroad and tyranny at home. He had lost a leg and an arm as a result of combat service in World War I and maltreatment in a Nazi concentration camp.

Schumacher believed that the Social Democrats had missed a great political opportunity, after the signing of the Treaty of Versailles, by standing for a policy of fulfillment at a time when the tide of public emotion was running in a strongly opposite direction. So he directed his parliamentary fire against Adenauer for being too subservient to the Western powers and he fought every proposal for European integration on the ground that Germany's interests were being neglected. On the same basis he opposed German rearmament, since, in his opinion, the Western powers were not making a big enough contribution to assure the success of this rearmament.

What Schumacher failed to grasp was the complete change in the German mood as an aftermath of the two great wars. In the wreckage of Hitler's Third Reich old nationalist slogans sounded empty and meaningless, and association with the free nations of America and Western Europe looked distinctly attractive. Nor did the Social Democrats have any more success with their argument that Adenauer, by his pro-Western orientation, was sacrificing the prospect of German reunification. Soviet willingness to consent to a merger of its zone with West Germany on tolerable terms was extremely dubious, to put it mildly. The issue whether alliance with the West or unification should have the priority was never put to a direct vote, although Adenauer's electoral victories in 1953 and 1957 might indicate the answer. But it is my impression, gained from repeated visits to Germany in the years of decision, from 1949 until 1954, that most Germans preferred the secure protection of America and the Western alliance to the uncertain prospect of a neutralized status, with all the possibilities this would have opened up for Soviet pressure and Communist subversion.

The rapid improvement in the economic situation also worked in Adenauer's favor. This was reflected in the Bundestag election of 1953, when the percentage of votes cast for the CDU leaped from 31 to 45.2, while the Social Democrats sustained a slight loss.

For a time the system of dual authority between the German government and the high commissioners almost inevitably worked with a good deal of friction. The habit of interfering in German internal concerns, developed under Military Government, was hard to outgrow. Some of the special privileges of the early occupation, increasingly incongruous as Germany moved toward self-government, were hard to forego. There were moments when Adenauer's normal attitude of coolheaded patience threatened to give way and the old chancellor threatened to resign and leave all responsibility to the high commissioners, rather than submit to petty meddling from the Petersberg.[6] But time was on Adenauer's side. As early as November, 1949 he obtained the exemption of some important factories from dismantling, and he secured permission to set up consulates abroad and authorization for Germany to join such international organizations as the OEEC (Organization for European Economic Co-operation), set up to co-ordinate the distribution of American aid under the Marshall Plan.

The profound change in the American attitude was reflected in the altered positions of two men who were closely associated both with the harsh and the mild phases of the American occupation. John J. McCloy, in the War Department, had been the author of the JCS 1067, of which Secretary of War Stimson says: [7]

"Rereading this order two years later, Stimson found it a painfully negative document. Although it contained no orders for economic destruction, it was certainly not designed to make the rebuilding of Germany an easy task, and instead it explicitly ordered the American military governor to 'take no steps (a) looking to the economic rehabilitation of Germany or (b) designed to maintain and strengthen the German economy'—with the exception that he might act to insure reparation payments and to prevent starvation or rebellion. Yet in the spring of 1945 JCS 1067 seemed so much less punitive and destructive than earlier proposals that Stimson found the final draft 'a fairly good paper.' "

Yet as high commissioner, McCloy was the pacemaker in hastening the release of Germany from occupation restrictions and paving the way for the return to full German sovereignty.

There was a similar evolution in the stand of Gen. Lucius D. Clay. It has already been pointed out that the image of Clay changed from a "hard" occupation commander to that of a hero in the eyes of the Germans during the blockade of Berlin. Clay also became a vigorous advocate of giving the German Government more freedom of action and eliminating artificial economic restrictions. In his memoirs he complains frequently of the negative, obstructive attitude of the French. But he found one high French political figure, Robert Schuman, at various times prime minister and foreign minister, who shared his viewpoint. Clay gives the following summary of a talk with Schuman, then foreign minister, at the Quai d'Orsay on March 20, 1949: [8]

"I repeated that French lead in rapprochement of the West to

West Germany was most desirable; that we could not hope to attract Germans to the West if each time they turned westward we 'kicked them in the face.' He agreed.

"Meeting was most friendly and cordial. I hope M. Schuman will carry out his views. His subordinates in France and Germany may be expected to try to defeat his efforts."

Schuman made a conspicuous contribution to Franco-German rapprochement when he pushed through a new organization, the Coal and Steel Community, under the plan that bears his name. This Community provides for the integration of the coal and steel and iron industries in six nations, France, Germany, Italy, Belgium, the Netherlands, and Luxembourg, under an international High Authority. Customs barriers for these products were abolished and cartels and other combinations in restraint of free competitive trade were declared unlawful. The High Authority was given power to impose fines in cases of proved violation of the conditions of this agreement, which came into force on July 25, 1952.

Although some German industrialists have long complained that France still enjoys a competitive advantage in steel export because of differing French and German methods of calculating and levying excise taxes, the Schuman Plan, on balance, was of distinct advantage to Germany. It meant the end of the clumsy foreign control of the Ruhr steel and coal industries. The limitation to 5.8 million tons a year of German steel production was dropped, and all other limitations on German industrial output were also tossed on the scrapheap. The Coal and Steel Community and the institutions which it created furnished a pilot project for the bigger and more ambitious scheme of a European Economic Community, which went into effect in 1958.

The intensification of the cold war by the invasion of South Korea by a North Korean army outfitted by the Soviet Union speeded up the transition from occupation to alliance. Winston Churchill, as leader of the Conservative Party in the House of Commons, raised his powerful voice in favor of German rearmament on March 16, 1950. Mr. Churchill, not for the first time, was ahead of public opinion. But a conference of American, British, and French foreign ministers in New York, in September, 1950, discussed seriously the buildup of European defense forces with German participation. This conference was also marked by a declaration in favor of "unification of Germany on a basis which respects fundamental liberties. . . . Pending the unification of Germany the three governments consider the Government of the Federal Republic as the only German Government freely and legitimately constituted and therefore entitled to speak for Germany as the representative of the German people."

Steps to terminate the state of war with Germany were announced and the three powers agreed to treat any attack on the Federal Republic or on West Berlin as an attack on them. So, five years before the Federal Republic received recognition of its full sovereignty, the three Western powers unilaterally extended guaranties which were later repeated during the final stages of negotiating Germany's membership in the NATO alliance. These were the obligation to defend West Germany and West Berlin and the designation of the Federal Republic as the sole legitimate representative of the German people. By implication this ruled out any recognition of the satellite regime in the Soviet Zone.

French Prime Minister René Pleven on October 26, 1950 came out with a scheme designed to overcome the reluctance of many Frenchmen to see Germans in military uniforms again. This envisaged the creation of a closely integrated European army, in which French, German, Italian, Belgian, Dutch, and Luxembourg units would be so closely mingled that no nation could play a dominating role. There was much talk of European integration, economic and political, at the time; the EDC (European Defense Community) was conceived as a suitable supplement of the Coal and Steel Community and the European Common Market, then still in an embryonic stage of discussion. Optimists even drew up a blueprint for a European parliament to fill out the picture of unity. But it proved impossible, in the end, to overcome the French psychological aversion to close military association with Germany. After long delays and after the five prospective partners had ratified the plan, the French Chamber of Deputies rejected it in August, 1954. The adverse vote was due to a combination of followers of General de Gaulle, who objected to "denationalizing" the French Army, and

Communists, who opposed any move toward unity among non-Communist nations.

But the impetus to a German military partnership had gone too far to be reversed. Great Britain consented to associate itself with a new military establishment called Western European Union, in which the six continental powers were also members. At the end of the year a very reluctant Chamber of Deputies ratified by small majorities German admission to NATO, German rearmament, and German association with the Western European Union. These had been the decisions of a nine-power conference in Paris in October.

It was obviously impossible to treat Germany on a basis of inferiority while inviting her to take a large part in the defense of Europe. So, once the principle of a German defense contribution had been accepted, restrictions and discriminations began to fall like ninepins. A considerably modified and much milder Occupation Statute came into force in March, 1951; this was quickly followed by the establishment of a German Ministry of Foreign Affairs. On May 2 Germany became a full member of the Council of Europe, an organization with merely consultative functions but a useful forum for the interchange of ideas between Europeans of varying political viewpoints.

The Schuman Plan took care of limitations on steel output and foreign controls in the Ruhr, and the prohibitions and limitations on shipbuilding, aircraft, chemicals, and other industries gradually disappeared. When the stage of full sovereignty was reached in May, 1955, the only important reservation was Germany's voluntary obligation not to manufacture nuclear, chemical, or biological weapons. There were also some provisions about maintaining anticartel regulations, directed largely against the reconstruction of the Krupp properties in their full extent; but there has been no effort to enforce these.

As the attitude of the Western powers shifted more definitely from domination to friendly co-operation, the German government, under Adenauer's forceful leadership, took one step after another to prove that a new German state, willing to honor moral and material obligations, had emerged in the aftermath of Hitler's tyranny. Reference has already been made to the hearty German co-operation in the visitors' exchange program with the United States, and similar contacts were established with other Western nations.

The world economic crisis that began in 1929 had caused a suspension of payment of Germany's obligations in foreign currencies. The Nazi regime would doubtless have repudiated these altogether if it had won the war. Following negotiations between German and foreign bankers and financial experts, an agreement was reached in London on February 27, 1953, providing for the settlement of Germany's foreign obligations at a cost to the Federal Republic of about $3.3 billion. Thanks to Germany's long series of favorable payment balances, much of this debt was paid off ahead of the scheduled dates. Advance repayment of German government obligations in the early sixties helped to relieve the strain on the United States gold reserve due to a succession of balance of payments deficits.

The Bundestag on March 18, 1953, again under vigorous prodding from the chancellor, ratified an agreement to pay to the state of Israel about $800 million as a kind of collective indemnity for the genocidal crimes of the Nazi leadership against Jews of many nationalities. Individual restitution grants to surviving Jews who had suffered at the hands of the Nazis brought the total payments of expiation to over $4 billion. The reparation transfers to Israel were mostly in the form of German machinery and equipment, a very useful asset for the industrial build-up of the new state. Threats of Arab boycott of German goods (threats that were not carried out, incidentally) failed to swerve Adenauer from a course which he regarded as right and just.

One of Adenauer's hardest struggles was to win German endorsement of the rearmament which was contemplated first under the European Defense Community, later under the Western European Union, under which a much looser form of integration was set up, troop units of the various countries remaining under their national officers. The psychology reflected in the expressions *ohne uns* and *ohne mich* ("count us out" or "count me out") was strong.

The extreme demilitarization measures in the first years of the occupation left some psychological effect; still more important was the widespread feeling of utter nihilistic frustration after the total defeat of 1945. General opposition to taking up arms was fused in some cases with concern for German unity, with fear that the new weapons might be used against other Germans in the Soviet Zone. The Social Democratic Party fought the measures for a new German military establishment by every means—agitation, legal appeals, and speeches in the Bundestag. The CDU lost ground in some local elections. But Adenauer, with a parliamentary majority enlarged by the second national election, pushed through the necessary legislation. The decisive vote came on February 27, 1955, when the Bundestag ratified the Paris treaties, approving Germany's entrance into NATO 314 to 157.

In the same session of the Bundestag there was a closer vote on one of Adenauer's least popular decisions. This was acceptance of an autonomous status for the Saar, a region with a solidly German population of a little over one million, adjacent to Alsace-Lorraine and long coveted by France for its rich coal reserves and developed steel industry. Ever since the end of the war the French had made a point of keeping the Saar detached from Germany. They did not include the territory in their occupation zone and they promoted an unrepresentative local collaborationist administration headed by Johannes Hoffmann. The Saar, as a visiting journalist remarked, was the most civilized police state in Europe; the French and their local agents confined themselves to little pinpricks and economic discrimination against local businessmen of outspoken German sympathies. But a police state it was; a trip to the area in 1953 convinced me that the majority of the inhabitants resented a separation from Germany that was unnatural on national grounds and that seemed less tolerable as economic conditions across the border steadily improved.

Adenauer, willing to make considerable concessions for the sake of reconciliation with France, accepted a French scheme which proposed not direct annexation of the Saar, but an autonomous "European" status for the territory. The chancellor obtained from a very unwilling Bundestag endorsement of this arrangement by a vote of 262 to 202. On this issue many Free Democrats joined the Social Democrats in opposition. There was a feeling, even among

Adenauer's supporters, that he had gone too far in renouncing the right of the Saar Germans to rejoin the Federal Republic.

But Adenauer was prepared to pay even this high price for Germany's admission to the European club. And in the end it turned out that the Saar price did not have to be paid, after all. For when the Saar population had a chance to vote on the proposed autonomous status, on October 23, 1955, they voted it down by a majority of more than two to one. Perhaps the Saarlanders could have been won for some such settlement when physical conditions in Germany were extremely bad, immediately after the war. But by 1955 the economic miracle was in high gear, while France suffered from chronically shaky governments and an even shakier currency. Under these conditions the pull of nationalist sentiment was irresistible.

There had been some talk in France of reversion to the former system of French administration with a puppet local government if autonomy should be rejected. But wiser counsels prevailed; it was realized in Paris that what might have been legally admissible was no longer politically possible. The local pro-French administration resigned. Following further Paris-Bonn negotiations an agreement was reached on June 5, 1956, under which the Saar was to be reincorporated with Germany politically on January 1, 1957, and economically not later than the end of 1959. Among the economic problems to be solved was the changeover from French to German currency. This treaty was enthusiastically and unanimously ratified by the Bundestag, and the last serious irritant in postwar Franco-German relations disappeared. Indeed, following the agreement on German rearmament and the retrocession of the Saar to Germany, the whole previous French policy of delay and obstructionism seemed to melt away. The stage was set for such further developments as the training of German troops on French soil, the ceremonial exchange of visits between Adenauer and de Gaulle in 1962, and de Gaulle's greeting to " the great German people."

The climax of Germany's political recovery was reached on May 5, 1955, when the Occupation Statute was terminated, the high commissioners became ambassadors, and the German government began to operate with no shadow of external restraint. It had been a long, steep climb from complete dependence under Military Government through the intermediate stage of supervision by the high commissioners; but the summit had been reached at last.

Adenauer had regained for Germany both its proper frontier in the West and the political and economic advantages of close association with the United States and Western Europe. If reunion with the sundered part of the country in the Soviet Zone was still out of reach, the chancellor had made the Federal Republic a partner in a powerful military alliance which offered the best, indeed the only effective guaranty against a Soviet effort to force communism on the whole country. And it is arguable that, with the larger, more populous, and more productive part of Germany a member of such an alliance, the ultimate prospect of reunion, distant at best, is brighter than it would have been if Germany had elected a status of weak neutralism. At any rate Adenauer's decision for the Western course in foreign policy was made, and even his political opponents, the Social Democrats, now recognize that this decision is binding for Germany's future.

NOTES TO CHAPTER III

1 As described later in the chapter, the Saar finally returned to Germany.

2 See Lucius D. Clay, *Decision in Germany* (Garden City, N.Y.: Doubleday & Company, Inc., 1950), p. 79.

3 *Ibid.,* p. 361.

4 A current German joke is that the initials DFU stand not for Deutsche Friedens Union ("German Peace Union") but *Deutsche Freunde Ulbricht* ("German Friends of Ulbricht," Communist dictator in the Soviet Zone).

5 On this point, and for other details of the emergence of the CDU as a force in German politics, see Arnold J. Heidenhammer, *Adenauer and the CDU* (The Hague: Martinus Nijhoff, 1960), p. 180.

6 See Fritz René Alleman, *Bonn ist nicht Weimar* (Cologne-Berlin: Kiepenheuer and Witsch, 1956), p. 161.

7 See Henry L. Stimson and McGeorge Bundy, *On Active Service* (New York: Harper & Row, Publishers, 1948), p. 582.

8 Clay, *op. cit.,* p. 427.

CHAPTER IV

The Economic Miracle—and Afterward

"WHAT has taken place in Germany during the past nine years is anything but a miracle. It is the result of the honest efforts of a whole people who, in keeping with the principles of liberty, were given the opportunity of using personal initiative and human energy. If the German example has any value beyond the frontiers of the country it can only be that of proving to the world at large the blessings of both personal and economic freedom." [1]

Despite this modest disclaimer by Ludwig Erhard, the principal architect of the German economic recovery and growth after the war, there is something miraculous about the transformation of Germany from a desolate shambles, a land of seemingly hopeless poverty, hunger, and gloom into one of the most prosperous countries of Europe, a pacemaker in realizing the goal of an affluent society.

The rapid process of recovery had great significance, politically as well as economically. More, perhaps, than any other factor, it accounts for the almost complete absence of left-wing and right-wing extremism in postwar Germany, for the virtual extinction of Nazi sympathies, and for the failure of communism to regain anything like its prewar following. Adenauer's policy of moderate conservatism at home and unconditional orientation toward the West in foreign policy went into effect more smoothly and with less opposition because every year the Germans could see visible improvements in everything that affected their standard of living: in food, clothing, housing, employment, and opportunities for travel abroad.

Mainly the phoenixlike emergence of a prosperous West Germany from the rubble and dust and ashes of the lost war was an impressive assertion of the German will to live and willingness to work without watching clocks and counting hours. Every industrial town in Germany has its little epic of workers, receiving little or no pay, clearing up damage, salvaging machines that had been only partly damaged, restoring factory buildings sometimes almost with their bare hands. Then, in their spare time, they went about repairing and rebuilding their own homes, so far as this was possible.

An important factor in the recovery, which Germans are perhaps readier than other Europeans to acknowledge, was American aid, mainly through the Marshall Plan, from which Germany benefited to the amount of about $3.2 billion. (Liability for repayment of $1.2 billion was assumed by Germany as part of a general foreign debts settlement.)[2] The timing of the Marshall Plan aid, mostly in the form of American machinery, equipment, cotton, and other raw materials, from 1949 until 1952, was precisely right. It came after the immediate postwar hunger and prostration had been outlived and gave a powerful stimulus to a process of reconstruction that was already in full swing. And it was accompanied and made more effective by a progressive abandonment of dismantling and restrictions on the output of German industries.

Two developments immediately after the end of the war which Germans regarded as social and economic disasters, and which were certainly not designed to help Germany, curiously enough in the end brought some benefits.

One of these was the flooding of Germany with some twelve million destitute refugees. At first they lived rather miserably in barracks, shacks, and improvised housing, although German efficiency helped to make their reception less chaotic than it might have been in some other countries. But the majority of these newcomers were hardworking people with a passionate desire to find jobs and regain their former living standards, and as industry expanded, the refugees began to represent a valuable source of labor power.

I saw an illustration of this point in Stuttgart, where I became acquainted with a group of Germans who formerly lived in Yugoslavia. They had gotten out with the retreating German armies later looking back with sympathy to less fortunate relatives and friends who had ended in Tito's concentration camps. When I first met them, in 1949, they were living in very rough, primitive quarters. But when I returned two years later almost all the men had found work, mostly in the booming building industry, and the children were getting on well in the local schools. Some families had already moved into new apartments and desire to return to their homes, now under Communist rule, was nonexistent.

"The refugees were pacemakers for all of us," said a Frankfurt banker. "Because they had lost almost everything they possessed, they were willing to take any jobs, to accept low pay, if necessary, to work long hours, just to make a new start. In a sense they took the places of millions of ablebodied workers who were killed in the war. We should never have come so far in economic buildup without them."

One constantly finds examples of how this influx of hand and brain workers, which continued until the separation wall was put up in Berlin because of the unfavorable conditions in the Soviet Zone, helped along the economic miracle. One German girl, who spoke excellent English and spent some of her vacation time reading British and American authors, remarked that of her entire graduating class in high school, in a town in the Soviet Zone, only one had remained. The others, above average young people in training and knowledge, had all come to West Germany in search of better opportunities. In Düsseldorf I met a prominent businessman, owner of a flourishing new cosmetics factory, a Mr. Schneider. His plant had formerly been in Dresden, in the Soviet Zone. Realizing that private business in the Soviet Zone was doomed, he had gathered a few of his trained specialists and his business blueprints and moved to Düsseldorf. His new factory there was yielding a good profit; his former plant in Dresden, as he heard from some of his old workers, was declining for lack of skilled management. Such cases, multiplied many thousands of times, help to explain the drive and impetus of the German economic upsurge.

Like the inflow of refugees, the dismantling program for German industry worked out better than might have been expected. The original Allied plan was to restrict Germany to about 65 per cent of the industrial output of 1936, the last year for which production was more or less normal, before the big Nazi drive for militarization. About 1,500 plants were to be destroyed, if they had military value, or transferred to Allied countries, if they were useful for peacetime production. There were successive cuts in this program and it ceased altogether after 1951. Even before that year it had become ludicrously at variance with the new policy of helping Germany through the Marshall Plan.

In the opinion of one of the ablest and most careful students of postwar German economic history,[3] the value of dismantled equipment and machinery was about $500 million. Probably no occupation policy aroused so much bitterness in Germany, where it was regarded as a wanton attack on the livelihood of communities which depended on the demolished plants. And the harm to Germany was out of all proportion to the benefit to the recipient countries, because the stripped machinery had often been constructed for the special use of the plant from which it was taken. Yet in this case also there was a silver lining, from the German standpoint. Much of the equipment removed was obsolescent. By way of replacement Germany obtained, either through the Marshall Plan or through the profits of its reviving industries, equipment of the most modern type. There were cases when after a factory had been stripped for reparations it was re-equipped in up-to-date fashion with the aid of the Marshall Plan.

Of all the forces that made for the German economic miracle the strongest was the bold reliance by Economics Minister Ludwig Erhard on the immense inherent vitality of economic free initiative. This daring experiment was made possible when the Economic Council (*Beirat*) of the united American and British Zones (at that time there was no German Government, only an Economic Council) on July 7, 1948 promulgated a law[4] giving the director of economic affairs, Ludwig Erhard, the right, as he puts it, "to throw into the wastepaper basket in one swoop hundreds of decrees promulgating controls and prices." Erhard took full advantage of this authorization, and almost with a wave of the hand, swept out of existence the system of rigid price controls which had been established by the Nazis and taken over practically unchanged by the occupation powers. As a logical sequel the existing freeze on wages was lifted on November 3.

At that time the German authorities had no right to change any single fixed price or fixed wage. But there was a loophole; the whole system could be swept away with impunity. Probably the feeling was that no German would dare to take such a drastic step. But Erhard made his wager on economic freedom. When General Clay informed him that all the American economic experts were gravely concerned, Erhard replied: "So are mine." But his experiment was allowed to stick and it produced one of the resounding success stories of postwar Europe.

Erhard was strongly influenced in his economic thinking by such neoclassical economists as the late Rudolf Eucken and the brilliant Wilhelm Röpke, an old-fashioned German liberal who went into exile during the Hitler period and became a naturalized Swiss citizen. It was and is Erhard's conviction, held with passionate intellectual and moral earnestness, that human beings will produce more if they are allowed to follow their own interest than if they are told by some state authority what they must produce and how much they may receive in compensation. This idea is more widely accepted now than it was at the end of the war, when economic regimentation because of military necessities was the rule, even in the United States, and socialist and planned economy theories were widely accepted in Western Europe. It was the brilliant success of Erhard's appeal to economic individualism, tempered by the recognized necessity to provide subsistence and care for widows and orphans, for the old and disabled,[5] that contributed to a fairly prolonged political eclipse of socialism in Europe, outside of Scandinavia.

A vivid passage in Margaret Mitchell's popular novel *Gone with the Wind* shows Scarlett O'Hara grubbing in the fields of her ruined plantation for enough vegetables to sustain life, vowing that, once this crisis has been outlived, she will never be poor again. Germany in 1945–47 was as flat on its back as Georgia after Sherman's march to the sea. And there was a mass impulse among the Germans to overcome this state of individual and national poverty as soon as possible, and at any cost in hard labor. It was this impulse that was touched off and given scope by Erhard's daring gamble that economic freedom was the formula that would pull Germany out of the depths most quickly, painlessly, and successfully.

It was a gamble, and the first years of the new free economy had their moments of danger and difficulty. Stunned by the possession of money that would really buy something, the Germans after the currency reform went on a purchasing spree that sent prices skyrocketing. There was talk of failure of the experiment; some bureaucrats dusted off old schemes of price control and rationing.

But as prices rose, so did production. The free market, as Erhard foresaw, proved a reliable instrument for keeping demand and supply in equilibrium. By 1949 prices had fallen appreciably and real wages were going up. Until the end of the fifties Germany enjoyed one of the most stable price levels in the world, another positive factor for the economic miracle. Balanced budgets and a tight money policy on the part of the central banking authorities produced this result. Between 1952 and 1957 the cost of living in Germany rose less than 5 per cent, as against about 15 per cent in Great Britain, Norway, and Sweden, and almost 20 per cent in the Netherlands.[6] This internal price stability was a mighty aid to the surging German drive for export markets.

In the first years of economic revival one of Germany's most serious handicaps was the necessity of operating on a very thin financial shoestring. The country was completely broke, possessing no means of paying for foreign imports. The new mark was viewed with some distrust abroad and sold at a discount of some 40 per cent in Switzerland. Its only backing was a small advance of American dollars. German exports at this time consisted mainly of such raw materials as coal and timber, and one of Germany's numerous disabilities was an obligation to sell coal at a controlled price considerably below that of the international free market.

Erhard was eager to get away from the clumsy method of barter in international trade, in which Germany was required to buy from every country just as much as it sold to that country. He wanted to open Germany's markets to foreign imports. He believed that the more Germany could buy abroad, comforts and luxuries as well as staple necessities, the more it would be able to sell abroad. He also repeatedly expressed the conviction that German industry, stiff and stagnant after a long period of state control and isolation from normal commercial contacts, would benefit from a breeze of foreign competition and that foreign imports would be an excellent check on profiteering.

All these contentions were to be strikingly vindicated by later experience, as the exports of the Federal Republic—minus the Soviet Zone and the considerable area annexed by Poland—far exceeded those of prewar Germany within its much more extensive frontiers. But in the beginning Germany was so short of foreign exchange that a wave of panic buying of raw materials after the outbreak of war in Korea in the summer of 1950 created serious difficulties.

As a final contribution to European financial stability in the wake of the Marshall Plan, the United States had furnished financial backing for a system known as EPU (European Payments Union). All members of the OEEC were eligible for participation and were entitled to draw specified amounts from the central fund of the EPU. This made it possible to get away from bilateral barter and to restore a limited amount of multilateral trade.

Germany's EPU allowance was on the verge of exhaustion in 1950 and it was necessary to borrow an additional $120 million. Free admission of imports had to be suspended, to Erhard's great regret. But this setback was only temporary. The international balance of payments soon swung heavily in Germany's favor, because the Korean War led to big arms expenditures in the United States and other Western countries. Here again a prohibition of maintaining armed forces, designed as a punitive measure, worked out to Germany's economic advantage. German rearmament was still six years ahead, and there was plenty of unused plant capacity to take care of orders for nonmilitary goods which poured in from all parts of the world.

The balance-of-payments crisis of 1950 was to be Germany's last. From this time Germany's reserve of gold and foreign currency began to swell like the legendary hoard of the Nibelungen, until it grew from zero to $8 billion, far more than any German government had possessed in the most prosperous prewar times. This was the result of a continuous lopsidedly favorable balance of exports over imports. In the late fifties the situation became positively embarrassing to the German financial authorities. There were bitter complaints, especially in Great Britain, that Germany was absorbing an unduly large share of the world's gold and dollars, and the piling up of huge reserves in the vaults of the Bundesbank, in Frankfurt was unhealthy for Germany's own monetary system and required drastic fiscal measures to avert inflation.

In recent years the German government has taken various measures designed to counteract Germany's Midas touch in international finance. Prewar debts were repaid ahead of time. The German contribution of aid to the economically less developed areas of the world was stepped up. To the great dissatisfaction of German manufacturers, interested in export markets, the value of the mark was raised by 5 per cent in the spring of 1961. This had the effect of making imports cheaper and exports more expensive, thereby counteracting Germany's tendency to build up a big surplus in international trade. As will be shown later in this chapter, wage increases and other inflationary pressures are now changing the economic picture from what it was when Germany had a classical type of smoothly functioning free enterprise economy and was consequently able to undersell its competitors in foreign markets.

The decade of the fifties was the golden age of the economic miracle. It was an interlude between the old problems of hunger, want, and wartime destruction and certain new problems that face Germany now, largely as a result of overfull employment. A few facts and figures point up what was literally a transition from rags to riches.

Between 1950 and 1961 German industrial output grew more than two and a half times, leaving far behind all comparisons with the prewar level, which was reached in 1950. By 1961 Germany had passed Great Britain and become the second largest exporting country in the world, surpassed only by the United States. The value of its sales abroad in that year was over $12.5 billion. The German automobile industry alone, thanks to the fantastic success of the Volkswagen, sold cars abroad to a value of about one and a quarter billion dollars. The national income increased from 75 billion marks to 230 billion marks—almost a threefold gain, even after allowance is made for a moderate rise in the price level. During this booming decade the German rate of economic growth was almost double that of the United States and well ahead of that of the Soviet Union, at least in the goods that make a difference in the standard of living. The industrial capacity of the Federal Republic now exceeds that of the undivided Germany which existed before the war.

It has been pointed out that certain measures which were applied in a spirit of retribution against Germany, the forcing of millions of refugees into the country, the dismantling of industry, the prohibition against armed forces, almost uncannily worked, in some ways, to Germany's advantage. This was also true as regards another measure of spoliation, the confiscation of German industrial patents, such as the formula for making the famous Cologne water. A German industrialist, referring to this, remarked to me, half defiantly, half jokingly: "You can steal our patents. But you cannot steal our brains."

And events were to prove him right. The loss of the patents, especially in the chemical industry, led to concentration on research for new formulas. Now over half the production of the chemical industry consists of products that have been developed since 1948. One of the targets of American crusading zeal in the first phase of the occupation was the German system of cartels, or trusts. There was a drive to break up large concentrations of capital, sometimes reasonably, from an economic standpoint, sometimes unreasonably. So the banking system was fragmented to a harmful degree, but it has been largely reintegrated into three big systems: the IG Farben, largest chemical firm in the world after Dupont, was required to split into three independent companies. Most Germans agree that the former organization of IG Farben was top-heavy and overcentralized. Now each of the three new branches does more business than the former parent firm.

Although businessmen, engineers, and technicians were the most obvious beneficiaries of the economic miracle, although some of the newly rich set patterns of extravagant living, the mighty wave of economic upsurge conspicuously raised the living standard of the whole population, and not least of the industrial workers. Real wages doubled during the fifties. Motor cars, television sets, refrigerators, washing machines, all sorts of household conveniences found more and more customers. By 1960 the shattered Germany of 1945, living from the crumbs that fell from the occupation tables, was well on the way to becoming an American-style affluent society—a goal that may be reached by 1970. There are innumerable examples of livelihoods regained, of devastated communities dramatically revived. The old ecclesiastical town of Würzburg, famous for its baroque architecture, was so thoroughly bombed out during the war that there was serious consideration of a plan to rebuild on another site. Würzburg was referred to as "the grave of the Main" (the river on which it is located). But the town has been rebuilt on its old site, and with an effort, so far as possible, to preserve some of the eighteenth-century atmosphere. In Hamburg in 1962 I talked with an old friend Max Brauer, a Social Democrat (of the distinctly undogmatic type) who returned from America and took out German citizenship in exchange for the American citizenship which he had acquired during the Hitler period. He was elected mayor of Hamburg and has devoted all his high-power energy to restoring the devastated city.

"At the end of the war," he said, "most of the shipping in the desolate port of Hamburg consisted of 3,000 ships which the Nazis had sunk to block the entrance. Last year 22,000 ships under many flags berthed at the new renovated port of Hamburg. Our foreign trade was greater than it has ever been, even though we lost our former hinterland in the East. There were equally impressive results in building schools, hospitals, houses, in laying out parks."

Germany has been building at such a tempo that it now possesses more housing units than it had before the war, although the new apartments are often smaller and less solidly built than the old. By 1961 a third of the population of the Federal Republic was living in new houses. Between 1950 and 1961 more than $25 billion was invested in new housing projects, half by state and local authorities, half by individuals. Germany has been adding over 500,000 apartments and small houses every year. Anyone who travels in Germany can bear witness to the feverish speed at which ruins are being removed, partially destroyed buildings renovated, and new housing put up. The sound of the bulldozer, the drill, and the hammer may be heard anywhere, day and night.

The boom extends not only to housing, but to the construction of big new office buildings which are changing the skyline of such cities as Düsseldorf, Cologne, and Munich. The building industry has been one of the prime movers in the permanent German boom. Indeed, to some of the experts in the Bundesbank and other financial institutions, building is something of a headache, because costs have shot up to levels unmatched in other fields.

A business opportunity on which Krupp and other German firms, large and small, were quick to seize is the demand for machinery and all kinds of industrial equipment from the economically retarded countries of Asia, South America, and to a lesser extent, Africa. In an early phase of the recovery I was shown over the big Krupp machine-building plant in Essen. The engineer who accompanied me spoke of a big order for locomotives from Indonesia. To a question whether Indonesia had acceptable means of payment he confidently replied: *"Wahrscheinlich, ja"* ("Apparently, yes"), and German firms could be counted on to make sure of being paid. Krupp also made a deal with Turkey on a semibarter basis, taking chrome and other valuable metals in exchange for machines, and German firms have been very active in India and the Near East. The fact that Germany has no colonial possessions, having lost its few African colonies after World War I, is a psychological advantage in lands which have been recently freed from colonial rule and are abnormally sensitive on the subject.

But the biggest German advantages have been the attractive prices and quality of its products, especially in heavy engineering, and in the intensity of its foreign sales methods. There is a story, no doubt apocryphal, that a South American country sent requests for certain machine installations to Great Britain, France, and Germany. From Great Britain came an old catalogue, from France no reply at all, from Germany the desired eqiupment, with a team of engineers and technicians to set it up. High-powered salesmanship and long-term credits, guaranteed by the government, have been two aids to German progress in foreign markets.

It is sometimes argued by critics of a free economy that Germany might have recovered just as fast, and with more social justice, if more plans and priorities had been maintained. Of course it is never possible to say with absolute certainty what would have happened if a different course had been followed. But there is one bit of impressive evidence indicating that freedom produced better economic results than planning. This is the comparison between what actually happened and the forecasts of the so-called Long Term Program (LTP), worked out in co-operation by German and American economic planners in 1948 and submitted to the Economic Cooperation Administration, which administered Marshall Plan aid.[7]

The LTP estimated that Germany would reach an industrial output about 10 per cent above that of 1936 in 1952–53. The actual figure achieved was about 50 per cent higher. The planners aimed at a standard of living 20 per cent lower than that of 1936 in 1952–53. This goal was reached in 1950. German export trade was supposed by the planners to reach a figure of $2.8 billion when the Marshall Plan came to an end in 1952. The actual accomplishment by that time had exceeded $4 billion. So it seems that Germany would have revived much more slowly if the national economy had been put in a straitjacket of tight economic planning, what the Europeans call "dirigism."

The results of Erhard's economic freedom policy also stand in very favorable contrast both with what happened in the Soviet Zone and also with British life during six years of Labor Party administration, from 1945 until 1951. The defects of British planning were vigorously denounced in the following terms by Winston Churchill: [8]

"The socialist planners have miscalculated and mismanaged everything they have touched. They have tried to substitute government control and direction for individual enterprise and skill. By their restrictions they make scarcity; and when scarcity comes they call for more restrictions to cure it. . . . 700,000 officials . . . have settled down upon us to administer 25,000 regulations never enforced before in time of peace."

Circumstances have helped to divert a large share of Germany's enormous reserves of natural ability and energy into the field of economic revival, development, and expansion. There was first of all the spontaneous national resolve never again to endure the privations of the last war and first postwar years. The armed forces have lost much of their former glamor, and this is also true, to a lesser extent, of the diplomatic service. So it is not surprising that some of the most brilliant reputations in the new Germany have been made in business and finance. Germany's captains of industries fall into two groups: self-made men who have come up from obscurity and owners or directors of well-established firms.

The most striking example of a technical and managerial genius who built up one of Germany's two biggest industrial firms out of the wreckage of an almost forgotten automobile works is Heinz Nordhoff, sixty-three-year-old director of the world-famous German Volkswagen Company. Volkswagen, unknown before the war, is now the third-largest automobile producer in the world, after General Motors and Ford. It turned out 1.1 million vehicles in 1962, an all-time record for Europe; of these 200,000 were sold in the United States. The basic model is the 1200, a beetle-bodied car without tail fins, lavish display of chrome, or superfluous gadgets, but sturdy and dependable in performance. Its oil consumption is low, which is especially important for Europe, with its high-priced gasoline, and it sells at the moderate price of a little over $1,000. A somewhat more roomy and expensive type is now also being produced; but the 1200 is the standard Volkswagen car.

Nordhoff has done for Europe what Henry Ford did for America; he has transformed the automobile from a luxury of the rich into a convenience for the many. One third of the 42,000 workers in the main plant at Wolfsburg (there are subsidiary works at Hannover, Brunswick, and Kassel) own their own cars, a figure seldom matched in European factories, and certainly never under "the dictatorship of the proletariat" in Communist-ruled countries.

The Wolfsburg plant, which I visited in the summer of 1962, occupies an area of about one and a half square miles, with about half a square mile under roofs and a fourteen-story office building as administrative headquarters. Going through the plant, one gets an impression of terrific speed in all operations, of widespread use of automatic devices, and careful testing at every stage of operations. The Volkswagen plant is a popular place at which to work. Accidents are few and the turnover is less than 5 per cent a year, exceptional in view of Germany's acute shortage of labor. This shortage is reflected in the yellow wooden barracks which house some 2,000 imported Italian workers, with Italian-speaking priests and doctors and cooks who know how to prepare spaghetti and other Italian dishes. Hourly wages have more than doubled during the last decade, from 1.54 to 3.80 marks (nominally 95 cents, although the mark in many ways buys more than the worth of 25 cents in America). This is low by American, high by German or European standards.

Nordhoff possesses the gift of keeping in close personal touch with the workers, explaining management decisions and persuading the workers to go along, instead of operating by remote control orders. There has never been a strike at Wolfsburg. The town itself, with a population of some 80,000, is, like the works, a brand-new creation, built where there were formerly only a couple of straggling villages. It is eminently a one-industry town; even its electricity and heat are supplied from the factory power plant. With a more variable industry this might be dangerous; but there has never been lack of employment, and the squat cars have been pouring off the assembly lines and into the railway station in an ever-increasing stream.

Wolfsburg is only a few miles from the Soviet Zone border. A short drive brings one to a village which, like Berlin, is sundered by barbed wire on the Soviet side. Near this village is a memorial plaque to "a German who was treacherously killed by other Germans at the order of Ulbricht." This refers to a German journalist who was shot when he stepped over the demarcation line to talk with peasants on the Soviet side.

Before the war the Nazi labor welfare organization Kraft durch Freude opened subscriptions for a *Volkswagen* or "people's car." This movement had not led to much production before the war broke out. The plant at Wolfsburg, much smaller than the present one, turned to manufacturing military vehicles and was bombed almost flat.

Educated as an engineer, Nordhoff, the architect of the Volkswagen enterprise, became a car designer at the factory of Opel, a General Motors subsidiary in Brandenburg, not far from Berlin. This plant fell into the hands of the Russians at the end of the war. Nordhoff was in the American Zone. Here, although he had never been a Nazi Party member, he was banned from any work but that of a common laborer under the early rigorous denazification policy. He had been an industrial executive.

For a time Nordhoff eked out a living as a garage employee in Hamburg. Then the British occupation authorities gave him his chance. They had no great expectations from the shell of the Volkswagen plant; a British commission had passed it up as not worth dismantling. But they believed a few vehicles might be turned out for their own use, incidentally providing employment for some hungry Germans. So the wheels started turning in what could be salvaged from the buildings and equipment of a badly bombed plant. Then, surpassing by far the tempo of the general German economic miracle, the few thousand cars of 1948 multiplied until the figure of one million a year was reached and surpassed. What emphasizes the quality of Nordhoff's personal achievement is that for many years the factory was an orphan, without a legal owner. The original proprietor, the Kraft durch Freude, had been liquidated with other Nazi institutions and there was a prolonged dispute as to whether the works properly belonged to the central government in Bonn or to the provincial government of Lower Saxony, where Wolfsburg is located. Meanwhile the factory continued to turn out more cars, ploughing back profits to produce still more cars for a constantly growing market.

Finally an arrangement was worked out under which the stock was distributed 20 per cent to the central government, 20 per cent to the *Land* of Lower Saxony, with the remaining stock sold to private owners. It is safe to predict that, so long as he retains working capacity, Heinz Nordhoff, an industrial superman who combines the gifts of engineer, designer, manufacturer, salesman, and expert in labor relations, will be the spark plug of the enterprise.

Nordhoff's tastes include rare furniture and Oriental and impressionist art. But he conveys the impression of being a dedicated man, mainly concerned with making better Volkswagens and selling more of them.

It is a far cry from the selfmade Nordhoff, son of a bank employee, to Alfried Krupp, heir of one of the oldest industrial dynasties of Europe; from the new town of Wolfsburg to the old Ruhr city of Essen, headquarters of the far-flung Krupp business empire.

And Alfried Krupp, like Heinz Nordhoff, experienced his reverses of fortune in the early revengeful period of the occupation. Gustav Krupp von Bohlen, the head of the firm, had become mentally and physically incapacitated, and since the prosecution in the war crimes trials was determined, it is said, to get "a Krupp," it sentenced Alfried to twelve years of imprisonment with confiscation of his property. This verdict was reviewed and quashed by General Clay, and Alfried Krupp was released and given back his property, with the provision, later bypassed, that he was to divest himself of some of his holdings. He is now the possessor of some two score enterprises, big, medium, and small, ranging from the two largest, the machine-building plant at Essen and the steel mill at Rheinhausen, to some chain stores and a variety of miscellaneous undertakings.

The Rheinhausen works, which I visited in 1957, was built before the turn of the century in an ideal natural location for a steel plant. Ruhr coal is available within a radius of a few miles. Located on the Rhine, the plant has its own port to facilitate the importation of ore and the shipment of its finished steel. It conveyed the impression of a smooth-running typically German enterprise. Every part fitted into every other part as neatly as the pieces of a crossword puzzle. Everything seemed to have been thought of, from the training of young apprentices as future skilled workers to the utilization of slag, left over from the steel-making process, for the manufacture of bricks. What was not used for bricks was ground up for phosphate fertilizers.

At the time of my visit Rheinhausen was turning out 180,000 tons of ingot steel a month and was planning to expand to a figure of 2.5 million tons a year. It was the largest integrated steel works in Europe. Krupp was supposed to dispose of this plant to fulfill an allied decartelization scheme, but no purchasers were found and Rheinhausen remains part of the Krupp possessions.

The old residence of the Krupp dynasty is the Villa Hugel, a mansion outside the town of Essen, built in the gaudy style of the late nineteenth century. It is now a museum, because the present head of the house, a shy, retiring man, prefers to live in less ostentatious quarters. In the Villa Hugel are lifesize portraits of the early Krupps, who might have stepped out of the pages of Galsworthy's *Forsyte Saga*. One can see Friedrich, who founded the firm in 1811: his son Alfred, who installed the first Bessemer plant in Germany; his grandson Friedrich Alfred, who constructed the first working model of a Diesel engine and built up the business to a point where it was employing 40,000 workers by 1900. Then the heiress of the house, Bertha, married Gustav von Bohlen in a lavish ceremony attended by Kaiser Wilhelm II, who gave the bridegroom special permission to change his name to Krupp von Bohlen.

The picture story of this remarkable family recalls *Buddenbrooks,* Thomas Mann's novel of the rise, decline, and fall of a merchant patrician family in the old Baltic town of Lübeck. But unlike the Buddenbrooks, the Krupps show no signs of fading out. Their machinery, locomotives, turbines, buses, and quality steel are shipped to all parts of the world and also have a considerable market within Germany. And Alfried Krupp, twice married and divorced, has a son who may carry on the dynasty into the twenty-first century.

Krupp as representative of the old, and Volkswagen as the most brilliantly successful enterprise of the new German industry are two beacon lights of the economic miracle. But there have been many other business success stories, large and small, which have made their contribution. For example, there is Max Grundig, who ran a small radio sales and repair shop before the war and later made radio parts for the armed forces. He evaded an early occupation prohibition on the manufacture of radio sets by constructing radio kits as toys which the buyer might put together. As prohibitions were lifted, his business flourished and grew on a large scale. By 1952 he had turned out his one-millionth radio and he went on to the manufacture of television sets, portable tape recorders, and similar products. By 1960 his sales, which had expanded to the United States and other foreign markets, exceeded an annual figure of $200 million.

Two of the best-known names in Germany's industrial heartland, the Ruhr, are Hans Günther Sohl, managing director of the Thyssen Company, and Hermann Winkhaus, chief executive of Mannesmann, a big, closely integrated coal and steel combine, with sales of $842 million in 1960. Mannesmann has gone far afield in its business ventures, owning mines in South America and South Africa, a steel tubing plant in Canada, and a plastics firm in Easton, Pennsylvania.

Sohl, with whom I talked in his Düsseldorf office in 1962, evolved from a mining engineer into one of Germany's foremost industrial managers. He welcomed the Common Market and expressed the hope that Great Britain would also join. "The more fair competition in our business, the better," he said. At the same time he voiced a complaint one often hears from German industrialists in the Ruhr: that differing methods of calculating a manufacturers' excise tax gives French steel an artificial advantage in the German market. He scouted the idea that the heavy fall on the German Stock Exchange, which started earlier and went farther than the decline on Wall Street, was an omen of a coming recession. "Business is much better than the Stock Exchange," he said. Sohl has a reputation as an excellent amateur pianist and confessed to enjoying two diversions, hunting and swimming on the French Riviera. But, like most of Germany's industrial managers, he finds little time for recreation.

A rather gaudy and spectacular newcomer in German finance is Rudolf Muenemann, who started with a capital of 125 marks and developed an original idea into a fortune of more than $10 million. The idea was to act as a contact man between insurance companies with idle funds to invest and industrial firms hungry for capital. Muenemann worked out a rotating system under which he paid the insurance companies good interest rates for short-term capital loans, then re-lent the money at a much higher interest to industry and paid off his debts with new borrowing.

His methods and the fact that he is considered an upstart in the financial world have made Muenemann unpopular with regular bankers. The Bundestag once considered an "anti-Muenemann law" that would have cramped his style by forcing him to incorporate as a regular bank. But it failed to pass and Muenemann, whose first base of operations was in Munich, has now taken over a bank in Frankfurt to facilitate his operations. Meanwhile the new financier keeps himself in the public eye with his conspicuous style of living, which include a mansion in Munich, a yacht, and three Cadillacs, luxuriously equipped with all gadgets, including telephone and television. Among other features of the Muenemann ménage is Lord Stranz, an Irish peer who functions as his private secretary for matters involving a knowledge of English.

The business history of postwar Germany has its failures along with its successes. One of these was personable, articulate Willy Schlieker, in charge of German steel allocation during the war, in the shadows during the denazification period, then emerging as a new Ruhr magnate of substance by cornering the German market for importing coal from America at the time of the Korean War. More recently Schlieker went into the shipbuilding business in Hamburg, and this proved his undoing when he was unable to extricate himself from financial difficulties and went bankrupt in the summer of 1962. His failure was due to a common difficulty of German industrialists, trying to swing big operations with too little reserve capital.

The German business picture has changed by comparison with prewar times. Some of the old industrial families, like the Thyssens, are dying out, with the result that operating control passes from owners to managers. There are more newcomers in business, partly because changed conditions have created new opportunities and partly because of the breaking up into smaller units of some of the top-heavy cartels, like the United Steelworks in the Ruhr and the IG Farben. Most German industrialists and bankers stick closely to their specialized affairs. But one also finds a new type of West German businessman, with a broad interest in international political and economic issues, such figures as Günther Henle, Kurt Birrenbach, and Otto Friedrich.

Henle, director of the Klockner firm in the Ruhr, was for some fifteen years in the German foreign service and has been a leader in stimulating interest in German foreign relations through conferences and forums. He is convinced that Germany should do more in furnishing aid to underdeveloped areas of the world. Henle is convinced that free institutions are firmly installed in West Germany and that there is no danger that the country will turn toward the East, because the Communist threat is obvious and the Germans now know too much about the Russians. He is a little disturbed at the growth of welfare-state psychology in Germany and the preference of some Germans for security as against a risk-taking spirit of adventure.

Birrenbach, also a steel industrialist, has published a book on Atlantic Union, of which he is heartily in favor. Otto Friedrich, a leading manufacturer of tires and rubber products in Hamburg, served with distinction as government adviser on raw material imports during the Korean War and has undertaken other commissions, political and economic, outside his immediate business interests. There are a considerable number of businessmen in the Bundestag, where they naturally become more familiar with the details of home and foreign policies.

Germany's economic boom began to lose momentum in the early sixties. Erhard's free-enterprise, individual-incentive policies had registered a magnificent success in overcoming the very formidable postwar difficulties—hunger and goods shortages of all kinds, desperate lack of housing, refugees living in hard camp and barracks conditions. But the very success of these policies helped to bring on a set of new difficulties, not unknown in other countries, with which the Federal Republic was wrestling in 1962 and 1963. Unemployment, considerable when the economic miracle began, has long been completely wiped out. In its place has come an acute labor shortage. Some six to seven hundred thousand foreign workers, Italians, Spaniards, Greeks, Turks, and others, have been brought into Germany and there are still substantially more jobs than people to fill them. The results have been what always happens when no one can be fired: slackening of factory and office discipline, increased absenteeism and labor turnover, some letting down in intensity of work and quality of output. At the same time the trade unions have begun to press for wage increases that are out of line with improvements in productivity. Germany has visibly become a more expensive country. The specter of inflation has appeared on the horizon.

Erhard, usually a sturdy optimist, struck a note of serious warning in a nationwide radio address in March, 1962. "Have we lost our feeling for what is possible?" he asked. The economics minister pointed out that wages had risen by 10 per cent between 1960 and 1961, while productivity had gone up by only 4 per cent, and he painted a dark picture of a relentless vicious circle: weakening of competitive ability, slackening of economic activity, lower profits, less inclination to invest, and finally, a threat to full employment. Noting that other countries, trying to overcome inflation, had regarded Germany as a model and example, Erhard asked whether the Germans would be so foolish as to destroy by recklessness what they had earned by hard work and restraint.

Chancellor Adenauer spoke in similar terms of praise for past achievement and warning of future danger when he addressed the Bundestag in October, 1962. After reviewing briefly Germany's great accomplishments—building 6.5 million housing units, bringing up foreign trade from virtual zero to an annual figure of $12,750,-000,000 in exports and $11 billion in imports, raising almost $11 billion through a special tax called the *Lastenausgleich* ("equalization of burdens") for the benefit of special sufferers from the war—the old chancellor called attention to some recent facts and figures of less pleasant significance. The rate of industrial growth, for instance, which had reached 10 per cent and even a higher figure during the best years of the fifties, had sunk to 3.5 per cent. Imports were rising much faster than exports. The German price level was going up more rapidly than that of some other countries. German competitive capacity in foreign markets was declining.

Talking with German industrialists in 1962, one heard these warnings repeated in sharper form: "We have the shortest working week and the highest wages of any country in the Common Market," said Hans Günther Sohl. "Our economic difficulties would be over if we had one million unemployed," declared Berthold Beitz, right-hand man of Alfried Krupp. But as an afterthought, he qualified this statement: "No, that would help the Communists too much."

Steel industrialist and Bundestag member Kurt Birrenbach put the case as follows:

"Our industrial economy is taking more punishment than it can absorb at once: higher wages, out of line with growth of productivity, costly new social legislation, the 5 per cent increase in the exchange value of the mark, which handicaps sales in foreign markets. There is real danger of inflation unless something is done to reverse present trends."

One naturally hears a different viewpoint from Ludwig Rosenberg, the personable, articulate president of the Gewerkschaftsbund ("Federation of Trade-Unions") in the imposing Düsseldorf headquarters of this organization of 6.5 million members:

"For many years German wages lagged behind those of European industrial countries. Now they are catching up. It would be hard to prove that the German wage scale is the highest in the European Economic Community. There are differences from country to country which make accurate comparison in this field very difficult. For instance, France has a very generous system of family allowances, payments for children, which does not exist in Germany. The United States has a scale of money wages much higher than the European. But the cost of living in America is higher and the system of social insurance is less developed.

"I wrote to Economics Minister Erhard asking for a comparative statement of the income gains in recent years of wage workers and of employers, and the middle class generally. He replied that no accurate figures exist for such a comparison. But I am sure that it is not the wage workers who have been the principal gainers from what is called the economic miracle.

"The trade unions recognize that they have an obligation to make a contribution to economic stability and prosperity. But, while there is much criticism of allegedly excessive wage demands, there are abuses on the side of the employers that are apt to be overlooked: tax privileges, bloated expense accounts, a practice of financing growth out of retained profits, which means high prices for the consumer."

Putting together the statements of the industrialists and of Mr. Rosenberg, one gets the same contrasted viewpoints that one would be likely to hear from management and labor spokesmen in New York or London or Paris. The Federation of Trade-Unions is not uniform in outlook. Many of its leaders believe that the old program of the movement, with its flavor of Marxism, is outmoded, especially as the Social Democratic Party itself has moved far from Marxism in recent years. But a formal change is blocked by the opposition of the powerful Metal Workers Union (1.8 million members) which, under the leadership of Otto Brenner, remains a stronghold of what might be called old-fashioned conservative radicalism.

An important new feature in German industrial relations is the legal right of workers to *Mitbestimmung* ("codetermination") in factories. Every German plant of any size has two directing bodies, the Aufsichtsrat (supervisory council), which has advisory functions, and the Vorstand (executive board), which is the principal organ of management. In the first of these bodies the workers are entitled to parity, with five representatives together with five for management and a neutral chairman. In the coal, iron, and steel industries the workers are also entitled to a representative in the Vorstand.

In all factories employing more than a hundred workers there is also an economic committee, with joint representation for management and labor. This body is entitled to monthly reports on the economic development of the factory. Two ideals of "codetermination" are to give the workers more voice in everyday working conditions and to give them more understanding of management's side of the case by bringing them more closely in touch with such problems as raising capital and finding markets.[9]

The judgment one usually hears on *Mitbestimmung* is favorable, although a crusty old-fashioned boss finds that his power is somewhat clipped while a militant trade-unionist sometimes looks at it critically because it draws workers into an attitude of joint responsibility for the economic success of the factory. Certainly this experiment did not slow down the forward sweep of output; the retarded pace of recent years has been due to labor shortage and other causes.

The bloom is now off the economic miracle—for reasons which in no way discredit the philosophy of economic individualism which made this miracle possible. The very successes of Erhard's policy, in some ways, have made for a slower rate of advance. For one thing, the fierce determination to get away from want and poverty which made the Germans, especially the refugees, willing to work long hours in the beginning, has slackened, because there is today very little real poverty, at least among regularly employed workers. So there is a temptation to take life more easily, to go occasionally on a long weekend,[10] and this temptation is enhanced by another aspect of the miracle, the replacement of unemployment by an acute shortage of labor.

This may well be Germany's principal economic and social problem. For it is quite possible that, even if there were no trade-unions, the shortage of working hands, aggravated by the low birth rate of the war and postwar years and the stoppage of the influx of refugees from the Soviet Zone, would exert an inflationary upward pressure on wage rates. The outlook is for a lower annual growth rate, unless automation can replace manual labor on a large scale.

But a condition of labor shortage, while it creates frustrations and inconveniences, is far preferable, from a human and political standpoint, to mass unemployment which turns men's minds to bitterness and despair and predisposes them to listen to demagogues with quack remedies. The achievements of the economic miracle have been tremendous and offer a solid base for further advance. And the EEC may provide the stimulus for a further advance within the limits of available manpower. The swift leap from almost universal ruin to general well-being is perhaps the most impressive visual demonstration of the phoenix image of the new Germany.

The German Federal Republic entered the year 1963 with a somewhat decelerated rate of growth, but with no serious crisis symptoms. The total of goods and services produced in 1962 was $84,200,000,000, a gain of 4.1 per cent over the preceding year. German exports in 1962 reached the record figure of $13.2 billion;

but imports, stimulated by the appreciation in the value of the mark, grew more than twice as fast as exports and amounted to $12.4 billion. Thus the surplus in the balance of trade declined from $1.6 billion to $820 million and the balance of payments, for the first time in many years, showed a deficit of $200 million. However, this is something Germany could well afford, with its comfortable reserve of $6.4 billion in gold and convertible currencies, mostly American dollars.

Shipbuilding experienced a poor year in 1962, but the manufacturing of high-quality machinery and electrical goods continued to expand. Despite the complaints of businessmen and the real difficulties and problems posed by the acute shortage of labor, there were no serious storm clouds on the German economic horizon by the middle of 1963. The prospect was for slower, but steady, growth, limited by the fact that German labor power is fully employed.

NOTES TO CHAPTER IV

1 Ludwig Erhard, *Prosperity Through Competition* (New York: Frederick A. Praeger, Inc., 1958), p. 116.

2 See Chapter III, p. 64.

3 Henry C. Wallich, *Mainsprings of the German Revival* (New Haven: Yale University Press, 1955), p. 370.

4 Erhard, *op. cit.,* p. 12.

5 Erhard habitually uses the phrase *Sozialmarktwirtschaft,* which might be freely translated: "market economy with human considerations."

6 See Erhard, *op. cit.,* p. 21 for a table of comparative rises in the cost of living.

7 See Erhard, *op. cit.,* pp. 148, 149, and Wallich, *op. cit.,* pp. 55, 56.

8 Cited in Ray Vicker, *How an Election Was Won* (Chicago: Henry Regnery Co., 1962), pp. 200, 201.

9 A detailed study of *Mitbestimmung* in German is *Zur Theorie und Praxis der Mitbestimmung,* by Professor Fritz Voigt (Berlin: Duncker and Humoldt, 1962).

10 A German industrialist told me that some cautious buyers of automobiles insist on getting a car not put out on Monday, because of the possible consequences of the long weekend.

CHAPTER V

The Old Architect of the New Germany

THE new Germany that has emerged from the Nazi collapse is a product of many causes and many forces. But it is mainly the creation of one extraordinary man, octogenarian Chancellor Konrad Adenauer, who achieved international fame at an age when most men have retired from public life. Adenauer, although widely respected, is not a universally loved or admired figure in his own country, where some aspects of his methods in domestic policy evoke hot debate and criticism. Yet, measured by the results he has accomplished, he is certainly one of the foremost political figures of postwar Europe and easily the greatest German statesman since Bismarck.

Indeed Adenauer's achievement in some ways has been more remarkable than that of the Iron Chancellor, who created the united Imperial Germany that disappeared with military defeat in 1918. Bismarck operated from strength, Adenauer from weakness. Bismarck possessed such assets as the power of the Prussian army and the rising tide of sentiment for German unification. When Adenauer in 1949 took over as first (and up to 1963, only) chancellor of the German Federal Republic, Germany was at an all-time nadir, with much of its eastern territory annexed by Poland and the Soviet Union, hated and distrusted abroad, devastated by air bombing, the people hungry, apathetic, almost bereft of hope and ideals.

Whatever the future may hold for Adenauer and for Germany, the rugged crag-faced chancellor—the striking cast of his features is the result of a facial operation after an automobile accident—who in his eighties could outwork many younger men, who could stand patiently in a hot sun or a pouring rain if protocol required, who could always dominate the Bundestag by his remarkably deep, powerful voice and the measured, austere logic of his speeches, has earned his place in history by two striking accomplishments.

He has restored his country to a place of power, honor and equality in the councils of the West much sooner than would have seemed possible immediately after the end of the war. A German exchange student, one of many who have come to the United States, recognized this fact when he said: "I and my colleagues have reason to be personally grateful to Konrad Adenauer. If it had not been for the prestige and confidence which he won for himself and for Germany, we could not have expected such a friendly, hospitable welcome abroad as we have received."

Under Adenauer's administration—although here, as shown in the previous chapter, the direct credit belongs rather to the old-fashioned liberal economics of Ludwig Erhard—Germany achieved both a fantastically swift material recovery and a very rapid pace of economic growth. Distress during the world crisis of 1929–33 was a most important element in paving the way for the success of Hitler. Steadily increasing prosperity has been an equally important factor in keeping the politics of the new Germany on an even keel, in turning the minds of the German people away from the siren songs of right-wing and left-wing demagogues.

It is thanks to Adenauer's grand design of integrating Germany as closely as possible with the West that war between those traditional continental rivals, Germany and France, has become now as unthinkable as a war between the United States and Canada. For almost ten years after the end of the war France pursued a policy of trying to block or at least delay the creation of a centralized independent German administration provided with its own armed forces. It is a far cry from this atmosphere to the ceremonial sealing of permanent Franco-German understanding on the basis of equality by the exchange of visits between those grand old men of Europe, Konrad Adenauer and Charles de Gaulle, in the summer and autumn of 1962. The pealing of the bells in France's historic Rheims Cathedral, and the joint review of French and

German troops by Adenauer and de Gaulle found a response in the cheering throngs which greeted de Gaulle in his highly successful visit to Germany. It was symbolic of a big and most constructive change in the European political climate when de Gaulle, speaking in Germany, greeted Adenauer as *"Mein Freund"* and affirmed "the respect I feel for the great German people."

Here is the prospect of two great European nations devoting their energies to peaceful co-operation instead of following the deceptive paths of military glory to new Jenas and Austerlitzes, Metzes and Sedans and Verduns.

The continuation, almost two decades after the end of the war, of the arbitrary and unnatural partition of Germany and of Germany's former capital, Berlin, has been the only failure of Adenauer's foreign policy. But the line of military demarcation between the Western and Soviet lines of military advance was drawn long before Adenauer came into power. There is no reliable evidence that the Soviet Government at any time would have been willing to scrap its puppet regime in its zone of occupation and accept the only basis on which German reunification would be tolerable, free all-German elections. In view of these circumstances Adenauer seems to have chosen the wiser course in concentrating on the political and economic recovery of free Germany and in knitting this part of Germany into the framework of the Western community.

Adenauer's roots in the Rhineland, historically more open to French influence and sympathy than other regions of Germany, have made it easier for him to give German foreign policy a pro-Western and pro-French orientation. To a Rhinelander Berlin may seem as far away as Paris, and sentimental feeling for East Prussia and other lost areas in the East may be rather weak. The chancellor was born in the Rhenish city of Cologne; he picked Bonn as the capital of the Federal Republic, and he lives in Rhöndorf, a picturesque hillside village overlooking the Rhine, within convenient driving distance of Bonn. It is these Rhineland roots that made it psychologically more natural and acceptable for Adenauer to abandon the traditional policy of trying to balance between East and West and to commit himself unconditionally to the close identification of Germany, politically, economically and militarily, with Western Europe and the United States.

The first postwar leader of the Social Democratic Party, Kurt Schumacher, himself an East Prussian, was in the habit of accusing the chancellor of losing sight of the goal of German reunification. Once, in a hectic Bundestag debate, he called Adenauer "the chancellor of the Allies." The insinuation was unjust. Adenauer has never been a puppet, but a thoroughly patriotic German; and it is doubtful whether any other leader would have regained German sovereignty as quickly.

Germany, in Adenauer's view, is too weak to bargain with the Kremlin on its own. So the best guaranty against Soviet aggression and the only possible road to reunion lie through close and strong ties with the United States and Western Europe. At the present time neutralism in Germany is virtually dead and could only be revived if there were some disgraceful betrayal of Germany by its allies, in regard to West Berlin or some other subject of vital German interest. Almost all Germans, even the Social Democrats who for a time were sharply critical of Adenauer's pro-Western foreign policy, have now been convinced by experience that the only united Germany in which Soviet dictator Khrushchev is interested is a Communist Germany.

Adenauer has been as successful in domestic politics as in foreign policy. He has led his party, the Christian Democratic Union, to four successive victories in national elections. After being elected chancellor by the narrow margin of one vote in 1949, he reaped the reward of improving conditions by a more substantial margin of victory in 1953. In 1957 he perhaps reached the peak of his political prestige when his party won an absolute majority of seats in the Bundestag. (This is very unusual in the multiparty politics of Europe.) *Der Alte* ("the Old One"), as Adenauer is often called, although not to his face, might well have repeated this success in 1961 if the wall sundering the two parts of Berlin had not been erected on the eve of the election. This rough confirmation of the partition of Germany was a severe shock to German public opinion. And for once Adenauer, usually a consummate student of popular psychology, seems to have missed his cue. His reaction seemed to many voters too cautious and mild. He was slow in visiting West Berlin and he allowed his chief opponent in the political campaign, Socialist Mayor Willy Brandt of West Berlin, to take the spotlight as the defender of the freedom of the city. The result was that the CDU lost its clear majority, although it came out of the election as the strongest single party. The FDP, weakest of the three competing political groups, held the balance between the CDU and the SPD.

This election setback brought to a head all the elements of personal and political dissatisfaction with the long reign of Adenauer. Some members of his own party, recognizing his past services, felt that he had become too old and set in his ways to function as an effective leader. There was much dissatisfaction among the Free Democrats with their former experiences as coalition partners with the CDU. Adenauer's brusque authoritarian ways were not calculated to ingratiate him with the junior partner in a political combination. The chairman of the FDP, Erich Mende, declared that he would never serve in a cabinet headed by Adenauer. However, after protracted maneuvering and bargaining over the allotment of cabinet posts and over the part the FDP should play in determining policy, Adenauer entered a fourth term as chancellor, as head of a coalition CDU-FDP administration in which Mende did not personally hold office.

This coalition creaked along a little uncertainly until the autumn of 1962, when a second-rate incident, very ineptly handled by the government, produced a first-rate crisis. *Der Spiegel,* a weekly which is a cross between a news magazine and a confidential scandal sheet and which specializes in exposures of real or alleged corruption and incompetence in high places, devoted an issue to a severe criticism of the efficiency of the German armed forces, with special reference to recent maneuvers in which the Bundeswehr had participated with other allied forces and allegedly received a low efficiency rating. This was followed by a police raid on the office of *Der Spiegel* in Hamburg and the arrest of the editor, Rudolf Augstein, and members of his staff. A *Spiegel* editor named Ahlers, who was vacationing in Spain, was arrested there by the Spanish police at the request of the German Defense Ministry and extradited to Germany.

The charge was that *Der Spiegel* had somehow obtained from the Defense Ministry and published secret documents. Adenauer spoke in the Bundestag of "treason," as if the accusation had been proved. Almost every conceivable error was made in carrying out the arrests. The Free Democrat minister of justice, Wolfgang Stammberger, was bypassed by some of his subordinates. Defense Minister Franz Josef Strauss first denied, then admitted sending a telegram to Spain which had led to the arrest of Ahlers. Strauss had been a favorite target of *Der Spiegel* and there was widespread suspicion that the whole case against the magazine had grown out of the resentment of the burly Bavarian Defense Minister. A widely circulated cartoon showed Strauss angrily smashing a mirror. (The word *Spiegel* means "mirror.")

As the ramifications of the *Spiegel* case unfolded, the Free Democrats, who at first had been placated by the dismissal of two high officials, one in the Defense Ministry, the other in the Justice Ministry, went further in their demands and clamored for the political head of Strauss, with whom they had old scores to settle from the past. Again the clouds of crisis hung over Bonn, but Adenauer finally remained chancellor with the same coalition and a reshuffled cabinet, Strauss being replaced by Kai-Uwe von Hassel, prime minister of Schleswig-Holstein. The chancellor also gave what was widely interpreted as an indication that he would retire from office in the autumn of 1963. This is not the first time the chancellor has contemplated retiring from his exacting office. This occurred in the spring of 1959, when the election of a new president of the republic was due. Adenauer proposed to become a candidate; [1] with the balance of political power as it was at that time he would certainly have been elected. His design was apparently to remain politically dominant in a post which would make less demand on his powers in day-by-day administration, but would leave him a decisive voice in appointing the head of government. He wished to turn over his office as chancellor to Fritz Etzel, at that time minister of finance, who had previously represented Germany in the Coal and Steel Community.

But Etzel, although an able administrator, was a rather colorless personality, little known to the public, not a leader with whom the CDU could confidently hope to win the next election. A public-opinion poll showed negligible support for Etzel, a heavy predominance in favor of Ludwig Erhard, the chubby minister of economics whose very name was considered a symbol and guaranty of prosperity. But Adenauer distrusted Erhard's political flair. As I was told by one of the old chancellor's closest confidants, he considers Erhard "a man of the Muses" because of his interest in music, a competent economic specialist, but a man of little experience and aptitude in the workaday details of home and foreign policy. This is not a capricious judgment. Many Bonn political observers believe that Erhard, while he is easily the best potential votegetter for the CDU, is not necessarily the best qualified for the office of chancellor.

When Adenauer realized that he could not transfer his office to Etzel he reversed his decision and remained in his post. The presidency went to a CDU politician with an agrarian background, Heinrich Lübke.

Those who know Adenauer best say that his instinct for retaining power is very strong, that it is hard to conceive his voluntary retirement into private life. I have visited Bonn many times since the end of the war, most recently in 1962. Previously Adenauer had seemed as fixed and immovable as the Drachenfels, the rocky cliff that towers above the Rhine near his home village of Rhöndorf. But the atmosphere in 1962 was different; one felt that the end of the Adenauer era was in prospect. Almost everyone with whom one talked had a date for *Der Alte's* retirement. Although Adenauer is sometimes referred to as "a biological miracle" (he celebrated his eighty-seventh birthday with a patriarchal gathering of his seven children and many grandchildren on January 5, 1963) there are persistent rumors, difficult to verify or disprove, that advanced age is finally catching up with him. The elderly statesman is still capable of performing magnificently under the stimulus of an important political occasion, a CDU party congress, a visit from Dean Rusk, a ceremonial meeting with General de Gaulle. But there are said to be intervals of relaxed concentration, of forgetfulness, of near apathy, and these have a slackening effect on the conduct of public affairs.

During his long term of office Adenauer has done more than win elections. He has witnessed the abandonment by his arch-enemies, the Social Democrats, of what were at one time their two most distinctive opposition policies. In the first years of the Federal Republic the Social Democrats advocated the nationalization of big industries and extensive state economic planning. They also fought to the last ditch the rearming of Germany, carrying this issue to the Supreme Court in Karlsruhe.

Now they have decisively shifted ground on both these points. After their crushing defeat in 1957, when the CDU won many of their former strongholds in the industrial Ruhr, the Social Democrats at a conference in Bad Godesberg tossed Karl Marx overboard and came out in favor of a free competitive economy, claiming that they would run such an economy more effectively than the party in power. Somewhat later, after two of their parliamentary leaders, Carlo Schmid and Fritz Erler, had visited Moscow and found Khrushchev unwilling to consider German unification on any terms compatible with freedom, the Social Democrats swung over to accepting Germany's rearmament as a member of NATO. In their Hannover program, adopted before the 1961 election, there was a significant omission of any protest against the arming of German troops with nuclear weapons. And in the economic field this program called for a government "whose economic policy combines freedom and social responsibility, creates prosperity for town and country and gets to work on the creation of a property-owning democracy." These aims are little different from those of the CDU, indicating that even after Adenauer passes from the scene, two of his achievements are likely to remain unchallenged, the forging of the military link with the West and the economic restoration of Germany on a predominantly free-enterprise basis.

What personal qualities and what circumstances have made Konrad Adenauer—chiefly known in the past as an efficient German civil servant, an energetic, authoritarian mayor of Cologne—the leader of his own country and an outstanding figure in the new

Europe? The answer is that in the case of Adenauer the man and the time have met.

His gift of leadership in the light of the record, is obvious. He is what the Germans call a *zielbewüsste Mensch,* a dedicated man sure of his goals and firm and consistent in pursuing these goals. Because of this he has inspired confidence, both in his supporters at the polls and in the American and other foreign statesmen with whom he co-operated. Never for a moment did he yield to the temptation to play off the Soviet Union against the West. His abhorrence of communism, as a devout Catholic with old-fashioned ideals in ethics, politics, and economics, was deep and unfeigned. He never gave his partners in NATO the least reason to suspect his loyalty to the Western orientation, even though his tendency to speak out his mind rather bluntly when he felt some other member of the alliance was behaving unwisely created awkward moments, and not least for his own foreign minister.

His leadership was not indicated by Gallup polls. He always told the German people not what they might want to hear but what he thought they ought to hear. Before German sovereignty had been fully restored, the British high commissioner, Sir Ivone Kirkpatrick, ordered the arrest of Werner Naumann, a former high official in the Nazi Ministry of Propaganda, and other members of a ring of ex-Nazis who were trying to infiltrate the German political parties. Adenauer, on the eve of an election and with complete disregard of possible German nationalist feeling, gruffly declared: "I will take the word of the British High Commissioner in preference to that of the former state secretary of Dr. Goebbels." In pushing through bills for restitution to Jews and other victims of Nazi tyranny, Adenauer was leading rather than following German public opinion.

Adenauer's style of leadership was just what the German people, recovering from a long orgy of emotional propaganda, wanted—fatherly, cool, unsentimental. An editor of *Der Spiegel* with whom I talked in 1962, no admirer of Adenauer's regime, recognized the chancellor's popular appeal and offered the following explanation:

"Adenauer, with what we sometimes call his 'chancellor-democracy,' democratic in form, authoritarian in content, has helped to reconcile the German people, most of whom are not, at heart, enthusiastic democrats, to a democratic form of government. They see *Der Alte* getting his way almost all the time, not much hampered by the Bundestag or by his ministers, whom he sometimes treats rather contemptuously. And they say: 'If this is democracy it isn't so bad, after all.' "

To the German masses Adenauer is a patriarchal father or grandfather figure, stern in laying down the law when necessary, but with human sides to his personality, and above all, with the sure touch of success in home and foreign policy. There is far more criticism of him in sophisticated political, journalistic, and intellectual circles than there is among the rank-and-file Germans, so many of whom have been regularly voting for him.

It was not from talking with the supposed professional experts in Bonn, but rather from casual chats with Germans whom I met on mountain walks in the Black Forest before the 1957 election that I gained the impression, which proved correct, that Adenauer would win a landslide victory. Typical of the general run of comment was this remark of a married couple, both doctors:

"We are Protestants, so we might be expected to vote for the Free Democrats, mainly a Protestant party. But we shall vote CDU; it is simply too risky to put anyone but Adenauer in power."

Adenauer has showed tact and skill in handling relations with the Protestant wing of the CDU and in avoiding the suggestion of religious favoritism in making appointments. The first president of the Republic, the economist and scholar Theodor Heuss, was a Protestant, as is the president of the Bundestag, Eugen Gerstenmeier.

There is nothing glamorous or spectacular about Adenauer's typically German middle-class background. His father was a *Beamte,* a public official, an occupation that yielded more in status than in pay in the time of the German Empire. He incurred considerable sacrifice to send Konrad to the University of Cologne, where he completed the law course, but he took up public administration as a profession. Adenauer handled rationing in Cologne during World War I and later acquired the reputation of an able town planner during his long term of service as mayor. One of his old associates in the Center Party, which furnished much of the Catholic core of the CDU, suggested to me that Adenauer's background as mayor of Cologne influenced his later conduct as chancellor.

"He is still the same type of man we knew as mayor of Cologne," said Heinrich Krone, minister without portfolio in the Adenauer Cabinet of 1962. "Immensely industrious, conscientious, head-strong—and very sure his decisions are the right ones."

As a devout Catholic and an authentic conservative, Adenauer looked on Hitler's rabble-rousing movement with instinctive contempt and disgust. He refused to hang out the swastika flag when Hitler came to Cologne; he was therefore dismissed as mayor and lived as unobtrusively as possible during the Nazi period, sometimes finding shelter in monasteries. He was shadowed by the Gestapo and was lucky to get off with a short term in prison.

After the downfall of the Third Reich, German political life was fragmented and paralyzed. Some former political leaders had been killed; others remained abroad, where they had found asylum. The impulse in the first occupation years was to distrust all Germans; communication between various regions of Germany was slow and difficult.

Adenauer had been reinstated as mayor of Cologne after the fall of the Nazis, but a British general dismissed him for alleged incompetence. Whether this incident influenced the chancellor's occasional sharp comments on British policy is a matter of debate. More probably, as one of his collaborators suggested to me, Adenauer, with his Rhineland birth and upbringing, feels more at home with the French than with Anglo-Saxons. At any rate, the judgment of the British general may be ranked with that of an insurance company which found Adenauer "too delicate" and a bad insurance risk.[2] Thirty years later the chancellor celebrated his eighty-fifth birthday with a large and festive gathering of members of his family and invited guests.

Adenauer, although a conservative, is not a Prussian aristocrat with the prefix Von before his name. Goosestepping military pomp and ceremony are alien to him, although he accepted German re-armament as a regrettable defensive necessity.

The British general who dismissed him as mayor of Cologne rendered him an unconscious service. Out of office he had more time for conferences with other West Germans interested in forming a party along the lines of the Christian Democratic Union. At first these lines were rather uncertain and blurred. Some Catholic groups were prepared to support a considerable amount of state economic planning, even the nationalization of basic industries. Adenauer is not a doctrinaire mid-Victorian capitalist in outlook; he has sometimes used higher salaries and pensions as election bait. But from the beginning he stood on the right wing of the CDU; one of his most trusted advisers was a Cologne banker, recently deceased, Robert Pferdmenges.

At first there were three more or less independent centers of the new party, in the Rhineland, in Berlin—where a Catholic trade-union leader, Jacob Kaiser, undertook the hopeless task of trying to keep the CDU alive in the Soviet Zone—and in Munich. But Adenauer outlasted and outmaneuvered all his political rivals. Not for nothing does he sometimes tell the story on himself that a letter addressed "The Old Fox, Bonn" was promptly delivered to the chancellor's office. His political shadow lengthened as the Allies, with America leading the way, relaxed occupation restrictions, and as living conditions, under a *laissez-faire* economic policy, began to improve visibly.

In several ways the impressive old chancellor fitted the spirit and needs of the time in which he functioned. The sharpening of the cold war enhanced the appeal of a convinced, uncompromising anti-Communist at the head of the German Republic. Moreover the decade of the fifties witnessed at least a mild swing to the right in the Western world. There was a reaction against such aspects of a state-managed economy as minute government economic planning, rationing, and barter trade between nations.

In Great Britain the Conservatives displaced the Labour Party, and Dwight D. Eisenhower headed the first Republican administration in Washington in twenty years. Throughout Western Europe socialist participation in governments diminished. Adenauer fitted in with both these trends, with anticommunism in politics and more freedom of private enterprise in economics. He was the perfect partner in the Western alliance, and an increasingly important one as Germany gained in political and economic stature.

In everyday life Konrad Adenauer is a man of strict, regular habits and simple tastes and pleasures. Up at six punctually every morning, he takes time out to enjoy the roses which surround his villa and which grow luxuriously in the damp, humid climate. Then he is driven to his Bonn headquarters, the white eighteenth-century Schaumburg Palace, near the Bundestag building in Bonn. His normal working day is ten hours, often extended in times of emergency. There are two breaks, for a frugal lunch and for a brisk fifty-minute walk in the park around the palace. Almost the only trait Adenauer shares with Adolf Hitler is that he does not smoke and dislikes the odor of tobacco. He eschews strong liquor but enjoys an occasional glass of the more select Rhenish wines. He relishes chocolate and there is a story that the duration of a cabinet meeting is more or less determined by the length of time required by the chancellor to consume a bar of chocolate.

Adenauer is not a sophisticated intellectual. He has a taste for painting and will sometimes mark the end of an interview by showing his guest some of the paintings of the German and Flemish schools which hang on the walls of the Schaumburg Palace. He enjoys classical music, especially Mozart and Haydn. In art and music, as in politics, his slogan would probably be: *Keine Experimente* ("No Experiments"). He is an inveterate reader of detective stories. His favorite vacation spot is Cadenabbia, overlooking Italy's beautiful Lake Como, although he has also gone to the Black Forest and to Mürren, a picturesque cliff-hanging resort in Switzerland's Bernese Oberland.

Adenauer's manners are grave, dignified, almost courtly. One can understand Eisenhower's reaction after a visit to Bonn: "A grand old gentleman." But he also has a good sense of humor, which, on occasion, may be caustic.

Adenauer is probably admired abroad (except by Communists and left wingers) more unreservedly than in his own country. This is not altogether unnatural or illogical. The chancellor combines in his personality the qualities of a great European statesman and of a ruthless, hard-hitting German politician. The foreign observer can perhaps see more clearly the bigness of Adenauer's vision. The German is more apt to be rasped by some instance of his political sharp practice. One of the ablest and best informed foreign observers in Germany offered this judgment of the personality of the old architect of the new Germany:

"A remarkable combination of big advanced ideas on such subjects as German participation in a united Europe with readiness to resort to very petty tactics in order to outwit or beat political rivals and opponents at home."

And an editor of one of Germany's most respected newspapers, discussing the same subject, remarked: "Adenauer? A great man? Certainly. A good man? No."

The two reproaches that are most often directed against Adenauer, even by some who recognize his great services to Germany and to the free world, may be summarized as follows:

(1) His methods of administration have not promoted real democracy in depth in Germany.

(2) He has created the danger of a future political vacuum by giving his ministers too little independence and responsibility and by failing to designate a "crown prince," or successor. Here, of course, his lack of harmony with the most probable candidate for the succession, Ludwig Erhard, enters into the picture.

There is a story that may or may not be accurate but that certainly contains an element of symbolic truth, to the effect that Adenauer's reply to an associate who had suggested that "we must be fair to the opposition" was "Yes, certainly, after the election is over."

Social Democrats still smart over an incident in an early election campaign, when two of their members were widely accused, on the basis of material that was later proved false, of connections with the Communist regime in the Soviet Zone. When this was brought up in the Bundestag, so they say, Adenauer blandly brushed it off with the remark: "If this incident cost the Social Democrats a few hundred thousand votes, I don't think this was any great misfortune."

The chancellor sometimes carries campaign oratory rather far, as when he declared in 1957 that a victory for the Social Democrats would mean the ruin of Germany. And in the 1961 campaign he delivered a below-the-belt blow when he referred to his opponent as "Herr Frahm, alias Brandt," a reference to Willy Brandt's illegitimate birth.

Adenauer's prodigious working energy and his habit, as mayor of Cologne, of personally overseeing every detail of administration have sometimes led him to interfere unduly in the operation of ministries and to take important decisions with little consultation or discussion in the Bundestag. And this tendency, not without justification, to regard himself as indispensable in his post, to cling to power to the last possible moment may conceivably prepare a sad ending for a most brilliant and fruitful career. It has yet to be proved that the old veteran of so many political battles knows how to step down gracefully at the right moment.

Adenauer undoubtedly possesses the defects as well as the virtues of a strong national leader. There is something aloof and cold in his nature, more calculated to inspire respect and esteem than warm friendship and devotion. In West Berlin one can meet critics who believe that Adenauer, with his roots in Cologne and Rhöndorf, cares little what happens to Germany east of the Elbe.

Perhaps it is too soon to assess the historical significance of the Adenauer era. And yet, if the venerable chancellor should take time for a few moments of self-appraisal during one of his walks in the garden of the Schaumburg Palace, he could summon into memory a list of achievements that has rarely been equalled by a man whose political career began at an age when most men are in retirement:

He has raised Germany from a bankrupt pariah to an affluent ally of the free nations. He has replaced Nazi despotism with free institutions and the rule of law. He has built up and led from one victory to another a party unique in German history, with appeal to all groups of the German people. He has ended Germany's tragic quarrel with France and brought the Germans into new close relations with the West. He has done what was possible to atone for the crimes of the Nazis.

Surely this is no mean record of statesmanlike accomplishment. If a phrase from the Latin lessons of his remote school days recurs to Adenauer's consciousness, he might say, comparing Germany now with the Germany which he took over in 1949:

Si vis monumentum, circumspice.

NOTES TO CHAPTER V

1   The German President is elected not by direct vote, but by a Federal Convention, composed equally of the members of the Bundestag and of an equal number of representatives of the legislatures of the states.

2   Terence Prittie, *Germany Divided* (Boston, Little Brown & Co., 1960), p. 210.

CHAPTER VI

Adenauer's Political Heirs

AFTER Adenauer, what? This question acquires additional urgency as the end of the long Adenauer era approaches, even though the precise date of the chancellor's retirement is not certain. The Free Democratic Party, unfriendly junior partner of the CDU in the uneasy coalition that has governed Germany since the autumn of 1961, through its leader Erich Mende, has been pressing for the autumn of 1963 as the terminal date of Adenauer's long chancellorship. Some members of Adenauer's own party, with full recognition of his qualities of greatness, privately express fears that he may remain in office too long for his own dignity and reputation. But the wily and tenacious old statesman has weathered many political storms, and retirement before the end of 1963, while most probable, will be certain only when it occurs.

Certainly the atmosphere of Bonn will never be quite the same after Adenauer quits the Schaumburg Palace; a monumental landmark in the political scenery of the capital will have disappeared. However, the idea that a chaotic vacuum will follow the chancellor's retirement seems unduly pessimistic. It is true that Adenauer's highhanded methods of running the administration on a personal basis have somewhat diminished the responsibility of the Bundestag and delayed the development of full-fledged parliamentary democracy. Yet it would be unwise to overlook the great progress toward free orderly government which Germany has made since emerging from the twelve-year paralysis of Hitlerism.

National and local representative bodies have been set up and have been functioning smoothly. There has been practice in political debate and experience in administration. Elections have been free and orderly. Rowdy disorders on political or ideological grounds have virtually disappeared from German life.

Moreover, there has been a substantial, significant change in the nature of German politics which makes for future stability and moderation, a change in the direction of larger parties with less extreme positions. This was pointed out to me in an interesting conversation with Heinrich Krone, one of the veterans in the CDU leadership, formerly head of his party's parliamentary group in the Bundestag, more recently minister without portfolio. In this capacity he handles any problem which Adenauer may wish to assign to him and is available for general consultation. Before the eclipse of political life under Hitler, Dr. Krone, a Berlin lawyer by profession, was an active figure in the Catholic Center Party, so that he is able to speak of German political development in a fairly long perspective. His personality is of the fatherly, conciliatory type and his services are often used in mediating inner party disputes and smoothing the ruffled feelings of individuals who feel affronted as a result of some controversy.

"The Christian Democratic Union," said Dr. Krone, "is something new in German politics—a party of broad national appeal, not restricted to followers of any one economic group, or religious faith, or regional residence. We have members of all social and economic groups. There are bankers and businessmen, like Robert Pferdmenges, Kurt Birrenbach, Günther Henle. But there is also a working-class wing, headed by Catholic trade-unionist Katzer, with quite advanced social ideas. There are also peasants, and middle-class people. And our party unites Catholics and Protestants with similar political ideals.

"This was not true in Germany under the kaiser, or during the existence of the Weimar Republic. There were more parties then, and they were identified with some group interest or ideology. The Center was an avowed Catholic party. The German National People's Party represented conservative landowners, the German People's Party business interests, the Social Democrats the industrial workers, except for the more radical who joined the Communists.

"Now differences are fought out within one big party, instead of causing clashes between several small parties. The CDU includes people of differing backgrounds and viewpoints; on social legislation, on taxation, on other subjects we have arguments. But in the end a compromise is reached, so that we continue to function as a united party."

The CDU represents a coming together of most nonsocialist German voters, and it is considerably more moderate and social-minded than conservative parties of the past. At the same time, and partly because the CDU developed so much voting strength, the Social Democrats have displayed a marked tendency to broaden the basis of their appeal. Their leaders lay stress on the idea not of a workers' party, but of a people's party. The old rigid Marxist doctrines of class war have now been quite generally discarded.

The Social Democrats are trying to cast themselves in the image of a pragmatic progressive party, with no intention of "liquidating" or expropriating the middle classes or setting up any dictatorship of the proletariat. They even use the argument that a free market economy would be better safeguarded under their administration—because they would bear down harder on cartels and other devices for keeping up prices.

This pattern, very noticeable in Germany, of conservatives becoming more welfare-state-minded and socialists becoming quite unrevolutionary, is characteristic of Western Europe. This was brought to my attention once by a talented young Dutch economist whose father had been the Laborite prime minister of the government of the Netherlands.[1]

"Both liberalism and socialism have changed profoundly since the war," he said. "Most liberals now admit that the state must intervene in economic life, if necessary, to prevent mass unemployment and industrial stagnation. Most socialists are prepared to drop such goals as all-out nationalization of industry, minute state planning, rationing. We had enough of that sort of thing under the Nazis. And socialists both here in the Netherlands and in other countries of Western Europe have been impressed by postwar American prosperity and by the remarkable recovery in Germany—both on the basis of a free enterprise economy. With each side giving up its more extreme positions and moving toward a middle-of-the-road attitude, the old romantic idea of fighting out a socialist revolution on the barricades is as dead as the nineteenth century."

Germany offers an excellent example of prewar extremes becoming softened and moderated. So an important feature of Adenauer's political legacy to Germany is two big political parties, opposed to each other on various matters of detail but not likely to fly at each others' throats in irreconcilable conflict. Indeed the Social Democrats are willing, even eager to accept a share of power in a coalition cabinet with a CDU chancellor. Their prospect of winning a clear electoral majority is dubious; their high-water mark in a national election, in 1961, was 36 per cent of the total vote cast. It is unlikely that a coalition between the two big parties will be formed under Adenauer, although the old chancellor was so exasperated by the attitude of the Free Democrats during the cabinet crisis late in 1962 that he put out feelers to the Social Democrats through one of his trusted advisers, Baron von Guttenberg. This, however, came to nothing; Adenauer lost interest when he learned that the Social Democrats were just as insistent as the Free Democrats on a date for his retirement.

A post-Adenauer coalition between CDU and SPD is not to be ruled out, especially in the event of a national emergency. Such an arrangement would duplicate the permanent coalition between two very evenly matched big parties (the Socialists and the conservative People's Party) in neighboring Austria. It would be open to the objections that the voters would, in effect, be deprived of any choice in an election, and that government posts would have to be parcelled out on a basis of party parity rather than merit. But unless the Free Democrats can work more effectively in harness as coalition partners, the alternative of a CDU-SPD coalition— which might mean a change in election laws that would wipe out smaller parties altogether—is not outside the range of possibility.

The personal problem involved in the Adenauer succession is complicated because of the long unwillingness of the chancellor to give his political blessing to the most probable immediate candidate for the chancellor's post, Ludwig Erhard. Adenauer distrusts Erhard's capacity to handle foreign affairs and also to hold together the disparate factions and groups in the CDU. Of all the Bonn political figures Erhard is perhaps most passionately devoted to an ideology, with his faith that honestly enforced competition, with no favors to big combinations of capital or of labor, is the key to enduring economic well-being. This has more than once brought him into conflict with Adenauer, who is more willing, for political reasons, to make concessions to special interest groups and who takes little interest in economics anyway.

Erhard has lost some prestige by not resigning in protest against the sharp-tongued chancellor's occasional open attacks on him; he has been nicknamed "the rubber lion." Erhard is not a militant political figure, and his temperament and his preoccupation with economics have kept him out of the rough-and-tumble of party infighting. Although his popularity as the visible symbol of Germany's regained prosperity won him the majority vote of CDU members of the Bundestag as Adenauer's successor in April, 1963, Adenauer himself would probably prefer his friend and political confidant, Heinrich Krone. Politicians in Germany, as elsewhere, like to nominate a winner. Erhard looks like the most hopeful winner of the 1965 election for the CDU.

His accession to power may have important consequences in foreign policy. Erhard has favored a united Europe not as an end in itself, but as a means to removing trade and tariff barriers in an important part of the world. Maximum free trade is part of his economic credo. He will almost certainly oppose General de Gaulle's conception of a "tight little Europe" and will wish to attract as many countries as possible into the low-tariff or no-tariff club.

Erhard has passed the age of sixty-five, and, as his rotund figure would indicate, he is less abstemious in his habits than the somewhat austere Adenauer. His term of office will probably be much shorter than that of his famous predecessor, and speculation is already revolving around the names of younger men in the CDU who may take over when Erhard dies. Among those who are often mentioned as possible candidates for the long-range succession to Adenauer are Foreign Minister Gerhard Schroeder, former Defense Minister Franz Josef Strauss, and CDU party chairman, Josef Hermann Dufhues.

Schroeder's political stock went up and that of Strauss declined during 1962. But this is a situation which could change after the passing of years. Born in 1910, Schroeder studied law, philosophy, and history at several German universities and also at Edinburgh. His career as a lawyer was interrupted by military service in World War II. After the war he became a prominent figure at the bar in the Ruhr and he helped to work out plans for reorganization of the coal and steel industries. He left private practice to become federal minister of the interior in 1953, and was appointed foreign minister in November, 1961, when Adenauer found himself obliged to sacrifice his old favorite in this post, Heinrich von Brentano.

As minister of the interior Schroeder acquired the reputation of being an efficient administrator, precise in detail but rather cold and aloof in personality. He began to be mentioned as a possible future chancellor only after he became foreign minister and struck out along more independent lines than his predecessor, who had always been something of a yes man for Adenauer. Schroeder furnished a counterweight to Adenauer's rather strong pro-French orientation. The foreign minister's patience and understanding in the tedious and sometimes irritating exchanges between Washington and Bonn during the exploratory talks with Moscow on the Berlin issue offset the chancellor's occasional outbursts of suspicion and resentment. Schroeder's attitude found expression in the question with which he answered some Bundestag critics who felt he was going too far in accepting the United States position:

"Do you know of any power that can protect us—except the United States?"

Schroeder seemed to develop a new personality image as he showed himself determined to run his own Ministry without too much interference from the Schaumburg Palace. He encouraged debate on foreign affairs in the Bundestag. His political prestige rose with the opposition Social Democrats, with the often balky coalition partners, the Free Democrats, and also with those members of the CDU who have reservations about Adenauer's coolness toward the Anglo-Saxon powers. He accomplished more for himself politically in eight months as foreign minister than in eight years as minister of the interior.

Before the *Spiegel* crisis, [2] of which he was the principal casualty, Franz Josef Strauss, for many years head of the Defense Ministry, would perhaps have headed the list of candidates for the future chancellorship, assuming that Erhard becomes Adenauer's immediate successor. And even at a time when Strauss is temporarily down, it would be dangerous to count him out. Of all the younger men in political life, he is the most vivid and strongly etched personality, applauded by his partisans, obnoxious to his opponents.

A big, bluff, hearty Bavarian, son of a Munich butcher, Strauss almost from the beginning has been closely identified with Germany's new military establishment. His enormous energy and ability are conceded even by his enemies; one of his Bavarian political friends characterized his future potentiality as "incalculable." His exceptional proficiency in Latin as a boy won him a scholarship which paved the way to a good classical education.

He fought what was long a hard fight to persuade German public opinion to accept the necessity for German rearmament. A quick and vigorous debater, he gave and took hard knocks in Bundestag debates with the Social Democrats. In a conversation with me he once referred to a campaign against German nuclear arming which was being waged under the slogan *Gegen den Atom Tod* ("Against Atomic Death"):

"Of course we are all against atomic death. We are against death with conventional weapons. We are against death in general. But should we send our troops to fight against tanks with bows and arrows? This is just what it would mean if we were to renounce nuclear weapons while the enemy has these weapons."

Strauss has been insistent that the German Bundeswehr should receive the same weapons as its allies, both for the sake of morale and in the interest of an efficient defense of Europe. He once told me he was satisfied, on the whole, with the present system, under which German troops are trained in the use of nuclear weapons, but with the warheads under American lock and key, to be released only in the event of an ultimate emergency. However, he wished the system were less time-consuming. And he has expressed himself in favor of an independent European nuclear deterrent.

Born in 1915, a power in the politics of his native Bavaria,

Strauss seems certain to leave his mark in German political life. His worst stumbling block, which he may overcome with increasing maturity, is his habit of getting involved in incidents which place him in an unfavorable light. Finesse is not his strong point. Even before the *Spiegel* affair Strauss was under a cloud because of a long parliamentary airing of a recommendation given by him to American military authorities for a firm that was supposed to put up buildings for the use of American soldiers. The project was dropped and there was no indication of personal corruption. But in this case the former defense minister seems to have acted hastily in a desire to do a favor to a fellow-Bavarian, who employed an unqualified contractor.

To his admirers Strauss is potentially the greatest political leader in post-Adenauer Germany. His detractors find him too impulsive, too brusque, too dictatorial—a possible danger to democracy. Just because of his fiery temperament, not a quality widely shared among the political figures of Adenauer's Fourth Reich, Franz Josef Strauss seems a man to watch, despite his temporary eclipse late in 1962.

One of the newer names in the list of possible future chancellors is Josef Hermann Dufhues. He came into national prominence early in 1962, when he received the longwinded title of *Geschäftsführender Vorsitzender* ("managing chairman") of the CDU. In this capacity he was supposed to relieve Adenauer, who had previously functioned as party leader in addition to administering government affairs, of part of his burden. His functions include looking after party organization, planning political campaigns, and supervising the regional and local organizations of the CDU.

Dufhues is a lawyer who from 1958 was minister of the interior in the rich and populous state of North Rhine-Westphalia. A Catholic, brought up in the tradition of the pre-Hitler Center Party, he has taken over in his new post the strategic task of party management which Adenauer had previously kept in his own hands.

One of his first acts was to visit London and study the organization of the British Conservative Party, which is similar to the CDU in much of its political philosophy and program. He was impressed by what he learned and is expected to wield a new broom in the offices of the CDU. In a radio statement he suggested a more active political role for the party:

"I don't want the responsibility for political development to be entirely in the hands of the government, and thus largely in the hands of the administrative offices with which the government co-operates. I should like to see the party approach the government with constant suggestions about important political questions, and the government take these suggestions into consideration in making its decisions."

Defense Ministry, Bavarian politics, Foreign Ministry, direction of the CDU machine—these are all springboards from which there might be a leap to the highest office in the land. Among other possible candidates in the CDU camp are Heinrich Krone, Eugen Gerstenmeier, Heinrich von Brentano, and Kai-Uwe von Hassell. And in politics, there is always the chance of a "dark horse" not at present in the public eye.

Gerstenmeier is president of the Bundestag. He is prominent in Protestant church circles, is an eloquent speaker, and narrowly escaped with his life after the unsuccessful conspiracy against Hitler of July 20, 1944. His name was often mentioned in the autumn of 1961, when there were rumors of a combination of the two big parties, the CDU and the Social Democrats, without Adenauer. One of his close friends described Gerstenmeier's attitude as too passive for political competition, and summed up his position as follows:

"If it be God's will that I become chancellor, so be it. But I will not lift a finger to bring this about."

Krone, Adenauer's probable choice, is a politician's politician, highly esteemed in the upper circles of the CDU for his sagacity, experience, and ability in conciliating opposing points of view, but little known to the rank-and-file voter. He would very probably make an excellent chief executive—if he could be elected. But doubt on this point seems to place him rather low on the list of candidates for the Adenauer succession.

Kai-Uwe von Hassel has gone to the Defense Ministry in Bonn after a markedly successful term of eight years as prime minister of Germany's northernmost state, bordering on Denmark—

Schleswig-Holstein. When he took over the administration, Schleswig-Holstein was sometimes called the poorhouse of Germany. It was flooded with refugees, natural resources were limited, and there was a nationality problem with the Danish minority. Now Schleswig-Holstein is rated among the better governed states, economic conditions have much improved, and a good deal of the credit goes to its earnest, serious, fabulously hardworking prime minister.

Von Hassel faces new difficulties in Bonn, especially at a time when NATO is rent with differences of opinion, some political, some military. However Von Hassel's notably calm, equable disposition, rooted in a basically conservative attitude toward life, may have a desirable effect after the tempests which were sometimes unloosed by his more temperamental predecessor.

The new defense minister has come up the hard way. As he once remarked: "Nothing has been given to me. I have had to work hard for everything." Forty-nine years old when he shifted his office from Kiel to Bonn, Von Hassel is the son of a German plantation owner in Africa, expelled after the German colonies were lost following World War I. Kai-Uwe returned to Africa in 1935, and established himself again in Tanganyika, only to be deported after the outbreak of World War II. He served in the armed forces through five years of war, thereby getting some practical initiation into the military affairs for which he now assumes responsibility.

There is some talk in Germany of a triumvirate—Schroeder, Dufhues, Von Hassel—which may function as an advisory council to Erhard, in view of his relative inexperience in details of home and foreign policy.

There is no assurance, not even much likelihood, that the office of chancellor will remain a CDU monopoly during the post-Adenauer period. Where voting is free there is usually a tendency for the political pendulum to swing after one party has been in power for a long time. In Adenauer the CDU will lose a big political asset. Intellectuals may storm and politicians may fume over some of *Der Alte's* special methods of governing, but a good many Germans have been steadily voting for Adenauer as a leader of stature and proved ability to achieve his aims. No comparable towering figure is visible on the German political stage today.

There are internal stresses and strains in the CDU, personal, regional, and ideological, that might lead to schisms after Adenauer's commanding authority is no more. But a breakup seems unlikely, because of the common interest in remaining the governing party. It is not impossible, however. There is also the possibility that the votes of the two big parties may become so nearly even that it will become difficult for either to govern alone. This might bring in Germany the Austrian solution of a permanent coalition of the two large parties, with a meticulously measured sharing of posts in public service, from top to bottom.

Certainly some of the leading personalities of the Social Democratic Party should be considered in any sketch of perspectives after the passing of the Adenauer era. The front man of the Social Democratic Party, its presumptive candidate for chancellor, is Willy Brandt, very much in the public eye in Germany and abroad because of his post as burgomaster of harassed West Berlin. For the first time he carried the standard for his party in the 1961 election, and he raised the increase in the proportion of socialist votes cast from 31.8 per cent to 36.2 per cent, with a gain of some 20 seats in the Bundestag.

Brandt is a handsome man in middle age, with an attractive family, a sympathetic, outgoing manner, and an apparently inexhaustible capacity for hard work—a German characteristic that knows no party lines. Despite his exacting official duties, he makes time available to receive many foreign visitors to Berlin, convinced as he is that the widest possible understanding abroad of Berlin's position is an important element in the city's struggle for freedom.

West Berlin's mayor was an illegitimate child who grew up in a working-class socialist atmosphere. He took refuge from the Nazi terror in Norway, was active in socialist underground activity, and found asylum in Sweden when the Nazis overran Norway. He acquired Norwegian citizenship and returned to Germany as a member of the Norwegian mission in Berlin. Rejoining his old party comrades, he became a lieutenant of the militant Social Democratic mayor of West Berlin, Ernst Reuter, who led the struggle of the people of Berlin against Communist infiltration and terror and the attempted starvation of the city which was frustrated by the airlift. Some time after Reuter's death, Brandt, now a German citizen, succeeded to the office.

It is not altogether accidental that a Berlin Social Democrat should have become his party's most hopeful candidate for national leadership. Especially in the first years after the end of the war there was a distinct psychological difference between Social Democrats in Berlin and in West Germany. This was partly because in Berlin Social Democrats had the practical responsibility of carrying on the administration, while in the Federal Republic they could permit themselves the luxury of negative opposition.

I first met Brandt in the corridors of the Bundestag in the early fifties. (He was a deputy from Berlin, with the right to sit and speak but not to vote.) I was impressed by the fact that he did not talk like a typical West German socialist. At that time the Social Democratic Party was opposed to German rearmament and distrustful of the Western powers, yet Brandt was already convinced that Germany must make a contribution to its own defense, and in alliance with the West.

The special situation of West Berlin, an island in a Communist sea, made its Social Democrats pragmatic, not dogmatic, in their approach to questions of policy. Their two primary objectives as the dominant party in the administration of the city were to rebuild Berlin and to preserve its freedom against the threats and pressure of the Soviet Union and its German satellites. Neither could be achieved without close co-operation with and help from the West, especially from the United States. In a larger sense this was equally true for West Germany also, and the German people gradually swung around, following Adenauer's leadership, to accept this view. But Berlin's location directly on the firing line created a clarity of perception that was slower in developing in the Federal Republic. So it was easier for a man with Brandt's background to discard old shibboleths of inevitable class warfare and point the Social Democratic Party in the direction of aims not very dissimilar to those of America's New Deal and New Frontier.

I had another experience of Brandt's independence of party

dogma when I called on him in 1959 at the Schöneberg Rathaus, the administrative center for West Berlin. At that time the Social Democrats had put forward a so-called Germany Plan, which offered far-reaching concessions to the regime in the Soviet Zone in the hope of making a start toward German unification. Brandt was visibly embarrassed when I referred to this, remarked that the plan was a matter for discussion, and personally dissociated himself from it. The whole idea was dropped as it became clear that Khrushchev was interested only in a Germany united under Communist rule.

Two aspects of Brandt's image hurt him to some extent with the more conservative Germans: his illegitimate birth and the fact that he returned to Germany in the uniform, or at least in the service, of a foreign country. But he seems to be the party's best vote-getter, with a wider popular appeal than the average socialist functionary who has not fully achieved the psychological transition from a "workers'" into a "people's" party.

Perhaps the ablest of the Social Democratic parliamentarians, a man who will almost certainly receive a high post in a Social Democratic or coalition cabinet, is Fritz Erler, who took advantage of a term in prison under the Nazis to learn fluent and excellent English. Erler is a leading Social Democratic specialist on national defense. During an hour's conversation in his office in the Bundestag he expressed a viewpoint much closer to that of the Kennedy Administration than one is apt to hear from some CDU spokesmen.

Only America, Erler feels, represents a genuine shield for Germany and for Europe. There can be no effective nuclear weapons base in such a restricted area as Europe. France's independent nuclear deterrent he dismissed as "not enough to threaten the Soviet Union, just enough to create a quarrel within the NATO alliance." Nuclear weapons in the direct possession of the Bundeswehr? "Too dangerous. The power to touch off an atomic war should not be in the hands of a company commander. This is the gravest kind of political decision. And, given the present balance of power, only one man in the world, the president of the United States, is qualified to take it."

Erler believes there should be more advance consultation with America's European allies and more precise advance information about America's military dispositions and plans. But he conveyed the impression that the Social Democrats are generally satisfied with America's leadership in the defense of the free world.

On domestic affairs Erler declared that the German Social Democrats stand about where New Deal Democrats stand in the United States. Taxation with a sharper edge against the well-to-do, and increased social services? Yes. Nationalization and comprehensive planning of the details of individual life? No.

"Remember," said Erler with a smile as the interview came to an end, "there were two persons who made the German people familiar with ration cards. The first was Kaiser Wilhelm II. The second was Adolf Hitler. Neither was a member of the Social Democratic Party."

Another member of the inner circle of Social Democratic leadership is Herbert Wehner. During the war years he was apparently very close to the Communists and his name is often used as a bogey by conservative orators warning the Germans to be alert to the siren songs of a new non-Marxist socialist party. But Wehner seems to have thoroughly outlived his radical past. It was he who announced the shift in favor of supporting Adenauer's foreign policy. His name also figures among the negotiators for a CDU-SPD coalition late in 1962. Sometimes it is the ex-Communist or ex-Communist sympathizer who becomes the most principled anti-Communist, because he has a clear idea of what communism is.

Carlo Schmid, vice-president of the Bundestag, is an unusual type of Social Democrat, a somewhat bohemian intellectual of broad aesthetic interests, an early sponsor of the movement for united Europe, a coiner of witty sayings. If the German political pendulum should swing more to the left, Schmid some day might be an excellently qualified president of the Republic. Temperamentally he is not well suited to the rough-and-tumble of party politics. A popular speaker, especially before university audiences, he does not seem fitted for executive posts.

Wedged in between the two larger parties is the third political group which has maintained its representation in the Bundestag.[3] This is the Free Democratic Party, usually referred to by its initials as the FDP. Its leader is Erich Mende, a former officer with a brilliant war record who took up the practice of law after the end of the war. Mende, like any leader of this minority party, faces two difficult tasks. He must maintain his party's individual image while playing the role of junior partner in a coalition dominated by the more powerful CDU. And he must hold together in his own ranks some rather disparate elements.

The FDP is pre-eminently a middle-class party, in contrast, of course, to the SPD and even by comparison with the CDU, which has a substantial contingent of Catholic industrial working-class voters. The FDP is predominantly Protestant and liberal, in the European sense of the word, which means it is for a maximum of private enterprise and a minimum of state intervention in economic life. Its members do not always speak in the same language. In southwest Germany the FDP has attracted a number of old-fashioned liberals. In the Ruhr and in North Germany its accent is on nationalism and there is a group in the Ruhr composed of more or less reconstructed ex-Nazis.

The FDP has been a restive, not to say mutinous coalition partner. In the early fifties a group of "Young Turks" in the FDP branch in North Rhine-Westphalia broke with the CDU and for a time carried on a coalition with the Social Democrats. Later they returned to the more natural alliance with the CDU. When Adenauer lost his absolute majority in the Bundestag in 1961, there was a fairly strong movement in the FDP ranks to insist on Adenauer's departure from office as a condition for taking part in a coalition cabinet. The resistance of this group was finally overcome, but toward the end of 1962 the *Spiegel* case gave them occasion for a new rebellion, as a result of which they obtained the elimination of Franz Josef Strauss from the cabinet and a more or less firm promise from Adenauer to step down.

Ewald Bucher, one of Mende's lieutenants in the Bundestag, a lawyer who has specialized in defending the interests of small businessmen and who was appointed minister of justice in the cabinet shake-up of December, 1962, foresaw a prospect of growth for the FDP if the CDU should swing further to the left. Talking to me in the summer of 1962, he declared that his party could not remain in the coalition if decisions contrary to sound economic common sense were taken against its opposition. He mentioned especially the tendency of the government to grant wage increases that threatened to unbalance the budget and the effort to exert pressure against the decision of the Volkswagen Company to raise the prices of its cars.

The FDP lacks the solid mass support which the Social Democrats find in the trade-unions and the CDU in the churches. It would remain the only opposition, but a rather helpless one, if the two big parties should reach a coalition arrangement. Such a development might be quite disastrous for the prospects of the FDP, because it could lead to an elimination of the element of modified proportional representation in the German electoral law. There would be very few FDP deputies in the Bundestag if the American or British method of giving the seat to the winner in each constituency, with no consideration for the third party vote, should be adopted in Germany.

In all three parties there are a number of men who have proved in national and local offices that they could carry on a competent administration. Naturally the departure of Adenauer will be keenly felt. But it is quite possible that the passing of de Gaulle will create more difficulties for France than that of Adenauer will for Germany. Of the two countries Germany has the more placid political atmosphere. There is no large Communist Party in Germany, as there is in France, to form the nucleus of a possible "popular front" and thereby create a bitterly hostile reaction on the right.

The CDU and the SPD are opponents, but they talk the language of mutual understanding and compromise. Political fanaticism in Germany is at an all-time low ebb. There are no irreconcilable feuds on basic issues of foreign and home policy. A severe economic crisis might change this picture, and one should not underrate the potential danger implicit in the fact that the Federal Republic is not *das ganze Deutschland* ("the whole Germany") of the poem. Only reunion in freedom can bring a sense of ultimate permanence.

But, with no visible extremist movements of any consequence, with no very black economic storm clouds on the horizon, the political weather outlook for Germany seems generally fair. There seems to be an excellent prospect that the Federal Republic, so largely the creation of Konrad Adenauer, will survive its founding father in good operating condition and remain one of the more stable partners in the new, more closely integrated Europe.

A long step was taken toward the solution of the problem of the political succession to Adenauer when the parliamentary membership of the CDU designated Economics Minister Ludwig Erhard as their choice for the next Chancellor late in April, 1963. Although nothing in politics is quite certain, there is an apparently irreversible character about this decision. What remains uncertain is the exact date of Adenauer's retirement, and this is expected in the autumn of 1963.

Considerations of both foreign and internal politics hastened this vote (which was scarcely acceptable to the old Chancellor although he appeared to take it with fairly good grace). German public opinion was inclined to regret the accidental coincidence between General de Gaulle's veto on the admission of Great Britain to the EEC and the signing of a treaty of consultation between France and Germany. While virtually all Germans rejoice in the ending of the historic feud between Germany and France, very few Germans are enthusiastic over the idea of a German foreign policy oriented exclusively toward Paris, to the detriment of relations with the United States and Great Britain. And there was some feeling that Adenauer made no very strenuous effort to modify de Gaulle's anti-British stand.

Moreover, local elections in a number of states, in North Rhine-Westphalia, in West Berlin, and in the Rhine-Pfalz had been going badly for the CDU, and one cause was believed to be uncertainty as to leadership after the retirement of Adenauer. In the first weeks after his specific designation as political heir-apparent, Erhard brought off several successes, which helped to enhance his prestige and perhaps his self-confidence. He was instrumental in pushing through a compromise settlement of a serious strike in the metal industry. His participation in a state election in Lower Saxony broke the political losing streak of the CDU, which registered an increase in its vote over the preceding election. (The Social Democrats also gained; both these big parties seem to have profited from the decline and disintegration of some small political groupings.) And Erhard also functioned as a successful mediator in negotiations between the United States and the EEC representatives on trade and tariffs.

The Erhard administration will presumably come into office before the end of 1963, and will most probably continue if the CDU comes out of the 1965 national election the strongest single party. It may be expected to remain loyal to Adenauer's policy of close political, economic, and military ties with the West. On one occasion, before an audience of African political and economic visitors to Germany, Erhard enraged Soviet Ambassador Smirnov by declaring, "I hope the African peoples, who have obtained their independence, are fully conscious of the fact that there is no worse type of colonialism than totalitarian Communist imperialism."

Although Erhard is an individualist rather than a team man by temperament (he pretty much let his economics ministry run itself), he is not likely to run such a one-man political show as did his predecessor. As a German diplomat privately remarked to me, "Adenauer was his own foreign minister, his own defense minister, his own finance minister." Under Erhard there will probably be a more normal balance between the head of the government and the members of his Cabinet. Erhard's instincts will be against a closedoff "Little Europe," although Germany by itself cannot counteract General de Gaulle's views about British unsuitability for membership in a European community. From his past record he may be expected to support moves for the widest possible area of free trade with a minimum of tariffs and other barriers.

One temperamental difference between the first and the prospective second Chancellor of the Federal Republic is that Adenauer takes a pessimistic and Erhard an optimistic view of human nature. It remains to be seen which will prove the better basis for enlightened statesmanship.

NOTES TO CHAPTER VI

1 The Dutch economist was using "liberalism" in the European, not the American, connotation of the word. The European liberal is for as much free private enterprise as possible, while the American-style liberal is a champion of state intervention to cure real or alleged economic defects.

2 This was described in the preceding chapter, pp. 97–98.

3 A party that fails to win either 5 per cent of the total vote or a plurality in any single constituency loses its right to representation in the Bundestag. This is why small "splinter" parties, so numerous in the Weimar Republic, have, as a rule, quickly passed out of existence in the new Germany.

CHAPTER VII

Germany Divided

THE enforced, artificial, and unnatural partition of Germany is one of the most disastrous consequences of World War II, if only because it might well become a contributing cause of World War III. It is hard to believe that a people as energetic, nationally conscious, and highly educated as the Germans can be kept divided forever, especially at a time when the right of self-determination is being claimed by primitive African peoples who scarcely know what the word means.

Yet the twenty-two divisions of the Red Army stationed in the Soviet Zone of Occupation constitute an impressive warning that the reunification of Germany in freedom is apparently not possible without a major war. The Allied forces in West Germany and in West Berlin offer an equally clear warning that a Soviet military attempt to extend to all Germany the satellite Communist regime which has been set up in the Soviet Zone will mean all-out war. The Western powers will certainly not initiate a war for German reunion. The balance of probability, despite Khrushchev's threats and brinkmanship in Berlin, is that the Soviet Union also will refrain from such a desperate course.

The military establishment of the Federal Republic is so closely tied in with NATO as regards logistics and supplies that it could not touch off a war, even if the public opinion of a Germany that shudders at the memory of the non-nuclear bombings of the last war would support such a move. The Soviet Zone administration is still more completely bound to the Soviet Union.

So the partition of Germany creates the most difficult type of political problem—a situation that cries aloud for a remedy, but that cannot be changed without risking even less tolerable disasters than the status quo. Some American politicians and publicists, notably Senator Mike Mansfield and Walter Lippmann, have proposed that the West and East Germans should negotiate between themselves for a basis of unity. It is also the Soviet viewpoint, set forth in a number of official statements and diplomatic notes, that there are two German states, and that unification is a matter for these states to work out between themselves.

If it were true that there are two independent German states, one in the West, committed to political freedom and private enterprise, the other in the East, more inclined to a state-managed economy, a formula for reunion could probably be found. But no such situation exists. There is only one German government which derives its authority from freely elected representative bodies and the rule of law. This is the Federal Republic, with its capital at Bonn.

The so-called DDR (initials for German Democratic Republic) is neither German nor democratic nor a republic. It is a totalitarian police regime, completely subservient to the will of a foreign power, the Soviet Union. Not since 1946 has there been a semblance of a free election in the Soviet Zone. Many of East Germany's leaders, notably the dictator Walter Ulbricht, have been trained in the Soviet Union, and as indoctrinated Communists, owe allegiance not to the German people but to Moscow. In the past some have assumed Soviet citizenship. It is difficult to see how any benefit could come out of talks between spokesmen for this made-in-Moscow regime and representatives of the Federal Republic. On the Communist side there would be no independence, no maneuverability. Ulbricht could not accept a comma in any agreement without the approval of Khrushchev.

The German governors of the Soviet Zone can have few illusions as to the amount of popular support they possess. On this point there are two incontestable decisive proofs. A Berlin workers' strike against excessive speed-up demands in June, 1953 quickly developed into a general work stoppage that paralyzed the whole administration of the Zone. The DDR would have ended then and there if Soviet troops with tanks had not moved in to restore Ulbricht's Humpty Dumpty rule. (There has never been a case when Allied troops intervened to put down a revolt in the Federal Republic.)

With outright revolt hopeless, with no means of protesting through the press or the ballot, some 3.7 million inhabitants of the Soviet Zone registered their emphatic negative vote by taking to their heels and fleeing to the West. This was always at the price of leaving behind all they owned, except what they could carry, and often at the risk of arrest or shooting by frontier guards.

Free discussion with the people of the Soviet Zone is obviously impossible, as anyone can see by going up to the barbed-wire entanglements which mark the Eastern—not the Western—side of the interzonal frontier. Since August, 1961, these have been supplemented by the wall that cuts the city of Berlin in two. The refusal of the Bonn government to recognize this foreign satellite tyranny, its insistence on breaking relations with any government which does accord such recognition (with an exception only for the Soviet Union) is not, as critics sometimes allege, an ostrich-like unwillingness to face reality, but a realistic appraisal of the futility of any such concession.

The demarcation line between the Soviet and the Western zones was worked out in negotiations in London among the United States, the Soviet Union, and Great Britain during the winter of 1944–45. At that time it was believed that American and British troops might not reach this line by the end of the war. But the swift collapse of German resistance, especially in the West [1] in the last months of the war, enabled American troops to overrun considerable areas of Saxony and Thuringia which had been allotted to the Soviet Zone. These areas were handed back to Soviet administration as arrangements were completed for the Western powers to take over their previously agreed sectors in the city of Berlin, a little over a hundred miles inside the Soviet Zone and surrounded by it.

It would have been militarily feasible for the American and British forces to have reached Berlin ahead of the Russians. Winston Churchill, with his keen political instinct, recommended that this be done. But General Eisenhower rejected the idea on the ground that "Berlin itself is no longer a particularly important objective." [2] Militarily this may have been true, because the German will and ability to fight on were in an advanced state of collapse. But the possession of Berlin would have been a political asset of the first value. Eisenhower suggests in his memoirs that, in any event, the demarcation line was fixed well to the west of Berlin. But the fixing of the demarcation line was only one of a number of Soviet-Western agreements. One of these provided for "free unfettered elections in Poland"—of which there has been no sign up to the present time. Berlin in Allied hands could well have been treated as a pledge for the implementation of free elections in Poland—or as a compensation for the breach of this engagement.

The interzonal frontier starts at the Baltic Sea, just east of the old Hanseatic town of Lübeck, and runs in a general north-south direction, turning eastward so as to leave Bavaria entirely in the American Zone of Occupation. The boundary in the main follows the frontiers of the former German states of Pomerania, Brandenburg, Anhalt, Saxony, and Thuringia. But in some cases, as I have seen, there are little Berlins, villages sundered by slashes of barbed wire, perhaps because the line was drawn just where the military operations ceased. The erection of the Berlin wall made escape from East Berlin, formerly fairly easy, extremely difficult, and in 1962 the Soviet Zone frontier was strengthened by clearing a wide strip along the border, by laying mine fields, and by setting up new stronger barbed-wire fences.[3]

The possibility of breaking up Germany into two or more states was discussed at the Yalta Conference of the Big Three in February, 1945. But the decision at the later Potsdam meeting (July-August, 1945) was to treat Germany as a political and economic unit. In practice, however, the Soviet Government handled its zone as an area of exclusive exploitation, detached from the remainder of Germany. At the same time the Soviet authorities tried to obtain and for a time did obtain reparations, in the form of dismantled machinery and equipment, from the Western zones.

The Soviet plan for the communization of its zone unfolded gradually, both in economics and in politics. Industrial plants in the key industries and those whose owners had fled to the West were declared *volkseigen* ("owned by the people") and operated by state trusts, as in the Soviet Union. But for some years a fair amount of industry and trade was left in private hands. The first agrarian legislation provided for confiscating the larger estates, which mostly belonged to Junker families and dividing up the land among the peasants. This was explained as a punitive measure against "Nazis and militarists."

Politically, also, there was at first a show of moderation. The military administration in the Soviet Zone permitted the existence not only of the Communist Party, but of the Social Democrats, the CDU, and the Liberal Democrats. In April, 1946, some of the Social Democrats, under strong pressure, consented to merge their party with the Communists. This was the origin of the ruling group in the zone, the SED (Socialist Unity Party of Germany). However, Social Democrats in West Germany and in the western sectors of Berlin refused to recognize the merger and maintained the separate identity of their party.

There were reasonably honest elections in the Soviet Zone, for the first and last time, in the autumn of 1946. The newly organized SED naturally received preference from the Soviet occupation authorities in such matters as newsprint and transportation facilities, and no independent Social Democratic candidates were permitted, as it was assumed that the whole party was bound to accept the fusion with the Communists. However, the SED won only about half the seats in the provincial parliaments. And in Berlin, which voted as a unit, West and East, the Soviet-organized party sustained a crushing defeat, receiving only about 20 per cent of the vote, as against 48.7 per cent for the independent Social Democrats, the remainder going to the CDU and the Liberal Democrats. Wolfgang Leonhard, a young Russian-trained German Communist, was quick to analyze the reasons for the defeat: [4]

"To the man in the street we were known as the 'Russian party'. . . . The result of the election was a logical consequence of our dependence on the Soviet occupation authorities. I told myself that the population of Berlin had not voted against us because we were in favor of socialism. . . . They voted against us because they saw in us a party dependent on the Soviet Union; and unfortunately they were not wrong."

Leonhard, something of a German Titoist [5] before Tito had asserted his independence of Moscow, hoped that the SED would improve its image with the German people by dissociating itself from too close an identification with the Russians, who were hated because of the savage brutality with which the Red Army had raped, looted, and smashed everything in sight during the sack of Berlin and other German cities. But just the reverse happened. The links with the Soviet Union and the Soviet occupation authorities were strengthened. Soviet holidays were observed with servile tributes to Stalin. And the efforts of the SED to procure a stoppage of dismantling were ineffective.

Indeed Soviet policy in the Zone in the first postwar years suffered from a kind of schizophrenia. While the head of the political administration, Colonel Tulpanov, and his aides tried to create a basis for pro-Soviet sympathy, other Moscow agencies persisted in extensive dismantling, sometimes removing machinery and equipment more than once, after a plant had started up again. Many finished products were also siphoned off for Soviet use by placing some plants under Soviet control and earmarking their output for reparations. No accurate record of the value of Soviet appropriations was kept; but the figure may have easily reached $10 billion,[6] the sum in German reparations which Stalin demanded at Yalta.

The levying of reparations ceased in 1953, long after dismantling and other measures of exaction had ceased in the West. There was no Soviet equivalent for the Marshall Plan aid which the United States extended to the Federal Republic, although the Soviet Union, in special crisis situations, has granted credits to prop up its satellite regime or to promote industrial construction considered useful for Soviet purposes.

After beginning with a show of political and economic moderation, the DDR evolved steadily toward complete totalitarianism. All signs of independent thought, even within the framework of the dominant Marxist philosophy, were ruthlessly stamped out. So the Communist philosopher Wolfgang Harich and some of his associates were arrested in 1956 and Harich was sentenced to ten years in prison on the charge of "forming a conspirative group hostile to the state." What Harich had apparently favored was the injection of some elements of personal and intellectual freedom into a socialist society.

There was a purge of three high party functionaries, Ernst Wollweber, Karl Schirdewan, and Friedrich Oelssner, in 1958. Wollweber had been a prominent figure in the secret police, Schirdewan and Oelssner in the party and state administration. Through these and other shifts Ulbricht became steadily more powerful, easily eclipsing the president, Wilhelm Pieck—a corpulent veteran Communist who was approaching senility before his death and the prime minister, Otto Grotewohl, who suffers from chronic poor health.

Born in 1893, Ulbricht is a native of Leipzig and speaks with the strong local Saxon accent. A joiner by trade, he became a member of the Social Democratic Party at the age of nineteen, sided with its more extreme wing during World War I, and was one of the early members of the German Communist Party. Going into exile after Hitler came into power, Ulbricht spent some time in France, and like many other prominent Communists, turned up in Spain during the civil war, becoming notorious for "liquidating" anti-Stalinists in the republican armed forces. He possesses a remarkable memory and enormous capacity for work. Completely devoid of pity or of any moral sentiment, with no capacity for original thinking, Ulbricht is the perfect type of Communist *apparatchik,* or operative bureaucrat. Sometimes hopeful rumors get about that he may be shelved and replaced by a milder Soviet proconsul. But from the standpoint of the Kremlin he is extremely useful for his ability to sit on the lid of seething discontent and to create a machinery of repression which can extract from his subjects a maximum of work for a minimum of reward. With the bright, magnetic example of the Federal Republic just across the zonal border, a milder type of ruler—a German Gomulka—might be too great a risk.

The DDR was formally instituted on October 7, 1949 as a response to the establishment of the Federal Republic in West

Germany. On its tenth anniversary, in 1959, the Association of Free Jurists in West Berlin, which has collected voluminous material about violations of personal rights and liberties in the Soviet Zone, published a summary of significant developments during its existence. In abridged form this summary gives a picture of the steady march toward the totalitarian state: [7]

1950. A Ministry of State Security [8] was created to take over the police powers formerly exercised by the Russians. There was an "election" in the Russian style, based on a single list of candidates, for a legislature, the Volkskammer ("People's Chamber"). The list was allegedly endorsed by 99.7 per cent of those who voted.

1951. Arrests multiplied. In a single trial 19 young people (some below the age of 18) were sentenced to a total of 130 years of imprisonment. The workers lost the right to bargain freely; "collective agreements" were henceforward to be drawn up by the factory management.

1952. A security zone and a "death strip" were established along the zonal border. All property belonging to people who flee was declared confiscated.

1953. The Soviet Zone administration raised compulsory work quotas by 10 per cent with no increase in pay. This led to a strike of building workers in East Berlin's Stalin-Allee and to the general uprising which paralyzed the zonal authorities until Soviet troops moved in with tanks. Eighteen persons were sentenced to death; 4,000 years of imprisonment were meted out to about 1,200 people. There was a record flight of 331,390 persons to the West.

1954. A campaign was launched against religious teaching in homes and schools. There was intensified effort to regiment the young people in Communist organizations.

1955. A drive was started against private industry and in favor of state co-operatives among the peasants.

1956. First trials of persons who "encouraged flight from the People's Republic." Two men and one woman were sentenced to life imprisonment for this alleged crime. The regime introduced a new method of destroying private business firms by "offering" state participation in financing and management.

1957. Ulbricht proclaimed that anyone leaving the German Democratic Republic was a traitor to the working class. A new passport law decreed three years of imprisonment for everyone making an unauthorized journey outside the DDR. Travel to West Germany was drastically curtailed.

1958. Ulbricht announced a new law under which any criticism of the regime was punishable as a slandering of the state. Nineteen students of Jena University were sent to prison for breaking this law. In imitation of the Soviet Union, "polytechnical" education was introduced. All school children were required to work in industry and agriculture for stated periods.

1959. The Ministry for Cultural Affairs ordered a purge of the universities and technical colleges. In Dresden five students were sentenced to a total of 37½ years of imprisonment. Members of the People's Chamber were instructed that their duty was not to represent the wishes of their constituents, but to explain and justify every act of the government.

The chronicle of the Free Jurists ended with 1959. But the march toward totalitarianism went on. The last individual peasant farm was liquidated in 1960. About a million peasants who had kept their own land were forced to join some 20,000 collective farms, which were completely dominated by the government. There was a marked stepping up of peasant flight to the West, although shortage of unused land made it difficult to set them up there on individual homesteads.

Collectivization brought its own retribution to the rulers of the Soviet Zone. The small and medium peasant farming that had replaced the large estates of the Junkers had proved more successful than many Germans expected, and by 1958 the food situation had improved sufficiently to permit the abolition of rationing, which had been scrapped in the Federal Republic eight years earlier. Ulbricht and his henchmen began to boast that by the early sixties the DDR would be giving its people a better diet than the citizens of the Federal Republic enjoyed. These boasts now sound as hollow as Khrushchev's prediction (also in 1958) that the Soviet Union would soon exceed the United States in per capita output of meat and dairy products. Since 1960 the DDR has been plagued with persistent shortages, not only of meat, butter, and milk, but of such a staple item, for Germans, as potatoes.

Rationing, abolished with a flourish of trumpets a few years earlier, was, for practical purposes, reimposed, either by direct regulations or by the impact of shortages. Citizens are required to register in stores for meat, milk, and butter, and the butter ration was set at a quarter of a pound a week for each family member. But this quota is often not available. Restaurants in the Zone were urged to introduce potatoless days. Peasants were even encouraged to ask friends and relatives in the West for potato seed.

The cause-and-effect relation between collectivization and food shortage was admitted in the leading zone newspaper, *Neues Deutschland,* which lamented: [9] "Every good individual farmer used every hour from daybreak until late evening to sow, plow, and harvest. Today the collective farmers take time off from 5:00 P.M. and are farmers only until Saturday afternoon."

People who escaped from the Soviet Zone in 1962 unanimously reported long queues at food shops and poor quality of what fruits and vegetables were obtainable. If 1960 in the Soviet Zone was marked mainly by the enforcement of collective farming and the beginning of a prolonged food crisis, the dramatic event of 1961 was the erection of the wall which shut off communication between West and East Berlin, except at a few carefully guarded checkpoints.

The construction of this wall (the Wall of Shame, as the Germans call it) was a tremendous shock to Germans, West and East. Previously it had been fairly easy for those who found conditions in the Eastern Zone intolerable to go to East Berlin and cross into West Berlin by subway. With the wall this escape hatch was abruptly closed. Walled in by barbed wire along the zonal frontier and through the city of Berlin, the DDR was revealed as a huge concentration camp for its 17 million inhabitants.

For the West Germans also the putting up of the wall was a severe blow, indicating the limitations on the power or will to act of the Western powers and dimming very much the prospect of reunion.

The sundered sections of Germany represent the largest and

fairest experiment in competitive coexistence, which Soviet dictator Khrushchev professes to welcome. Here are people of the same nationality, language, education, and culture, living under two radically different political and economic systems. As this experiment has now gone on for almost two decades, some conclusions may reasonably be drawn. In terms of general well-being and satisfaction the result is clear beyond a shadow of reasonable doubt. Such developments as the decision of about one fifth of the population of the Soviet Zone to flee to the West, the continuing death-defying efforts, some successful, others not, to escape from the Ulbricht penitentiary, the very necessity of sealing off the Soviet Zone in order to stop a population drain that was taking away badly needed working hands and a high proportion of doctors, engineers, teachers, and other educated professional people—these developments speak for themselves.

Precise wage and salary comparisons are difficult, because the "East mark," the Soviet Zone currency, has no value in free international exchange. However, the German Industry Institute, in the summer of 1962, published a comparison of living costs in the two parts of Germany, based on the number of hours of work required for this or that object of consumption. On this basis butter was twice and beef three times as expensive in the East as in the West. Women's nylon stockings cost nine times as much, refrigerators five times, automobiles four times, television sets more than twice as much. The only things that were listed as cheaper in the Soviet Zone were haircuts and movie tickets. These comparisons are confirmed by visits to stores in both sections of the city. Books, musical instruments, and sports gear are also comparatively inexpensive in East Berlin.

As regards housing, the DDR made some progress in the later fifties, but it remains far behind the Federal Republic. In 1959, for instance, 597,000 housing units were built in the West, 77,300 in the East. It takes only a very casual comparative view to see that West Berlin is far more advanced in rebuilding and new building than East Berlin, although both sections of the city were impartially demolished by air bombing. And virtually every journalistic visitor to the Soviet Union reports a strong impression of strained, sullen faces, of uniform drabness, of curious emptiness in what were once the lively bustling streets of Leipzig and Berlin (East). So Robert Alden presents the following vignettes of Soviet Zone life: [10]

"The arrival at Leipzig is weird, a trip into a surrealistic dream world with nightmarish overtones. The buildings are old and brown and very German. The streets are cobbled and broad and there are trolley-cars moving along the tracks. But there are hardly any people in evidence—just the bare streets, the closed shutters on the windows and empty shop windows. Once the trolley-car has passed down the line, a stillness prevails, an absolutely eerie stillness. . . .

"One soon learns that the strange quiet experienced on entering Leipzig, the empty streets, the empty shops, the closed shutters, are the mark of East Germany to-day. Because this is Fair time in Leipzig [11] and many foreign visitors are here, the shops in the center of town, unlike those on the outskirts, are stocked with the best that the communist world has to offer. But one does not have to be particularly astute to learn the facts. Save for the dedicated party members, almost any Leipziger will supply the detail that a week or two after the close of the Fair the shops will be empty and once again there will be shortages of everything—potatoes, eggs, sauerkraut, beef, pork, sausage, dresses, shoes, cloth.

"Through a supreme effort Leipzig has now been made a showcase. But the East German authorities do not want Fair visitors roaming about the East German countryside and, except for a conducted bus tour of Buchenwald and Weimar, permission to leave the city is not granted."

The British correspondent Michael Wall, who visited the Soviet Zone in the spring of 1962, summed up his impressions with the observation: [12] "Cross the border into East Berlin and you have stepped back, in time, fifteen years or more." Along with many material deprivations, he found among the students "a desperate hunger for intellectual freedom" and cites one student as saying:

"You cannot buy a book or a newspaper, listen to the radio or television, or attend a lecture without hearing the party line. There are no new ideas, there is no experimentation in drama or art, no chance to travel and find out how others live and think."

All this is typical of a totalitarian regime. And the totalitarian technique of tyranny, unlimited terror plus unlimited propaganda, accounts for such strength as the DDR possesses, but it makes it repulsive to the inquiring minds among its subjects, even those who are willing to accept many of the tenets of Marxism. On passing through the passport inspection office at the Friedrichstrasse, crossing from West to East Berlin, the foreign visitor is offered a large choice of propaganda pamphlets in several languages. I noticed one in French, with a title calculated to provoke an explosion of indiscreet laughter against the background of drab desolation: *The DDR, An Economic Miracle.*

Yet, if one can forget for a moment the incredibly gray, drab, oppressive atmosphere of life on the other side of the zonal border, one must recognize that, like other totalitarian states, the DDR has registered some accomplishments. According to official figures, industrial output approximately doubled during the fifties. Especially during the period between the cessation of reparations in 1953 and the imposition of 100 per cent collectivization of farming in 1960, this growth of output was accompanied by some improvement in an extremely low standard of living. This improvement was not remotely comparable with what happened under a very different system in the Federal Republic. And it was much less than the bare statement "doubling of industrial output" would suggest.

Anyone who has lived in the Soviet Union for a considerable length of time can understand this apparent discrepancy. There also impressive figures of alleged growth of output have been accompanied by very modest, sometimes almost imperceptible gains in the bread-and-butter things of life—food, clothing, housing, consumer goods. And the reasons for the apparent contradiction are the same. Consumer demand and consumer preference play no part in the industrial development of a Communist-ruled state. In such states the people get not what they want, but what their rulers think is good for them. The consumer receives what is left after the government planners have siphoned off a tremendous amount of capital (labor power and raw materials) for the needs of heavy industry and military development. The number of East Germans in the uniforms of the "People's Army" and "People's Police" is strikingly large and represents a considerable subtraction from an already inadequate labor force.

While consumer-goods industries languish and the peasants sulk and work indifferently under the collective-farm yoke, the main energies of the Soviet Zone have been harnessed to building up big new industrial plants, some of which are not in operation, while others are of dubious utility. For instance, a construction project that has dragged on for years is the building of a petrochemical works at Schwedt on the Oder. Supposed to be the terminus of a pipeline extending over 3,000 miles from Kuybishev, on the Volga, it is apparently to come into production only in 1965.

Much work has been invested in enlarging the harbor of Rostock, one of the few DDR ports on the Baltic Sea. But Rostock's overland connections are undeveloped. The trade of its economic hinterland, Czechoslovakia and Poland, continues to flow mainly through Hamburg and Stettin, now incorporated in Poland. One of the biggest new enterprises in the Soviet Zone is located in the new center of Eisenhüttenstadt ("Steel Town") in the valley of the Oder. The original name was Stalinstadt; its renaming was Ulbricht's grudging concession to de-Stalinization. Its planned capacity is 1.7 million tons of steel a year and it was built with the idea of helping to compensate for the loss of the former economic contact with the Ruhr. But the new plant is dependent on a 1,400-mile haul of iron ore from Krivoi Rog, in the Soviet Union, and its supply of coke, from Poland, is inadequate. Its unit costs are extremely high.

An airplane factory, built in Dresden, was such an economic failure that it had to be closed down. This by no means exhausts the list of new undertakings which contribute nothing to the everyday well-being of the people in the zone and which are often run at big deficits because of faults in planning and location. Economic planning has been in the hands of a triumvirate, composed of Karl Mewis,[13] Alfred Neumann, and Bruno Leuschner, all veteran Communists, of whom only one, Leuschner, had any training in business methods. These men have obviously been guided in many of their decisions more by doctrinaire ideas than by practical considerations of efficiency.

It is a tribute to the German inheritance of technical efficiency and working discipline that despite these handicaps, the DDR has become the biggest economic partner of the Soviet Union and the countries of the Soviet bloc, just as the Federal Republic is a leader in the trade and industry of Western Europe. About half of the zone's exports of about $2 billion a year go to the Soviet Union, which is also heavily interested in the mining of uranium and other rare metals in the districts of the Soviet Zone which adjoin Czechoslovakia. As the economic links with the Communist bloc have increased (fresh and canned fruits and vegetables from Poland, Bulgaria, and other bloc countries help to eke out the meager supplies in the stores of the Soviet Zone), the prospects of German reunion may have become smaller.

Politically the methods employed by Ulbricht and his associates are strikingly similar to those of the Nazis, and of the Soviet Communists who put them in power in the first place. (It is remarkable that purported exposures of "Nazi revival" in Germany are usually restricted to the Federal Republic, where neonazism is very much the exception, and ignore completely the prevalence of the Nazi methods of terror and mass propaganda in the Soviet Zone. Perhaps this has some bearing on the origin and political motivation of these "exposures.")

Evidences of terror are not hard to find in the controlled newspapers of the Soviet Zone, with their frequent reports of prison sentences imposed for mere grumbling or criticism of the regime, "offenses" which would incur no punishment in the Federal Republic. In the larger towns every apartment house has its warden, whose main task is to spy on the views and associations of the tenants. School children are encouraged to denounce their parents. Almost everyone is under pressure to spy on almost everyone else.

The strong arm of this totalitarian system is the force of 78,000 Vopos ("People's Police").[14] The ruling party, the SED, numbers about 1.6 million members,[15] about one tenth of the population. Many have probably joined for opportunist reasons, but any SED member is a potential informer. Given this far-flung machinery of control and the complete absence of freedom of speech, press, and assembly, the chances of developing any widespread underground movement are obviously limited. There is also the softer, subtler, and more insidious instrument of mass propaganda.

A West German film, *Question 7,* built around the pressures for conformity that are directed against a pastor in East Germany and his son, conveys an excellent image of the means by which non-conformists are isolated, softened into submission, or, if necessary, broken by sterner means. The "Free German Youth" in the Soviet Zone is a close copy of the former Nazi youth organization; its members are trained to march and sing and are offered the attraction of picnics and sporting events. Moreover, young people soon learn that a record of service in the Free German Youth is essential in order to obtain admission to higher schools and training institutes.

With all political opposition silenced, the churches in the Soviet Zone have remained the only centers of passive resistance to the claims of the totalitarian state. The Soviet Zone is predominantly a Protestant area and the Lutheran Church has borne the brunt of an antireligious offensive that has varied from such crude methods as arrests of pastors and blasphemous parodies of religious rites to subtler means of winning away young people from religious faith. Teaching in the schools is Marxist and dogmatically atheistic. A direct challenge to the churches has been the arrangement of so-called *Jugendweihe* ("Consecration of Youth") ceremonies at times which coincide with confirmation in the churches. The *Jugendweihe* begins with special courses in the theory of communism and reaches its climax with a kind of secular catechism in which the children answer *"Ja"* to such questions as "Are you prepared to devote your lives to the building up of the socialist state?" "Will you do battle for the cause of peace?"

Formally there is freedom of religion in the DDR. But in a police state formal legality counts for little; there are all sorts of means of harassing pastors, priests, and active members of congregations. According to one prominent Catholic ecclesiastic with whom I talked in Berlin in 1962, the current policy was to avoid making martyrs of priests. Pressure is strongest against influential laymen, who may be arrested and sentenced on some false charge.

At first the churches excluded young people who had gone through the *Jugendweihe*. But so many youths agreed to go through with this conformist gesture that a compromise arrangement is now generally accepted. Those who go through the *Jugendweihe* may be admitted to the church after a period of probation.

How much genuine loyalty does the Ulbricht regime possess? This is obviously a hard question to answer with absolute certainty under a system where the first impulse of the critically minded is to conceal any public show of their real ideas. Undoubtedly there are some convinced Communists in the Zone, men and women who survived the Nazi concentration camps, young people who have more or less accepted the pervasive propaganda in which they have been brought up. The regime has made higher education free, with preference for children of workers and peasants, and this may give to some of the poorer classes a sense of greater opportunity, although, up to the time when the wall was put up, an embarrassing number of students, after receiving the free education, took to their heels and fled to the West at the first opportunity. Like the Nazis, with their Kraft durch Freude, the Communist rulers of the Zone offer much in the way of organized sport, recreation, and festivities. Sometimes even people who run away from the Zone find the way of life in West Germany alien; what they consciously or unconsciously want is a combination of far-reaching state welfare measures with individual freedom. The values in the West also seem to some of the refugees unduly materialistic.

Yet it seems unlikely that the SED rule has engendered as much genuine fanatical enthusiasm as nazism aroused in its first years. For while there are many similarities between Nazi and Communist methods, Hitler was a product of German conditions and emotions, while Ulbricht is a Soviet puppet. Most Germans regard the Russians with a mixture of fear and contempt. The horrors of the Red Army invasion and the first phase of occupation have not been forgotten and they help to discredit an administration that is clearly made in Moscow. A German visitor to the Zone told me of the remark of a father, an ex-Nazi, to his son, a student who was going through all the motions of zealous conformity with communism:

"Our generation, many of us, were tricked and fooled; we really believed in what we now see was the Nazi nonsense. But your generation doesn't even have the satisfaction of honest enthusiasm; you demonstrate for something that, in your hearts, you don't believe in."

In the Soviet Zone, as in the Soviet Union, contraband jokes help to make up for the absence of a free press. According to one, an international commission visits a factory in East Germany and notices very few parked cars in the vicinity. Asking to whom the factory belongs, it gets the reply: "To the workers."

"And to whom do the cars belong?"

"To the bosses."

A visit to a factory in West Germany, where the parking lot is crowded, elicits precisely the reverse answers. The factory belongs to "the bosses"; the cars to the workers.

There is also the tale of an old lady in Leipzig who sent this message of congratulation to Ulbricht on his birthday: "I wish you everything the German people have been wishing for you for many years." The next day she was arrested for incitement to murder.

The putting up of the Berlin Wall inspired the story of an East Berliner replying to a question what he would do if the Wall were taken down: "I would climb a tree, so as not to be crushed in the stampede of people running to the West."

The totalitarian apparatus of suppression and the failure of the West to give any help to the East German revolt of 1953 or to the Hungarian uprising of 1956 discourage any new violent effort to overthrow the Ulbricht dictatorship. (To be sure, the Wall closed a safety valve. People who find life in the Zone unbearable can no longer escape without great difficulty and danger.) But in terms of genuine internal support the DDR is probably the weakest of all the Soviet satellites, if only because of the example of a prospering free Germany beyond the barbed wire. Should the time ever come when the Soviet Union, for any reason, would decide to write off its annexation of East Germany, Ulbricht and his collaborators would be well advised to make early one-way reservations to Moscow.

Was there ever a chance of preserving German unity? The evidence seems to point to a negative answer. The issue of German reunification was batted back and forth between Moscow and the Western capitals in a series of notes and conferences too long and tedious to recapitulate here, especially as no positive results ever emerged.

The Soviet Government in the early fifties, alarmed at the prospect of alliance between the Federal Republic and the Western powers, made several proposals purportedly favoring German reunification. However, a study of the fine print of these proposals indicates that the true Soviet design was a communized Germany, or, at least, a neutralized Germany which would have been in a very weak position to resist Soviet pressures and demands.

A Soviet note of March 10, 1952 contained the draft of a proposed peace treaty with Germany. It was proposed that Germany be restored as a united state, "independent, democratic, and peaceloving." All foreign occupation forces were to be withdrawn within a year after the peace treaty came into effect. There was to be free activity for democratic organizations. Germany was to pledge itself not to enter into any coalition or military alliance against any power with which it had waged war. There was to be a German national army, with sufficient equipment from its own resources for defensive needs.[16]

The proposal for a German national army was rejected by the Western powers as "a step backward" and Chancellor Adenauer rejected the veto on alliances as a "neutralization" of Germany. Whether the Soviet offer was sincere in the sense that Germany would have been treated as an independent neutralized state cannot be determined with absolute certainty, because the offer was not accepted. However, although the note was phrased in a manner calculated to appeal to German nationalist feeling, its acceptance would have created several serious dangers for Germany's development in freedom.

The stipulation that all foreign troops should leave Germany within a year meant that United States troops would retire across the Atlantic, while Soviet troops would withdraw to the eastern frontier of Poland. The return of the Soviet troops would have been very much easier and the mere knowledge of this fact would have placed any German government under strong pressure to comply with Moscow's wishes, especially as Germany, under the terms of the note, would have been prevented from seeking support from the West against any future Soviet aggression.

The united Germany which was envisaged under the Soviet proposal would have come out of a fusion of the western zones with the Soviet Zone. But to mix free with totalitarian systems is as impossible as to mix oil with water. The very political anatomy of the Soviet Zone administration excludes the possibility of free elections, for unfettered voting presupposes freedom of speech, press, and assembly, opportunity for spokesmen of all viewpoints to present their case. Such conditions have always existed in the Federal Republic and they have been nonexistent, for more than fifteen years, in the Soviet Zone. It is most improbable that the Soviet Government, in 1952 or at any other time, was prepared to throw over its puppet government.

The Soviet note of March 10, 1952 makes no mention of free elections. In a note of August 15, 1952, the Soviet Government suggested that "the parliaments of the German Democratic Republic and the German Federal Republic, with the broad participation of democratic organizations, should form a provisional all-German government." Again no promise of free elections, along with an attempt to equate the appointed parliament of the DDR with the freely elected parliament of the Federal Republic. It should also be noted that the word "democratic," in Communist usage, means either Communist or at least pro-Communist.

Decisive proof that the Soviet Government has never been interested in German reunification in freedom (which would demand as a prerequisite the demolition of the totalitarian setup in the DDR) was furnished at a four-power conference on Germany which took place in Berlin from January 25 until February 18, 1954. At this meeting British Foreign Secretary Anthony Eden put forward the following scheme for German unity:

(1) Free elections throughout Germany.

(2) The convocation of a national assembly on the basis of these elections.

(3) The drafting of a constitution and the preparation of negotiations for a peace treaty.

(4) Adoption of the constitution and formation of an all-German government, responsible for the negotiation of a peace treaty.

(5) Signing and entering into force of the peace treaty.

The Federal Republic accepted these proposals. The Soviet Government rejected them. It is also noteworthy that Soviet notes proposing German reunion were regularly and obviously timed to obstruct the progress of the negotiations that led to German integration with the West. There was also an almost automatic series of responses, in Soviet official relations with its satellite administration in the Zone, to the various steps that culminated in full recognition of the sovereignty of the German Federal Republic by the Western powers.

The choice Adenauer faced in the early fifties was between insuring for the Federal Republic the powerful guaranty of alliance with the West or entering on the dubious road of neutralization, which might well have been a halfway house in the direction of becoming a Soviet dependency. He chose the first course and his decision is defended by two German diplomats of long experience in dealing with Moscow:

Gustav Hilger, a now retired veteran of the German foreign service, who served continuously in the German embassy in Moscow between the two wars, offers the following judgment at the end of his memoirs: [17]

"Only two alternatives are open to her [Germany]. She can either seek security against the Soviet threat by an alliance with the Western powers, or else she can ally herself with the Soviet Union. But in the event of the latter, West Germany, and probably the rest of Europe, would doubtless share the fate of the East European satellites."

This judgment is more significant because Hilger, born in Moscow of German parents, speaking Russian as a native language and warmly sympathetic with the Russian people, approved the policy of balancing between East and West pursued by Foreign Minister Gustav Stresemann under the Weimar Republic. But at that time German and Russian power were fairly evenly balanced. After World War II Russian power vastly increased as German power diminished. Germany was no longer strong enough to pursue with any prospect of success the policy of independence between its neighbors. It had to join one camp or the other.

Wilhelm Grewe, long the legal expert of the Bonn Ministry of Foreign Affairs, later ambassador to the United States, reaches the same conclusion from a somewhat different premise:[18]

"The goal of German foreign policy is not mere reunion, but reunion in freedom. A reunion which would lead to a Communist-ruled all-Germany, or to a type of all-German state for which Sovietization would be only a question of time would be no worthwhile object of German policy."

After the Federal Republic joined NATO, the Soviet Government ceased to pay even lip service to the desirability of a united Germany. One exception to this rule may be noted: At the Geneva conference of heads of government in July, 1955, Nikolai Bulganin, then Soviet prime minister, signed a joint direction to the foreign ministers of the four powers (the United States, the Soviet Union, Great Britain, and France) to settle "the reunion of Germany by means of free elections." But this promise was quickly broken. For at the subsequent conference of foreign ministers Molotov stubbornly adhered to the position that there are two German states, which must settle the problem of reunion between themselves. The Soviet Government also put up the demand that a united Germany should not belong to NATO. (The Western position is that an all-German government should be free to remain in NATO or to withdraw.)

Chancellor Adenauer's visit to Moscow in the autumn of 1955 was followed by a re-establishment of German-Soviet diplomatic relations, but led to no progress on the issue of German reunion. Its principal positive result, from the German standpoint, was the release of some ten thousand German war prisoners who were still detained in the Soviet Union. The Germans believe that there are many more who were never returned; but this is a subject on which precise evidence is difficult to obtain.

Some foreign commentators from time to time have predicted a German-Soviet rapprochement, political and economic, recalling the spectacular Treaty of Rapallo in the spring of 1922. But the possibilities of such a development seem very limited. Adenauer is unshakably committed to the Western orientation, even though in 1963 he faced a new problem of adjusting Germany's relations between the competing claims of Washington and Paris. And even after he passes from the political scene, any German chancellor will be unlikely to forego the advantages of an alliance in which United States nuclear power is the most powerful guaranty of German independence.

The idea that there is a vast market in the Soviet Union, waiting to be picked up by Germany or some other Western power, is an illusion. Soviet trade with the non-Communist world is little more than Switzerland's. What the Soviet Union can buy abroad is sharply curtailed by what the Soviet Union can sell abroad. Germany's important markets, as a glance at trade statistics will show, are in the Common Market countries, in the United States, in Great Britain. Germany's exports to and imports from the Soviet Union, Red China, and the East European Communist-ruled states, sometimes ignorantly or maliciously exaggerated, amount to a very small proportion of its total foreign trade. So there is little likelihood of a German turn toward the East, for political or economic reasons.

The unresisted construction of the "Wall of Shame" in Berlin was a severe shock to the West Germans. This grim warning of Soviet power and of the limitation of Allied responsibility to the defense of West Berlin, excluding any obligation to maintain freedom of communication between the two sections of the city, produced two reactions among politically minded Germans. Majority opinion supported the policy of the government: no concessions that would endanger the freedom and economic security of West Berlin, no departure from the Hallstein Doctrine [19] of breaking off relations with any state which extends diplomatic recognition to Ulbricht's DDR. Incidentally, the Hallstein Doctrine, sometimes criticized as negative, futile, and sterile, has in practice proved quite successful.

Despite strenuous propaganda efforts in Asia and Africa, the Ulbricht regime has received official recognition from only two Communist-ruled countries in recent years, Yugoslavia and Cuba; and Bonn promptly severed diplomatic relations with Belgrade and

Havana. West German trade and credits have proved a potent weapon in dissuading other states, even those neutral and uncommitted in foreign policy, from taking a step that would involve economic as well as political disadvantages. Because of the potential importance of possessing a direct line of communication to the Kremlin, one exception to the Hallstein Doctrine has been permitted. Moscow is the one capital where there are ambassadors both of the Federal Republic and of the DDR.

There is also a minority viewpoint in Germany that advocates a softening of policy toward the East, in the name of flexibility and realism. The issue was threshed out in an interesting public debate in Hamburg in the autumn of 1962 between Golo Mann, historian and son of the novelist Thomas Mann, and Baron Karl Guttenberg, a CDU member of the Foreign Affairs Committee of the Bundestag and consistent advocate of a hard line in foreign policy. The subject under discussion was: "Has Germany a Future?"

Mann started from the proposition that Germany could no longer use military force to support its claims to reunion and to return of the German lands east of the Oder-Neisse frontier which were annexed by Poland and the Soviet Union after the end of the war. Poland and the Soviet Union regard these annexations as an accomplished fact, while the Germans cling to the formal position that this territory is "under Polish and Soviet administration" until a peace treaty is signed.

"We can't achieve such aims as reunion or the recovery of our lost territories by force," said Professor Mann, "'without burning up both our neighbors and ourselves, thereby making the question of the German future purely academic." Proceeding from the premise that the existing situation could not be altered in any foreseeable future, Mann recommended that Germany, without loosening its ties with the West, try to cultivate bettter relations with the Soviet Union and its East European satellites, especially Poland; scrap the Hallstein Doctrine; and aim, by conciliation, at improving the living conditions of the Germans in the Soviet Zone.

Guttenberg vigorously denied that Free Germany had any alternative to a policy of close alliance with the West. "The cold war," he said, "is only another name for the Soviet offensive against the free world. . . . The Soviet Union up to this day has never been willing to give up its German war spoils. On the contrary, it has always tried to press forward beyond what it has already gained." And Guttenberg took issue sharply with Mann's hope, partly expressed, partly implied, that acceptance of the partition of Germany would lead to relaxation of tension and promote evolutionary development in the Soviet Union and its East European empire.

There are three aspects of the partition of Germany: the division of the city of Berlin, discussed in the following chapter, the simultaneous existence of the German Federal Republic and the dictatorship in the Soviet Zone, and the severance from Germany of an area of 44,130 square miles (between one fourth and one fifth) of its prewar territory, formerly inhabited by some 9.6 million Germans, now incorporated into Poland and the Soviet Union. These include the former German provinces of East Prussia, Lower and part of Upper Silesia, and parts of Pomerania and Brandenburg.[20]

From the standpoint of national self-determination, a principle emphasized so strongly in the Atlantic Charter, the annexation by Poland and the Soviet Union is outrageously indefensible. The whole area had been thoroughly German in nationality, loyalty, and culture for many centuries. Germany had already lost all areas with a Polish majority under the Treaty of Versailles. It is as if, following a defeat of the United States in war, the entire non-Mexican population of California, Texas, Arizona, and New Mexico had been driven from their homes as penniless refugees and the whole area turned over to Mexico.

As a matter of right and of national feeling it is easy to understand the reluctance of the Germans to admit the irrevocable loss of these lands, where even the architecture bears mute witness to historic German character. The millions of Germans who have been expelled from their homes have formed regional associations, and these operate as powerful pressure groups against recognition of the 1945 frontier.

Yet the demand for regaining these territories, because of the economic miracle, is not as strong and threatening as it would be if the expellees were sitting around in the sullen misery of emergency camps and mass unemployment. The younger people have been absorbed into the booming West German economy and have often forgotten their former homes. A public relations employee of the Volkswagen plant in Wolfsburg, a native of Silesia, frankly told me that he would not go back if he could; he was quite satisfied with his life and work in the Federal Republic. A rally of former residents of Silesia, such as I stumbled on by accident in Düsseldorf in the summer of 1962, was marked by speeches affirming the German character of Silesia and by a colorful display of traditional costumes. But the atmosphere was that of an Old Home Week, a get-together of people who liked to meet their former neighbors from Breslau and Oppeln and Glogau, not of a sinister gathering of "revenge-hungry militarists," to use a cliché of Communist propaganda.

Since the German Government and also the refugee organizations have repeatedly renounced any desire or intention to recover the lost territories by force, and since Poland, after resettling the area, will not relinquish it voluntarily, this issue does not represent a serious threat to peace. The partition of Germany by the zonal line of demarcation is much more potentially explosive, especially as the continual shooting of fugitives trying to escape from the Ulbricht penitentiary is a constant provocation to the emotional resentment of the West Berliners and West Germans. But, while the situation urgently calls for a solution, no practicable way out is visible.

An attempt, either by the Soviet Union or by the West, to change the existing condition by force seems improbable, because of the tremendous, almost suicidal risk of unloosing a nuclear war in which the Germans on both sides of the unnatural border would probably be the first and worst sufferers. "Negotiations between two German states" cannot lead to positive results because the Ulbricht regime, for sheer self-preservation, could not submit to the test of a free election. And German reunion, except in freedom, would be of no benefit to Germans, West or East. It would be no help to the Germans in the Soviet Zone to extend to all Germany the regime of tyranny, exploitation, and poverty under which they live.

So the status quo in Germany, unsatisfactory, uneasy, and liable to disturbance by incidents as it is, may continue for some time for sheer lack of any visible formula for agreed change. Perhaps, in the long run, such factors as the European Economic Community, with the enhanced power and prosperity it should bring to Free Germany and to its other members, or a serious threat to the Soviet flank in Asia from an increasingly aloof and hostile Red China may create a situation favorable to Germany's long overdue reunion—in freedom.

NOTES TO CHAPTER VII

1 German troops in the last phase of the war displayed an understandable preference to surrender to the Western Allies, rather than to the Red Army. The fate of German prisoners in the West was much easier than in the East.

2 Cf. Dwight D. Eisenhower, *Crusade in Europe* (Garden City, N.Y.: Doubleday & Company, Inc., 1948), pp. 399–401, and Winston Churchill, *The Second World War* (Boston: Houghton Mifflin Company, 1953), Vol. VI, pp. 456–461.

3 Cf. article by the Swedish correspondent, Sven Oesle, in the *Christian Science Monitor* for November 9, 1962.

4 Wolfgang Leonhard, *Child of the Revolution* (Chicago: Henry Regnery Co., 1958), pp. 359, 360.

5 The term Titoist seems a fair designation for a Communist who wished to achieve communism without dependence on Moscow.

6 *SBZ* (*Sovjetische Besatzungszone von A-Z*) ("The Soviet Occupation Zone from A to Z"), a publication of the Bonn Ministry of All-German Affairs (pp. 348, 349), estimates reparations exactions at $17.8 billion, much the largest item being the take from current production.

7 Cited in Terence Prittie, *Germany Divided* (Boston: Little, Brown & Co., 1960), pp. 341–343.

8 The principal function of "ministries of state security" in tyrannical governments is to make life insecure for many of their subjects.

9 Cited in an article on the crisis of supply in the Soviet Zone in *Der Spiegel* of July 25, 1962.

10 Cf. Sunday Magazine of the *New York Times,* April 8, 1962.

11 The annual Leipzig Fair is one occasion when the usual restrictions on travel in the Soviet Zone are relaxed.

12 Cf. *Manchester Guardian Weekly*, March 22–29, 1962.

13 Mewis was demoted at the SED Congress in January, 1963.

14 Cf. *SBZ, op. cit.,* p. 438.

15 Cf. *Report of the Central Committee to the Sixth Party Conference of the SED* (in German), p. 91.

16 Cf. Boris Meissner, *Russland, die Westmächte und Deutschland* ("Russia, the Western Powers, and Germany") (Hamburg: H. H. Nölke Verlag), pp. 270 ff.

17 Cf. Gustav Hilger and Alfred G. Meyer, *The Incompatible Allies: German-Soviet Relations 1918–41* (New York: The Macmillan Co., 1953), p. 342.

18 Cf. Wilhelm Grewe, *Deutsche Aussenpolitik der Nachkriegszeit* (Stuttgart: Deutsche Verlags-Anstalt), p. 173.

19 So called because it was formulated by Walter Hallstein as state secretary for foreign affairs. Mr. Hallstein later became executive head of the EEC.

20 For these and other details, cf. *Germany Reports,* a publication of the Press and Information Office of the Federal Government, pp. 182 ff.

CHAPTER VIII

Divided Berlin

BERLIN, capital of Prussia for centuries and of united Germany since 1871, is now a dramatic symbol of a divided Germany and a divided Europe. For many years West Berlin and East Berlin have been striking object lessons in the consequences of two philosophies and two ways of life, the free and the totalitarian. No one, driven at random blindfolded through the streets of the huge city, could feel the least doubt in which sector of the city he was, once the blindfold was removed. Seldom has there been a more impressive and instructive tale of two cities, formerly one city, inhabited by people of the same nationality.

Both parts of Berlin, the Western with some 2.2 million, the Eastern with about 1.2 million inhabitants, started in 1945 from a common level of general desolation, emphasized by the vast expanse of the former capital. (West Berlin occupies 186 square miles, East Berlin 156.) I visited the two cities five times, first in 1946, most recently in 1962.

West Berlin, at a slower pace and under greater handicaps, repeated the economic miracle of West Germany. After surmounting the Soviet blockade of 1948–49 the city experienced a fairly high rate of unemployment for some time after there were jobs for all in the Federal Republic. But this has disappeared during recent years. Full employment is the rule now in West Berlin, as in the cities of West Germany.

Recovery, sparked for a time by Marshall Plan funds and by continuous substantial subsidies from the Federal Government, has been evenly spread over all sections of the city. In the West

End the Kurfürstendamm, usually abbreviated by Berliners to "Kudamm," the boulevard of elegant shops, restaurants, cafés, and theaters, looks much as it did before the war, except for the much increased volume of motor traffic. In Kranzler and other well-known open-air cafés one finds the sign: "Destroyed in 1944, restored in 195—."

The bombed-out shell of the Kaiser Wilhelm Memorial Church, flanked by two new buildings, one a bell tower, the other used for worship, still stands as a solemn warning of the fearful destructive power of modern weapons. But restoration and new building are the general rule. The city landscape is constantly changing with new structures. A few blocks from the Kurfürstendamm is the highly modern Conrad Hilton Hotel, where one is apt to encounter delegates to some international congress. Not far away is the Congress Hall, one of the last United States gifts to Berlin, built by an American architect in an original style that according to irreverent Berliners suggests a pregnant oyster.

The Hansa Quarter, one of the worst destroyed sections of the city, now offers a view of new apartment houses, attractively varied in style and color. These are the results of a competition in which leading architects of Europe and America were invited to participate. Now what had been a mass of rubble is one of the more pleasing residential sections of West Berlin.

The famous Berlin Zoo was a conspicuous casualty of the war. Some of the animals were bayoneted to death by drunken Soviet soldiers. Others were cared for in improvised quarters or private homes. Now the zoo is one of the best stocked in Europe and attracts throngs of animal-loving visitors. The old University of Berlin is located on Unter den Linden, in the Soviet sector of the city. A new free university with 15,000 students, many of them refugees from the Soviet Zone and a considerable number from Western Europe and the United States, has been built up with considerable aid from the United States, notably in the construction of the library.

And many of these students have proved that they are not apathetic or indifferent in the face of a challenge to freedom and humanity. They have formed groups to dig tunnels under the "Wall of Shame," through which a number of East Berliners have escaped. Some, especially those with West German passports, go about the risky business of crossing into East Berlin to distribute false papers and otherwise promote breaks to freedom. German youth is sometimes criticized as cool, calculating, materialistic. But the dangerous work for freedom of the West Berlin students shows that this charge is not universally true.

The visitor to West Berlin is impressed by the many new apartment house projects, with their liberal allotments of green space. As Mayor Willy Brandt says, it is all the more necessary to have as many green plots as possible within the limits of West Berlin, because its people can no longer make excursions to the many lake and forest resorts around Berlin which are now in the barred Soviet Zone.

In some ways there has been visible social progress over prewar times. The bombings of Berlin destroyed impartially elegant apartment houses, villas, and poor tenements. One of the grimmest slums in old Berlin was Wedding, which, not unnaturally, regularly produced a big vote for the Communist Party. Now Wedding is almost unrecognizable, its grimy tenements replaced by attractive housing, gardens, and playgrounds. And West Berlin today harbors few Communists, in Wedding or anywhere else. The object lesson on the other side of the Wall is too plain.

Crossing into East Berlin, even before the Wall went up, one always sensed the atmosphere of being in another country. There, too, some reconstruction has taken place, but at a much slower pace. On one of my visits I was told that West Berlin was putting up about 20,000 housing units a year, compared with 2,000 in East Berlin. These figures seemed in line with the impressions of one's eyes.

New building in East Berlin is heavily concentrated on what was once Stalin-Allee, now rechristened Karl Marx-Allee. (The original name was Frankfurter-Allee.) Here are long rows of apartment houses, with shops on the ground floors, built in the heavy, tasteless style which appealed to the Soviet dictator. Apartments in these houses are usually rewards for faithful service in the SED.

What perhaps most sharply distinguishes East Berlin from West Berlin is the extraordinary lack of movement in the streets. There is little risk of traffic accidents. The buses and streetcars look shabby and run-down; private automobiles seem almost entirely reserved for high officials. I have never seen a passerby smile or laugh in East Berlin; faces are set in a tense, sullen, grim expression.

What makes the impression of shabby, drab decay stronger is the memory of what Unter den Linden, Wilhelmstrasse, Friedrichstrasse looked like before the war. Here was the heart of Berlin, with some of the principal government buildings, the opera house, the university and some of the finest European hotels, of which the Adlon was the best known. Now there are empty stretches along the Wilhelmstrasse which look as if they might be turned back to cow pasture. The Adlon is a pitiful shadow of its former self, approached through a dingy side entrance and serving inferior snack meals.

A striking negative feature of East Berlin is the absence, at least on a surface view, of public restaurants and hotels where a stranger set down by chance in the city can obtain food or shelter. Of course this situation would seldom arise; border and passport controls are so strict and the general prospect is so uninviting that tourists in East Berlin are almost exclusively groups and individuals under the chaperonage of the Soviet Zone authorities.

Two things which are abundant in East Berlin are uniforms and propaganda. The sense of continuation of Nazi methods is strengthened by the large numbers of young men in Vopo uniforms, employed in guard duty all along the Wall and at the few check points through which foreigners and West Germans may cross from one part of the city to another. Propaganda signs are everywhere: "Fatherland, peace, socialism," "Whoever attacks the German Democratic Republic will be annihilated," and so forth. The newspapers in the summer of 1962 were full of shrill propaganda against "the revengeful Bonn militarists," of confident predictions that West Berlin would soon become a "demilitarized free city," together with reports on the failures of the industrial and agricultural plans to come up to expectations.

One of the approved diversions of the East Berliners is to go in conducted groups to Treptow Park, where there is a Soviet war memorial, with a huge statue of a Soviet soldier holding a child and beating down the Hakenkreuz, emblem of the Nazis. Some five thousand Red Army soldiers, whose names are entered in a book, are buried here. On the stone monument is an inscription in Russian and German: "Eternal glory to the heroes who have fallen in the battles for freedom and the independence of the socialist fatherland."

Another Soviet war memorial stands near the Brandenburg Gate, in the British sector of Berlin. This figured in one of the minor crises of the post-Wall period. In August, 1962, a nineteen-year-old fugitive from East Berlin, Peter Fechter, was shot and allowed to bleed to death on the eastern side of the Wall in full view of a large crowd of West Berliners. So bitter was the feeling that a proposal was made to prosecute the American commandant, Gen. Albert Watson, for "failing to come to the aid of an injured person," and American prestige and popularity experienced a temporary nosedive. Naturally, however, Russian soldiers were the principal targets of this bitterness. Buses carrying these soldiers to the war memorial were stoned. The Soviet military authorities then began to send in troops in armored cars and for a time it seemed that this might represent an attempt to assert a Soviet right of military access to West Berlin. However, when the mood of the West Berliners calmed, the Russians yielded to firm representations and resumed transportation of their soldiers by bus.

The dominating impression after a brief visit to East Berlin is an overwhelming impulse to get away as soon as possible. It is not that people are starving or in rags. And it would be a rare accident if a casual visitor saw an incident of police terror.[1] What makes East Berlin the most depressing large city I have ever seen is the complete absence of all the little graces, amenities, and comforts of life. And this is emphasized by the existence, directly across the sector boundary, of a lively metropolis, with visible normal opportunities for recreation and amusement and generally having a good time.

Incredible as it may seem, East Berlin is considered the showcase of the Soviet Zone, far superior in provisioning to Dresden,

Chemnitz, Magdeburg, and other provincial towns. The test of coexistence, tried out in Berlin on a scale not matched anywhere else, has certainly not turned out favorably for the Communist way of life. Two simple figures are eloquent in this connection. Since the end of the war 3.7 million Germans have moved from the Soviet Zone to the West. As a result of this tremendous drain of one-way migration (movement from the Federal Republic, at all times free and unhindered, has been negligible) the Soviet Zone became the only area in Europe, perhaps in the world, where population during the fifties declined—from 19,066,000 in 1948 to 17,286,000 in 1959.[2] If, as Lenin said, the Russian Army in 1917 voted for peace with its feet, by running away, the German people, by the same method, have registered an emphatic vote against communism.

On several visits to Berlin before 1962 I visited the big refugee center of Marienfelde, where fugitives were put up in dormitories, given medical examinations, food, and shelter, and in most cases flown out to reception centers in the Federal Republic. The standard figure for new arrivals in Marienfelde, before the Wall choked off the outflow, was several hundred a day. All were put through a screening test before a three-man board, which finally retired, like a jury, and handed in a decision as to the genuineness of the plea for asylum. This procedure was designed to sift out secret Red agents and criminals. Members of the boards were themselves former refugees, able to check on the truthfulness of answers by their knowledge of East Zone conditions and institutions.

A writer in search of material for a novel or story could have profitably spent some time in Marienfelde. For there were many human dramas in the backgrounds of these people, coming singly, or in couples, sometimes, especially in the case of peasants, with several children, prepared to tear up old roots and seek new homes and living conditions. All the facts about the refugees were noted down with meticulous German thoroughness, and the veteran Marienfelde supervisors pointed out cause-and-effect relationship between actions of the Communist authorities and the tendency among various groups of the population to run away.

The peasants fled in largest numbers when private farming was made impossible. The year of unsuccessful revolt, 1953, showed a much higher than average number of fugitives. Years of purges, directed against the educated classes, were marked by an intensified flight of teachers, doctors, and other professionals. A veritable stampede, with thousands coming in every day, developed in the first weeks of August, 1961, when rumors got about that escape would soon be cut off altogether.

One frequently mentioned cause of flight was the pressure on young people to go through with the *Jugendweihe,* described in the previous chapter. Other parents declared they could not bear the indoctrination of their children with antireligious teaching, or the familiar practice of encouraging children to spy on their parents. A psychiatrist from an East German hospital reported that he had been expected to use his confidential relationship with patients for purposes of brainwashing and espionage. A woman cultural anthropologist reached the breaking point when she was instructed to inject a large dose of Marxist propaganda into an exhibition of the historical development of German culture. For her, escape had been easy. She walked out of her office with what she could carry in a handbag and got into the subway—which is still a connecting link between the two segments of the city, although it is now guarded closely at "frontier" stations on the East side—and got off in West Berlin.

I sat in at the examination of a twenty-five-year-old worker from Magdeburg named Hans Jung. He had always lived in the East Zone, had no contacts with West Berlin, was an ex-member of the People's Police. What had made him come over, leaving his wife and child behind? By his own story, it was resentment of dictation by his Communist superiors. He got into arguments that marked him as a suspicious character. He spoke contemptuously of the propaganda line that the workers in the East Zone "own" the factories in which they work. "That's all *Quatsch* ('rubbish') and the workers know it," he said.

But political discontent, in the case of Jung, did not seem to be the whole story. He spoke bitterly of looking about in vain for a year for material to fit out his kitchen. The fact that he left his wife behind indicated that marital difficulties might have influenced his decision. This was clearly the case with an older man, a maker of window frames, who had been born in Dresden, had paid a visit to West Germany once, but returned to his old home. He described life with his wife as unbearable, although he added a political touch by remarking that an "election" in the East Zone offered no real choice; it was merely a case of writing "Yes" on a prepared ballot.

For some refugees the move to the West was the equivalent of a trip to Reno. And a minority conveyed the impression of being unstable personalities, never satisfied and flitting back and forth between West and East. Few gave the impression of having been involved in organized anti-Communist activity. Nor were there many complaints of outright hunger, although women sometimes spoke of long waits in line for fruit and vegetables of inferior quality. This enormous migration, by far the biggest in Europe since the war, seemed to be a product of a combination of causes: principled objection to antireligious propaganda and various forms of thought control and the thousand petty irritations of a dull, austere way of life. There was also, especially for the younger fugitives (about one in four was under twenty-five) the hope of finding a more hopeful future in what was sometimes called "the golden West."

The Wall was the big new factor when I revisited Berlin, after an absence of three years, in the summer of 1962. This is a fantastic sight, the first time when a great city has been slashed in twain by a big ugly barrier eight feet high, built of concrete and cinder blocks, with strands of meshed barbed wire across the top. At more or less regular intervals are watchtowers, manned by two policemen armed with pistols and submachine guns, on the lookout for anyone trying to escape from what is now—brutally, nakedly, visibly—the huge penitentiary of the Soviet Zone. In places the demarcation line runs along the Spree and Havel and some of Berlin's canals. Some refugees have escaped, others have perished, trying to cross these streams, often under a hail of bullets.

On the Bernauerstrasse, in West Berlin, are the backs of houses which front in East Berlin. In the first weeks after the Wall was erected some East Berliners leaped to freedom from the back upper story windows of these houses, the West Berlin fire department supplying nets to catch them. Sometimes there are simple memorial plaques, often with wreaths of flowers, bearing such inscriptions as: "Bernd Lasse, driven to death by Vopos. Died for freedom. October 4, 1961."

The Wall usually comes into the news as a result of a shooting incident. But the visitor's normal impression is of an eerie silence, of an uncanny stoppage of movement in the heart of a great city. This is enhanced because the little shops in the immediate vicinity of the sector line, largely patronized by East Berliners, have for the most part gone out of business. With a view to making escape more difficult, people are barred from a considerable area on the East side of the Wall. The Potsdamer Platz was once one of the busiest spots in Berlin. Now it is a desolate wasteland. I saw a family of wild rabbits in the vicinity of the old Reichstag building, where before the Wall such a sight would have been as unlikely as at Fifth Avenue and 42nd Street.

Senator Heinrich Albertz of West Berlin stated on November 19, 1962 that 41 persons, including several women and children, are known to have been killed and 24 wounded in attempts to escape. The number killed in attempts to flee that were frustrated on the other side of the Wall is unknown. According to Albertz, 290 East German soldiers and police have fled to the West since the Wall was put up. They have the best opportunity to get away and this is why they always go about in pairs, each a spy on the other. The West Berlin authorities are unwilling to release figures of escapes, but obviously the former stream has dried up to a trickle.

Marienfelde had more supervisors and caretakers than inmates in 1962, in contrast to its former crowded condition. There was such a shortage of refugees that one of the rare couples that turned up was asked to put on a repeat performance for the benefit of an American mayor, in Berlin for a brief visit.

But although the outflow of fugitives has been brutally cut down to a minimum (the Negro in the American South trying to escape from slavery ran no greater risk than the German seeking to make his way over, under, or around the Wall), there has been no up-surge of productivity and prosperity in the Soviet Zone. One reason is the considerable investment of manpower and material required for building the Wall, which is in a state of continuous reinforcement, and the imposition of conscription early in 1962. There are also the difficulties and contradictions of a clumsily planned economy, discussed in the previous chapter.

West Berlin has proved that it can live with the Wall and function as a viable economic community, with aid from Bonn to the amount of about $500 million a year. This outpost of freedom behind the Iron Curtain has done much more than clear away its war ruins and present the appearance of a normal thriving city. Although its population includes an above-average proportion of elderly people [3] living on retirement pensions, it runs a neck-and-neck race with Hamburg as the biggest industrial center of the Federal Republic. Such famous names as Siemens, AEG, Telefunken, and other electrical equipment and electronics firms account for about 30 per cent of its industrial output, valued at about $2.5 billion in 1961. Berlin has regained its prewar status as a center of the clothing industry. There are a number of miscellaneous industries: food, cigarettes, liquor, machinery, pharmaceuticals. Sarotti is an old established chocolate firm, back in the market with its assorted chocolates and its bars with prewar wrapping designs of three Moors and of idyllic scenes (no longer, alas, remotely realistic) of rural life in the Prussian countryside.

There is a movement to bring all school children in Germany to Berlin for at least one visit, and the very perils of the encircled city have attracted considerable numbers of visitors from West Germany and from abroad. There is no city in Germany, or probably in Western Europe, where the foreigner from a Western country is more certain of a warmly hospitable reception. The Berliners feel themselves an isolated center of Western culture and civilization. All sorts of international meetings and conferences, film, music, and drama festivals help to break down the sense of claustrophobia that sometimes besets the Berliner. To live, as West Berliners do, pent up within a circle of barbed wire in an atmosphere of hostile threats, is nervous strain, from which any contact with the big free world outside is a welcome relief.

The West Berliner can make a telephone call to London or Paris or New York, but not to East Berlin. He is cut off from many of the natural outing places near the city. He can make a trip to West Germany or Western Europe; but even here there are dangers and difficulties. Only the airlines—American, British, French, Scandinavian—are entirely free from Communist control. This, incidentally, is an issue which can never be compromised if the freedom of the city is to be preserved.

The traveler on the Autobahn or on the railway, especially the former, may be picked up by the omnipresent Soviet Zone police for some real or alleged violation of the strict rules which govern travel through the Zone. It is *am strengstens verboten,* to use a German police expression for "strictly forbidden," to stop on the Autobahn to meet and talk with friends and relatives living in the Zone. And any former resident of the Zone runs a risk of being arrested if he travels by road or rail.

It is not surprising that some West Berliners, living in a semi-siege atmosphere, display a nervous sensitiveness as to whether their countrymen in the West are sufficiently concerned about their fate. Said one West Berlin journalist, who spoke amazingly good, idiomatic Americanized English, although he had never been in the United States:

"In the more progressive states of the Federal Republic, Hesse, Hamburg, Bremen, we find sympathy and understanding. But the more conservative Catholic regions, Bavaria and Rhine-Pfalz, for instance, regard us as something very far away. As for Adenauer, with his Rhineland background, everything east of the Elbe river is out of his world."

Some of this tendency to find fault with attitudes in West Germany is a result of claustrophobia; there is also a slight political coolness between conservative Bonn and Social Democratic Berlin. Still the Federal Government has been reasonably generous in responding to Berlin's needs, and financial aid, mostly in the form of tax abatements and investment incentives, has been stepped up since the building of the Wall introduced a new element of crisis.

In addition to creating the tense drama of fugitives crossing or burrowing under the Wall, swimming streams, crashing through barriers in trucks, hijacking river boats, the Wall has changed life in West Berlin in various ways. It has caused many family tragedies, since it was not unusual for members of the same family to live on opposite sides of the line of demarcation. Formerly large numbers of East Berliners came daily into West Berlin to shop, to see friends, to go to propaganda-free movies. Some 60,000 people who lived in East Berlin worked in West Berlin; this has been stopped by the Wall. It was the Communist calculation (there are differences of opinion as to whether Khrushchev or Ulbricht took the initiative in proposing the Wall) that the sealing off of East Berlin would paralyze the West Berlin economy, cause a mass flight from the city, and frighten the West Berliners into coming to terms.

These anticipations have been proved erroneous. Immediately after the appearance of the Wall there were a few symptoms of panic. Some professional people with established practices and reputations moved to the West. But West Berlin in the summer of 1962 gave the impression of having learned to live with the Wall. As Mayor Willy Brandt said to me in his office in the Schoenberg Rathaus:

"West Berlin can live with the status quo minus, as I call the situation that exists since communication with East Berlin was cut off. It has proved its ability to look the Wall in the face as an ugly fact of life and carry on. Last year Khrushchev told a foreign diplomat that Berlin would panic, with people leaving in droves and the economy collapsing. Nothing of the kind happened. Production is higher than ever. There are larger deposits in the savings banks. More young people are coming here to live and work. Plans are under way to make Berlin a still bigger industrial and cultural center, to attract foreign and German investment, to bring here museums, perhaps to open a third university."

Mayor Brandt described his relations with the Western commandants as excellent, although on some points he would have preferred a more vigorous policy. He would have liked to have seen West Berlin declared an integral part of the Federal Republic. (East Berlin was long ago made the capital of the German Democratic Republic.) And he believed that the West Berlin property of the Stadtbahn (city railway) should be taken over by the Western powers or by the West Berlin municipality. This is an overhead railway which crosses Berlin and is directed from a headquarters in

East Berlin. It has been a source of Western currency for the Ulbricht regime and, in Brandt's opinion, has been a convenient agency for infiltrating Communist agents into West Berlin.

Economically the Stadtbahn has become a heavily losing proposition because, following the erection of the Wall, the West Berliners have been systematically boycotting it, even when this involves some inconvenience in transportation. A few picket signs, "By using the Stadtbahn you help to pay for Ulbricht's barbed wire," were sufficient to touch off this boycott.

The courage of the West Berliners must be seen and felt to be realized. In this isolated city, surrounded by the Soviet Zone, its small garrison [4] hopelessly outnumbered by the Soviet and East German forces in the vicinity, its lines of access to the West exposed to harassment or stoppage, I have never met an advocate of appeasement. In direct confrontation with Soviet and German communism, having lived through the blockade of 1948–49, the Berliners have gained the conviction that the only way to survive in freedom is to be tough and unyielding. This is equally true for Mayor Willy Brandt, for the small boys who shouted *"Hinüber, hinüber"* ("Over, over"), when American tanks moved up to the boundary line in the autumn of 1961, for the ordinary citizen who shrugged his shoulders when Soviet supersonic jets carried out flights over Berlin to an accompaniment of earsplitting noise, and for the Free University students whose extracurricular activity is digging tunnels under the Wall.

There is no support in West Berlin for the idea that a soft, yielding attitude would preserve the freedom of the city. It is significant that Willy Brandt was one of the first European political leaders to endorse wholeheartedly President Kennedy's action against Soviet missiles in Cuba. There was fearful speculation in some quarters that Khrushchev, balked in Cuba, would retaliate in Berlin. Brandt had the sounder instinct: that strength in Cuba would be the best means of taking off Soviet pressure in Berlin.

In charge of Berlin's economic development is Senator Karl Schiller, who came to Berlin with a distinguished record in the reconstruction of the port of his native city, Hamburg. He visited the United States in the spring of 1962, trying to interest firms in placing more capital in Berlin. There is already a good deal of American investment there, symbolized by such well-known names as Woolworth and Goodyear and by the tallest hotel in the city, the Berlin Hilton. Up to the end of 1962 nothing very definite in the way of big new American investments had materialized, although Yale and Towne was considering a project for a new plant and there was a possibility that International Business Machines might locate one of its biggest computers there.

But Senator Schiller was optimistic about the economic future of the city. Industrial output was up 3.5 per cent in April, 1962 over April, 1961, a rate of growth not very different from that of the Federal Republic. And some 7,000 new workers came to Berlin in the first half of 1962.

"That is what we need, perhaps, most of all: young people who will marry and raise families here," said Senator Schiller. "West Berlin has an aging population. We need a net gain of 12,000 to 15,000 people to offset a death rate that is higher than the birth rate. To attract young people we have offered loans on easy terms to young couples who will settle here, and the response has been good."

Almost all West Berlin's trade with West Germany and with the outside world (68 per cent of its output is sold to Germany, 12 per cent to foreign countries) goes over rail, road, and water routes that are checked and controlled by Soviet Zone authorities. But according to Senator Schiller, there have been no unreasonable delays. The explanation may be found in part in an unobtrusive office on Berlin's Broadway, the Kurfürstendamm. In charge of this office is Dr. Kurt Leopold, in charge of interzonal trade for the Federal Republic. Interviewed, he conveyed the impression of a middle-aged civil servant with an exhaustive knowledge of the Soviet Zone economy and a good sense of humor.

"I am only a private man with no rank or title," he said with a wink and a smile, "and my job is to look after West German interzonal trade. This is far more important to the Soviet Zone than it is to the Federal Republic. But we like to keep it up as a small link with the other Germany."

Dr. Leopold is authorized by the Economics Ministry of the Federal Republic and by the Berlin Senate (the city parliament) to sign contracts as representative of "the West Mark Currency Area"; his opposite number in East Berlin signs as representative of the East Mark Area. The Bonn government is anxious to downgrade officially the status of trade relations with the unrecognized DDR.

Trade between West and East Germany increased during the fifties, but not spectacularly. In 1962 there was a turnover of about $500 million, exports and imports combined, balanced on a barter basis since the Soviet Zone currency has no value in international exchange. This is about 2 per cent of the foreign trade of the Federal Republic, about 11 per cent of the foreign trade of the DDR.

A difficult question was posed for Bonn when the Ulbricht regime intimated unofficially in the spring of 1962 that it would like a credit of $750 million for ten years, to be spent mostly on Ruhr coal. On the one hand there was no desire to strengthen a brutally oppressive tyrannny. At the same time there was the consideration that the granting of such a credit might be a restraining influence on the harassment of Berlin's lines of communication, since what was granted could be quickly canceled. Some German observers believe that the dependence of the Soviet Zone economy on certain types of high-quality West German steel may be a further restraining influence. The question has been allowed to drag on. When a decision is reached it will be for political, not for economic reasons. The Federal Republic would not miss the minute percentage of its foreign trade which is carried on with the Soviet Zone.

RIAS, the American broadcasting station which operates in West Berlin, received interesting proof that many of the people in the Soviet Zone strongly oppose the idea of credits to the Ulbricht administration. About eight hundred letters a month come into the RIAS office from the East Zone, of which about one fourth are on political subjects. Robert Lochner, the very competent director of RIAS, reported that practically all letters on the proposed credit were vehemently negative, the general consensus of judgment being: "Will the Federal Republic be so foolish as to help this gangster when he is at the end of his rope?"

Of course the issue is not quite so simple; the fate of Ulbricht depends on much bigger factors than the granting or withholding of the credit. But the demonstration of disaffection with his satellite rule was emphatic.

For almost a decade after the cessation of the Soviet blockade in 1949, frustrated by the gigantic American airlift, West Berlin lived in peace, with only sporadic minor incidents such as kidnappings of active anticommunists. Then, on November 27, 1958, Nikita Khrushchev presented the Western powers with a six-months' ultimatum to withdraw their military forces from West Berlin and consent to its transformation into a "free demilitarized city." The Western powers were invited within this time limit to conclude a peace treaty, either with "the two existing German states" or with "a confederation of the two." Unless this were done, the note stated, the Soviet Union would withdraw from the four-power administration of Berlin, sign a separate peace treaty with Ulbricht, and turn over to the DDR control of the routes of access to Berlin.

This was the first challenge by either side, apart from the earlier blockade of West Berlin, to the *de facto* partition of Europe along the military demarcation line set at the end of the war. The Western powers have never recognized the partition of Germany and the United States has repeatedly affirmed its desire to see freedom restored to the peoples who have been subjected to Communist dictatorships in Eastern Europe. But at no time has the West sought to change the existing situation by force or threat of force.

What Khrushchev demanded was that the Western powers give up, with no *quid pro quo,* established rights of military occupation in Berlin and that they dishonor solemn pledges to maintain the freedom of the city. An American-British-French declaration, issued in London on October 3, 1954, affirms this pledge in very unambiguous form:

"The security and wellbeing of Berlin and the maintenance of the position of the three powers there are regarded by the three powers as essential elements of the peace of the free world in the present international situation. Consequently they will maintain armed forces within the territory of Berlin, so long as their responsibilities require this. They affirm again that they will treat any attack on Berlin, from whatever side it may come, as an attack on their armed forces and themselves."

Article 6 of the North Atlantic Treaty, setting up NATO, specifies that the treaty applies in the event of an armed attack "on the armed forces of a treaty partner in Europe."

To have given way on West Berlin would have shattered the framework of the Western alliance, would have conceded to the Soviet Union the domination of Western Europe. It seems clear in the retrospect of later years that Khrushchev was not prepared to press his demand, stated in the form of an ultimatum, to the point of an actual collision. But there could be no certainty on this point in the winter of 1958–59. The governments stood firm, but there were some individual voices of defeatism and appeasement, especially in Great Britain. One quaint suggestion advanced by a former British diplomat was that West Berlin be evacuated and its population relocated in a new Berlin, to be built on the territory of the Federal Republic. Some publicists stressed the "indefensibility" of West Berlin without considering that an attack on Berlin would be no isolated episode, but a supreme trial of strength with all available weapons.

Khrushchev somewhat softened the impact of his November 27 demand by sending to America his smooth, ingratiating trade minister, Anastas Mikoyan, apparently on a mission of sounding out American opinion. There were no publicized results of the Mikoyan visit, but Washington was left a little less anxious that May 27 would be the beginning of Armageddon.

On January 10, 1959, the Soviet government proposed a twenty-eight-nation conference to discuss a peace treaty with "the two German states" and/or a confederation which these "states" should form. There was no favorable Western response to this suggestion. Khrushchev consented to put aside his original time limit when it was agreed that there should be a conference of the foreign ministers of the Soviet Union and the three Western powers at Geneva. Representatives of the Federal Republic and the DDR were invited to attend as consultants.

This conference opened on May 11 and proceeded, with one recess, until August 4, when it broke up in an atmosphere of complete disagreement. The Western powers on May 14 offered a "package plan" for solving the issue of Berlin within the framework of an all-German settlement. This plan envisaged a gradual reunification of Germany, with free elections to be held after two and a half years, a speedier administrative reunion of the city of Berlin, and several measures looking to an abatement of European military tension. The Soviet representative, Andrei Gromyko, rejected this proposal and offered nothing acceptable to the Western powers. He was willing to agree to a standstill agreement on Berlin for a period of eighteen months, but with no assurance that Western rights would be respected after the expiration of this period.

One point that was never made clear in Soviet notes and in declarations of Khrushchev and other Soviet spokesmen was what forces should replace the allied garrison in West Berlin. Sometimes there were intimations that the presence of allied troops might continue, on condition that Soviet forces be included in the garrison. In the summer of 1962 Khrushchev suggested a joint occupation by forces of two members of NATO, Belgium and Norway, and two members of the Soviet bloc, Poland and Czechoslovakia. On December 12, 1962, in a generally mild reference to the Berlin situation, Khrushchev suggested that a United Nations force should replace the American-British-French garrison. In all these proposals there was never a suggestion of a matching Soviet concession, such as the admission of Western troops to East Berlin. Khrushchev adhered to the time-honored Soviet formula: "What's mine is mine; what's yours is negotiable."

One of the more questionable decisions of the Western negotiators at Geneva was to discuss West Berlin in isolation, after no agreement had been reached on the general problem of German reunion. As the Soviet representatives refused to consider any change in the status of East Berlin, this made West Berlin alone the subject of discussion and placed the Western powers in an unfavorable bargaining position. In this situation any change was almost certain to be for the worse, from the Western standpoint, as it would be naïve to imagine that the Soviet government would consent to strengthen guaranties for the freedom and economic viability of West Berlin.[5] Also, two of the subjects that came up on the agenda of the Geneva talks, limitation of the Western garrisons and avoidance of "hostile propaganda," could have meant a serious weakening of the Western position by limiting discretion in military deployment and curtailing the freedom of the West Berlin press and radio.

So it was probably fortunate for the West that the Geneva conference, like so many other West-East meetings, ended in a blank, with no commitments by either side. There was no immediate renewal of pressure on West Berlin because Khrushchev accepted an invitation to visit the United States. This was a diplomatic and propaganda victory for the Soviet leader and was perhaps too high a price to pay for a mere temporary cessation of his threat to peace in Berlin.

The climax of Khrushchev's visit was a private meeting with President Eisenhower at Camp David. This was followed by the issue of a joint communiqué which characterized the situation in Berlin as "abnormal." The use of this word was unsuitable, since the context did not make clear that what was abnormal was not the situation in West Berlin, but such Soviet acts as refusal to permit German reunification by means of free elections and attempts by threat of force to upset a situation in West Berlin which, whatever its shortcomings, was no menace to international peace. This omission was later repaired in strongly phrased speeches by Secretary of State Christian Herter and Under Secretary Douglas C. Dillon.

Attention then shifted to a four-power "Summit" meeting, set for Paris in May, 1960. This, however, was disrupted in advance by a tirade from Khrushchev, accompanied by much personal abuse of Eisenhower, ostensibly because of the downing in Russia of an American U-2 high-altitude reconnaissance plane. It is possible that this was only a pretext, that Khrushchev, realizing from the tone of the speeches by Herter and Dillon that he could expect no surrender on Berlin, preferred no conference at all to a conference which promised him no success. There was some expectation that Khrushchev's temper tantrum in Paris might presage the signing of his long-threatened separate peace treaty with the DDR. But when he went to East Berlin his mood seemed to change from violence to caution. To the disappointment, no doubt, of his East German satellites, he announced no new ultimative date and declared that the Berlin question would be shelved until after the United States presidential election.

The next milestone on the long road of the on-again, off-again Berlin crisis was the brief meeting between Kennedy and Khrushchev in Vienna in June, 1961. Here Khrushchev took a tough, bullying, intransigent position, insisting that the Berlin question must be settled on his terms by the end of 1961.

In one of his finest state papers, delivered in late July, 1961, President Kennedy paid an eloquent tribute to the people of Berlin and affirmed American purpose to defend the city at all costs. The President referred to West Berlin as "a showcase of liberty, a symbol, an isle of freedom in a Communist sea . . . a link with the free world, a beacon of hope behind the iron curtain, an escape hatch for refugees. . . . Above all the great testing place of Western courage and will, a focal point where our solemn commitments and Soviet ambitions now meet in basic confrontation."

In words curiously reminiscent of Lincoln's First Inaugural, the President placed the responsibility for war, if war should come, squarely on the rulers of the Soviet Union:

"The world is not deceived by the Communist attempt to label Berlin a hotbed of war. There is peace in Berlin today. The source of world trouble and tension today is Moscow, not Berlin. For the choice of war or peace is largely theirs, not ours. It is the Soviets who have stirred up this crisis. It is they who have tried to force a change. It is they who have rejected an all-German treaty and the rulings of international law."

Strong words were followed by positive action. Reserves were called up. An increase of $3 billion in the military budget was asked by the President and voted promptly by Congress. And in the autumn Khrushchev again called off his latest deadline of December 31, 1961 without setting any new date, up to the spring of 1963.[6]

But on August 13, 1961 the construction of the Berlin Wall started, first with strands of barbed wire across points of communication between the two parts of the city, finally developing into the grim, bloodstained barrier of today. The building of the Wall was a flagrant violation of existing four-power agreements to maintain freedom of movement within the city of Berlin, West and East. Could it have been prevented by sending an American engineering unit to remove the barbed wire, politely notifying the Russians that this had been done to save them the trouble of doing the same thing themselves? A very able and experienced American official in West Berlin told me he was sure this method would have succeeded, if it had been promptly resorted to. He was convinced the East German troops and police would not have offered armed resistance.

A member of the American mission in Berlin took issue with this view. He believed the Wall would have been simply moved farther back, that the American forces would have found themselves faced with the problem—hopeless because of their small numbers and the size of East Berlin—of occupying the whole city, with increasing probability of an armed clash under unfavorable local conditions. Certainly the action, to be effective, would have had to be prompt. And prompt action in Berlin, with three governments and various military and civil agencies to consult, was not easy to obtain.

At first the unopposed erection of the Wall severely depressed the West Germans. The reinforcement of the United States garrison, the visit of Vice-President Johnson, and the temporary appointment of General Clay as the President's personal military representative in Berlin helped to restore morale. While there have been ups and downs in the West Berlin mood, the city has stood its ordeal successfully; normal life after the erection of the Wall was not interfered with as it was during the blockade of 1948–49. Apart from temporary holdups on the road communication and the occasional buzzing of commercial planes (without disastrous accidents), Berlin's communications across the Soviet Zone have remained undisturbed.

During 1962 there were prolonged but apparently quite futile talks between United States and Soviet representatives. Great Britain cordially favored this policy of keeping in touch with Moscow; France held aloof. The Federal Republic followed the course of the talks closely, with some concern that German interests might be adversely affected by some compromise formula for settlement.

However, the United States negotiators, or sounders, held themselves obliged to maintain three basic principles: the presence in West Berlin of Western garrisons, the self-government of the city, and its economic viability through assured communications with the outside world. This left little room for discussion, especially as the German Communists had sealed off East Berlin, even forcing foreigners to show passports at the checkpoints as if they were entering a foreign country. As regards West Berlin, there was nothing of substance that could honorably be given up.

A truly satisfactory settlement for West Berlin will only be possible when the whole city is reunited and the infamous Wall torn down, as part of a larger process, the reunion of all Germany in freedom. In the meantime the status quo, or status quo minus, as Mayor Brandt calls it, is far preferable to any deal which would imperil any of the three principles which the United States is committed to uphold. Nor should any blackmail be paid in the form of diplomatic recognition of the Ulbricht regime.

It cannot be emphasized too strongly that there are not today, as is sometimes loosely asserted, two German states. There is one legitimate representative German government. In the Soviet Zone there is an occupation regime with no semblance of representative character. To give any kind of formal sanction to what amounts to the annexation of a large part of Germany to the Soviet Union would be a disgraceful and humiliating procedure and would completely shake the confidence of the German people in the value of the Western alliance.

There are two lessons to be learned from the protracted Berlin crisis: The first is that Nikita Khrushchev is an inveterate bluffer, a practitioner of dangerous brinkmanship, but certain to draw back when he meets resolute resistance, provided no vital Russian interest is involved. The seizure of West Berlin is not a vital Russian interest. So, as usually happens, the policy of firmness in maintaining Western rights and Berlin liberties is also the safest policy, the one best calculated to maintain international peace. The second lesson is the urgent necessity of devising some means of advance preparation of effective concerted measures of resistance, should Khrushchev show a disposition to resort to Berlin brinkmanship again.

NOTES TO CHAPTER VIII

1 Some pro-Soviet visitors to Moscow at the height of Stalin's purges refused to believe that anything out of the ordinary was going on because they didn't see any arrests with their own eyes. This would have been equally true for a visitor in Berlin on June 30, 1934, when Hitler carried out sweeping arrests and executions. Such operations normally do not take place in broad daylight or in the presence of crowds of spectators.

2 Authority for these figures is *Statistisches Jahrbuch der DDR für 1960–61* ("Statistical Yearbook of the DDR"), p. 17. This yearbook is published by the State Central Administration for Statistics, Berlin (East), 1961. See also section on *Flüchtlinge* in *Soviet Besatzungs Zone von A-B,* pp. 123–125, and section on *Bevölkerung,* pp. 67–68.

3 Over 20 per cent of the inhabitants of West Berlin are over sixty.

4 The token size of the Western forces in Berlin is the best comment on the strident Communist propaganda about the city as an "aggressive NATO base." These garrisons could, with the West Berlin police, nip in the bud any attempt to take over the city by infiltration and provoked riots, but are obviously no military match for the Soviet troops in the zone.

5 A very influential American commentator succumbed to this form of naïveté in some of his writings on the Berlin situation.

6 Soviet conduct often recalls the prescient comment on Russian policy expressed by British Foreign Secretary Lord Palmerston to the Earl of Clarendon in 1853: "The policy and practice of the Russian Government have always been to push forward its encroachments as fast and as far as the apathy or want of firmness of other governments would allow it to go, but always to stop and retire when it met with decided resistance, and then to wait for the next favorable opportunity to make another spring on its intended victim."

CHAPTER IX

The Face of the New Germany[1]

Bonn.

The capital of the Federal Republic has nothing of the pomp and splendor of Berlin. Despite the many new buildings, severely functional in style, put up to house ministries and government offices, Bonn is still a solid *gemütlich,*[2] provincial town, with no big boulevards, elegant shops, or impressive hotels and restaurants. Government greeters and entertainers are likely to take guests to nearby Cologne. It is a popular story that Chancellor Adenauer picked Bonn as the capital because it is within easy driving distance of his home in Rhöndorf. Another reason is that Bonn, with no big industries, was a most unlikely setting for political demonstrations and disturbances.

Before it became a political center Bonn had two principal attractions: a renowned university and a fine view across the Rhine to the *Siebengebirge* ("Seven Mountains") which rise on the opposite side of the river. The university has an unusual building for classrooms and offices, a long, winding one-story building, facing on a large park, that formerly served as the electoral palace of the archbishops of Cologne. (In medieval times the archbishop was one of seven electors who, in theory at least, selected the German emperor.)

Late in June the students hold a midsummer festival, with a concert in one of the spacious courtyards; dancing in the streets; speeches from the mayor, the rector of the university, and other dignitaries; and all-night celebrations in the crowded beer and wine cellars. Talking with a group of students in a smoke-filled cellar, I got the impression that their main interests were their studies and careers. Their political views seemed to be usually determined by their homes; those I fell in with came from CDU Catholic families.

They were happy about the new cordiality between Germany and France and seemed to share General de Gaulle's suspicion of British motives in wishing to join the EEC, recalling that, in their opinion, it had always been British policy to keep the continental nations divided. America they were inclined to consider well-meaning but inexperienced, and they believed that stronger measures should have been taken when the Berlin Wall was put up. Their opinions were divided, however, when they were asked whether war should have been risked. Their ideal was a united Europe, not old-fashioned nationalism.

Before the war Bonn possessed an excellent hotel, the Königshof, which was completely destroyed. For a time the most comfortable place in which a visitor could stay was a converted villa near the site of the former hotel. A few years ago a new Königshof, with no decorative adornments and rather small rooms but with a fine outlook on the Rhine, was opened and became a center of entertainment and social life. A typical view of the lobby of the Königshof would shock a Nazi race fanatic; there are usually a number of delegates from the newly independent nations of Africa, hoping to profit from the more liberal German attitude toward aid for underdeveloped countries.

Near the Königshof is a little bluff, rising above the Rhine and surmounted by a statue of one of Bonn's more distinguished natives, the nineteenth-century nationalist poet Ernst Moritz Arndt. Near the statue are some old cannons from the time of the Franco-Prussian War and on the statue is engraved Arndt's famous saying: "The Rhine, Germany's river, not Germany's boundary." All this recalls a bygone age, when France was the hereditary enemy and the popular German song, never heard nowadays, was *Die Wacht am Rhein*. Now the Rhine is thought of not as an exclusively German river, but as an artery of European commerce, crowded with ships and barges under French, Swiss, Dutch, as well as German flags.

Bonn's Koblenzerstrasse, a section of the main highway along the left bank of the Rhine, has the dubious distinction of being probably the noisiest thoroughfare in Germany, as anyone can testify after trying to sleep in a room facing on it. From early morning until late at night big trucks come thundering up and down; the double view of the Koblenzerstrasse, on land, and the Rhine waterway offer a good illustration of Germany's economic miracle.

Walking upriver along the Koblenzerstrasse from the Königshof, one passes the Beethoven Gymnasium, an excellent German middle school which, by chance, one of my grandsons attended for a year; the modern-looking buildings of the ministries of posts and telegraphs and foreign affairs; the Villa Hammerstein, residence of President Lübke; and the Schaumburg Palace with its large attractive park, a white building which will long be associated with memories of Konrad Adenauer. Finally one comes to a converted former school building overlooking the Rhine, the seat of the German Bundestag, with its assembly halls and offices for individual members.

With new building stimulated by a hundred foreign embassies and the housing needs of a host of government employees, Bonn has spread out on all sides and now, to the south, almost merges with the comfortable-looking spa, Bad Godesberg, scene of the unsuccessful meeting between Chamberlain and Hitler in September, 1938, which almost touched off World War II a year ahead of time. Beyond Bad Godesberg are the spacious quarters of the United States Embassy, a small-scale Pentagon, with almost equal opportunities for confusion in the corridors. Nearby is the "American village" of Plittersdorf, built for the use of embassy employees and complete with American nondenominational church and American club and swimming pool. This is typical of the tendency of Americans stationed in foreign lands, to huddle together in special living quarters, with a minimum of contact with "the natives." Until the novelty wore off, Plittersdorf was an object of curiosity to Germans, who came in considerable numbers on Sundays and holidays to look it over.

In the narrow, winding streets between the Rhine and the railway station are the gay stone *Münster* (cathedral), topped by five towers, the Beethoven Monument, the old Rathaus, and the museum where music manuscripts and other relics of Beethoven—probably the most eminent citizen of Bonn—are preserved. There is also a large open-air market of fruits and vegetables, much of its produce brought in and sold by peasants from the adjacent Rhineland countryside. And in one of the unobtrusive confectionery shops near the market one can find the products of the finest recipe for making chocolate truffles I have ever discovered.

Despite its depressing climate, close and humid in summer, rainy in winter, the result of a location in a pocket between ranges of hills on each side of the Rhine, Bonn and its environs have their attractive features. The damp soil nourishes luxuriant rose gardens. There are delightful cruises up the Rhine to the little resort towns that dot the shores of the river. The basic impression of a provincial university town, with more than a normal share of bookstores and without the glitter and glamor of a great capital, remains. And this is perhaps symbolic of a Germany committed to seek its future destiny not in the revival of the Hohenzollerns and the more distant Hohenstaufens, but as a member of what Germans often call "the European club."

Cologne.

For first-rate opera and concerts residents of Bonn must usually go fifteen miles to its larger neighbor Cologne, with its miraculously preserved medieval cathedral. Recovered from its deep war wounds, Cologne has regained and enlarged its old position as a thriving center of West European industry and trade. It is one of the older German cities, with a history dating back to the time when it was an important frontier outpost of the Roman Empire. Its archbishop was, ex officio, one of the great princes of medieval Germany.

Even in Germany, always a leader in city planning, Cologne seems exceptionally well laid out, with a number of concentric ring thoroughfares bearing names of early German tribes such as the Salians and the Ubii, and of dynasties of the Holy Roman Empire. Two famous schoolmen of the Middle Ages, Albertus Magnus and Duns Scotus, are buried in this archiepiscopal city.

The University of Cologne is well known for its economics department, and one of the professors, Dr. Günther Schmölders, whom I had met at an economic conference in the United States, explained over tea and cakes in his home why the originally rapid rate of German economic expansion in the fifties was the result of "Victorian capitalism, modified by social legislation." Wage demands at first were modest and the industrial firms were sparing with dividends, plowing back the larger share of their profits for further investment. In recent years, with shortage of working hands strengthening trade-union pressure for higher wages, new problems have come up, of which erosion of the buying power of the mark is perhaps the most serious.

Another interesting meeting in Cologne was with Wolfgang Leonhard, whose personal story, *Child of the Revolution,* was unaccountably neglected in America, although it was a best seller in Germany and has been adapted for a film. Leonhard, a slight man in his forties, has gone through fascinating experiences in the making and unmaking of a Communist. Son of Communist parents, he was taken to the Soviet Union by his mother to escape Hitler's persecution. The choice of Russia as a place of asylum was unfortunate for her. She was almost immediately arrested in one of Stalin's paranoid purges and spent many years in a concentration camp.

Wolfgang, a boy of thirteen at the time of his mother's arrest, was educated in Soviet schools and given a thorough Communist indoctrination. After a difficult period of exile in the first years of the war, when he was treated as a suspect enemy alien, he was picked as a promising candidate for participation in a future German Communist government and sent back to Germany with Ulbricht in the spring of 1945. Increasing disillusionment with the inequalities of communism in practice and with the servile dependence of the German Communists on Moscow caused Leonhard to flee, not at first to the West, which he still despised as "bourgeois," but to Tito's Yugoslavia, which he had long secretly admired. Later he moved West as his political views became less extreme, spent some time at one of the colleges of Oxford, and settled in Cologne, where he reads a vast number of Communist publications from all over the world, when not on international lecture trips, and contributes regularly to the weekly *Die Zeit*. Professing to be a specialist only on the Soviet Union, Leonhard holds some nonconformist opinions about Germany, which he set forth to me in the course of a conversation.

"There is no danger of a Nazi revival in Germany. Such talk is ignorant, downright nonsensical. The real danger here is that the German people have not fully absorbed the spirit of democracy. There is too much clericalism, as in the recent appeal of the Catholic Church to the voters in the local state election, nonpolitical in tone, but clearly designed to help the CDU. And there is too much philistinism, indifference to ideas and intellectual subjects. The ruling group governs without much regard for public opinion. The German 'Meet the Press' is a pale shadow of the American. Answers to questions in the Bundestag are apt to be formal. It would be a good idea to form a CDU-Social Democratic coalition government until the parties learn to know each other better. Now the CDU is too self-assured; the Social Democrats are chronically frustrated because of their exclusion from power and responsibility in the federal administration."

This was an introduction to the views of Germany's alienated, critically minded leftist intelligentsia, of which more will be said in the next chapter.

Düsseldorf.

In 1949, when I first saw this city, located on the right bank of the Rhine downriver from Cologne, it was still badly smashed up, especially around the railway station. Capital of the rich industrial state of North Rhine-Westphalia, Düsseldorf lies at the entrance to the fabulous Ruhr Valley, industrial heartland of Germany. The whole Ruhr area was a preferred target of Allied bombing. Now this belongs to an already distant past, like the raids of the Norsemen into the Rhine valley in the ninth and tenth centuries. Düsseldorf is as handsome as ever, with its row of government buildings and foreign consulates on the Cecilien-Allee, facing the Rhine, its parks with artificial lakes, the elegant shops and fine restaurants which make local patriots compare it to Paris. Performances at its opera house are so crowded that it proved impossible to get a ticket for Wagner's *Die Meistersinger*. Both capi tal and labor in Germany have headquarters in Düsseldorf, where one finds the offices of many big Ruhr firms and national German banks and also the headquarters of the German trade-union movement. The varied interpretations of the economic situation which I obtained by calling at these offices have been reported in an earlier chapter.

The European Economic Community figures very much in the reckoning of Düsseldorf businessmen. One heard of many deals between German and French firms in the same line of business for specialization and division of activity. At the time of my visit, in the summer of 1962, General de Gaulle had not imposed his veto on the admission of Great Britain to the EEC and a delegation of British industrialists was visiting the Ruhr, in the expectation that British adhesion to the Common Market would make possible similar Anglo-German arrangements.

Hamburg.

This old Hanseatic mercantile city, its usually gray skyline marked by the gleaming green copper spires of some of its churches, is Germany's principal port and largest city, apart from West Berlin. With a small hinterland and an urban population of 1.8 million, Hamburg is one of the twelve Länder, or states, of the Federal Republic. Always a window to the outside world, with its merchant families cultivating friendships and contacts in many foreign lands, Hamburg showed more than average resistance to the Nazis. In the years of inflation and subsequent depression between the two great wars the Communists gained some following, especially among the dock workers. There were a number of dead and wounded in a Communist uprising in the autumn of 1923.

This atmosphere of sullen proletarian discontent has disappeared with full employment and increased prosperity. The Communists could not recruit a corporal's guard for an insurrection, even for a demonstration, today. The city has been under Social Democratic administration for most of the time since the establishment of the Federal Republic. But Hamburg's socialism has been of a very mild businesslike character. Its first postwar mayor, Max Brauer, who returned from exile in the United States and reacquired German citizenship, is an expansive, warmhearted personality, a German "Forty-Eighter" democrat with no trace of the doctrinaire follower of Karl Marx. Of his successor, the present Mayor Nevermann, a local journalist of conservative views remarked: "He is a very cultivated man. One would not know he is a Social Democrat."

The business life of Hamburg revolves largely around its harbor, fourth largest in the world, with an area of about 12 square miles. Hamburg is a river port; the open sea is over 100 miles distant at the mouth of the Elbe, but the inflowing tide is strong enough to bring ships of large tonnage to Hamburg. More than 20,000 freight and passenger vessels berth here every year, bringing a large variety of cargoes—coal from the United States, paper from Finland, grain from Canada, bananas from Central America and Africa. Hamburg has gained the reputation of being a "fast port," where loading and unloading operations are carried out with considerable speed, saving the charges of having a ship tied up in harbor.

A boat trip around the Hamburg harbor leaves a number of impressions: huge shipyards, employing the latest devices of automation; ships of all sizes and purposes and many national flags; a floating quay almost half a mile long; a giant tanker of 88,000 tons; two big cranes lifting loads of 100 and 200 tons; a huge shed for storing the bananas, which spoil in the open air. The shed holds 70,000 bushels of the perishable fruit and the transfer from the refrigerator ship to the shed is completely automatized. A feature of the port that adds to its popularity and turnover is the free trade area where goods may be shipped and stored without payment of duty—so long as they are not transferred to Germany. These goods may be transshipped to any other destination.

One of Hamburg's best-known tourist sights is the *Reeperbahn,* the red-light area, where off-duty sailors look for their customary diversions in an atmosphere of dance halls, sexy movies, and cheap restaurants. In one street of this area, forbidden to adolescents, women of easy virtue sit in the houses, exposing themselves in various degrees of undress to amorous passers-by. This is reminiscent of the Tokyo *yoshiwara* quarter. Helmut Schmidt, a prominent local Social Democratic political figure, wishes to clear up the more open manifestations of vice; it remains to be seen whether his crusading efforts will prevail against the city's old tradition of giving its transitory sailor population a rip-roaring time during shore leave.

Because of the partition of Germany, Hamburg has lost some of its former commercial hinterland. Some ships still come down the Elbe from Czechoslovakia; the crews are carefully forbidden to go on shore, for fear they might succumb to the fleshpots of capitalism. Still, the turnover of this renovated port is 30 per cent higher than it was in 1938.

Some Hamburg businessmen, such as Erik Blumenfeld (a prominent local leader of the CDU and member of the Bundestag), feel this rate of progress is not good enough. They point out that Rotterdam, Hamburg's principal rival, with its advantageous location at the mouth of the Rhine, has more than doubled its turnover in the same period of time. Blumenfeld believes that Hamburg is too dependent on its shipyards and a cyclical industry, and urges a program of attracting more diversified industries to the city. Whatever truth there may be in these criticisms, Hamburg seems to be thriving at the present time and certainly presents a favorable contrast to the stagnation of the depression years and outright hunger of the first years after the war.

There is a strong English influence in Hamburg, reflected in the prevalent custom of serving afternoon tea. And the mercantile character of the city, dating back to the medieval times of the Hanseatic League (a combination of trading cities to put down piracy and otherwise protect their interests), affects public opinion on political and economic questions. Nowhere in Germany does one hear so much sharp criticism of the idea that the EEC might become a closed trading area, with a discriminatory tariff wall against all outsiders.

"We want England in the Common Market," said one typical spokesman for a Hamburg import and export firm. "And we don't want to be forced to buy expensive French wheat, rather than cheaper Canadian wheat, or to eat inferior bananas and drink inferior coffee, just because these come from France's former African colonies."

One finds in Hamburg vigorous currents of intellectual activity. There is one of the largest of the German universities, and a smaller one in nearby Kiel. Hamburg is the publishing headquarters of one of Germany's two leading daily newspapers, *Die Welt,* also of its most pugnacious and controversial weekly, *Der Spiegel,* and of a widely respected weekly devoted to foreign and domestic politics, literature, and the arts, *Die Zeit.* It would be hard anywhere in Germany to hear more purposeful, informed discussion of the wide range of the country's internal and foreign problems than one encounters during an evening of talk with Countess Marion Doenhoff and some of her colleagues on the editorial board of *Die Zeit.* The Countess, who comes of an aristocratic East Prussian family, holds a Ph.D. degree and is a most energetic and indefatigable student of international affairs, traveling to the far corners of the earth to get material for her articles in *Die Zeit.*

Another highly useful source of information in Hamburg for the inquiring foreigner is Dr. Walter Stahl, executive director of the Atlantic Bridge, an organization devoted to promoting German-American understanding by publishing informative books and brochures on various aspects of German politics, economics, education, and culture. Dr. Stahl is a lawyer by profession, but devotes most of his time to work for the Atlantic Bridge.

Munich.

The trip from Hamburg in the north to Munich in the south is one of the longest that one can take within the shrunken frontiers of the German Federal Republic. And there is a substantial change of political and social atmosphere between outward-looking, politically progressive, seagoing Hamburg and the capital of landlocked, conservative Bavaria, seat of a monarchy which was swept away only by the defeat of 1918 and which, one suspects, is still yearned for by many old-fashioned Bavarians. The funeral of Crown Prince Rupprecht a few years ago attracted throngs of mourners.

Munich was long famous as a center of music, art, and literary café life; it is also associated, less pleasantly, with the early political ventures of Adolf Hitler. It was in the Bavarian royal opera house that King Ludwig II would sometimes listen alone to the operas of Richard Wagner. He was called "the mad king" and was eventually deposed, but he placed the whole international musical world immeasurably in his debt by coming to the aid of Wagner when the composer was in dire financial straits. And the memory of Ludwig, the ultraromantic, who loved torchlight rides over the *Fernpass,* which leads from Bavaria into Austria, still lives in the fairylike castles of Hohenschwangau and Neuschwanstein, built like eagles' nests in commanding heights of the Bavarian Alps.

Munich is also a considerable industrial city and it was frequently bombed during the war. Many fine buildings of the past, the royal opera house, the Residenz Theater, the royal palace, the Academy of Science, were obliterated. The Bavarian State Library was wrecked and two thirds of its books were destroyed. But the imposing Frauenkirche, the Rathaus, where there is a procession of little figures as the hours are struck, the Old and the New Pinakothek (famous art galleries) still stand. The damaged twin tower of the Frauenkirche has been repaired. And the time has long passed when the visitor to postwar Munich could scarcely recognize the outlines of the main streets because of ruins and debris.

Munich has risen from its ashes and now one of its principal problems is to regulate the traffic that grows more and more unmanageable as the population grows and more people own cars. Munich is also on the way to Austria, the Brenner Pass, and Italy. It is, according to a public opinion poll, one of the cities where Germans like best to live.

Old residents of Munich say that the city has lost some of its Bavarian character because of the heavy influx of newcomers from the North and refugees from the Sudetenland area of Czechoslovakia. Ten or fifteen years ago Munich was called the DP (Displaced Persons) capital of the world. The old city was then thronged with Russians, Ukrainians, Poles, Central Asians, people from the Baltic States, Hungarians, Yugoslavs, people of many nationalities and backgrounds united by one negative passion: a determination not to return to their Communist-ruled homelands. Among these uprooted exiles there were scores of rival political organizations and not a few Communist spies and secret agents; intrigue and violence were rife; cases of political murder were not unknown. There were also the people of German origin who were driven from their homes under circumstances of great cruelty by the Czechs after the end of the war. Now most of the ablebodied East European fugitives have begun new lives in the United States, Canada, Australia, and South America. The Sudeten Germans have been absorbed into the everyday life of Bavaria, like refugees in other parts of Germany.

But some cosmopolitan atmosphere remains in Munich, if only because of the presence here of the Free Europe Committee and the American Committee for Liberation. The former organization broadcasts to the Soviet East European satellite countries, the latter to the peoples of the Soviet Union, not only in Russian, but in Ukrainian, Georgian and other languages of the minor nationalities of the Soviet Union. Both groups are supported by American funds and employ on their staffs substantial numbers of the nationals of the countries to which they are directing their radio messages. Neither tries to encourage revolt behind the Iron Curtain. This would be cruel and stupid, in view of the failure of the West to give any aid to the fighting Hungarians in 1956.

The purpose of the two committees is more modest: to break little holes in the Iron Curtain by giving over the air news items and interpretations which would never appear in the controlled Communist press. There are also music and entertainment programs. Contents of heretical forbidden books like Pasternak's *Doctor Zhivago* and Milovan Djilas's *The New Class* are quickly communicated. Radio Free Europe is especially proud of its initiative in reporting the shocking revelations of cruelty and corruption by Josef Swiatlo, a prominent official of the Polish secret police who, for his own personal reasons, fled to the West. The Committee for Liberation keeps an exhaustive file of up-to-date information on Soviet developments, much of this derived from monitoring Soviet broadcasts. Both organizations receive an encouraging flow of letters of encouragement, comment, and criticism from listeners who write to code addresses in Western Europe, which are periodically changed to keep ahead of the censor.

Now, as always, Munich is a city of hearty eaters and drinkers, with epicurean restaurants and beer halls, some of enormous size and crowded to capacity on weekends and during the autumn and pre-Lenten festivals. It lies within easy reach of a fascinating vacation area, the mountains of South Bavaria, where Garmisch-Partenkirchen, Berchtesgaden, and Mittenwald are among the many centers for hikers in summer and skiers in winter.

I once spent a delightful three weeks exploring the countryside around Garmisch and feeling a sense of contact with a peasant Germany, far removed from the rush and bustle and sophistication of the cities. Bavarian peasant homes are often decorated with spirited if primitive paintings of religious subjects and scenes of farm life. The traditional Catholic faith of the region is reflected not only in the churches, with their spires or domes which dominate the villages, but in many roadside chapels and crucifixes. Once, at a spot with a very striking outlook on mountains and over valleys, there was a little admonition beside the crucifix, to reflect on how short are man's days on earth and to think of *Ewigkeit* ("eternity").

One house, built at the end of World War I, bore an inscribed prayer which was, unfortunately, not fulfilled:

> *In schwerer Zeit dies Haus erstand,*
> *Gott schirm' es und gib Friede ins Land.*

> ("This house was built in hard times.
> God keep it and give peace in the land.")

Oberammergau, the world-known peasant village where ever since the Thirty Years' War the natives have performed the Passion Play every ten years, is within walking distance of Garmisch. Nearby is the old monastery, Ettal, where there is a primitive painting of Swedish soldiers bayoneting the abbot—a reminder that there were atrocities on both sides in that savage and protracted conflict.

In the opposite direction from the Alps, in the hilly country of northern Bavaria, is Bayreuth, where Richard Wagner was able to build his ideal theater on top of a hill and where he found ease from his cares and struggles in Villa Wahnfried. Here, every summer, German and foreign admirers of the Wagnerian music dramas gather for the festival, where an orchestra recruited from the finest musicians in Germany and a cast of leading Wagnerian singers of all nationalities perform the *Ring* and other Wagner operas in the abstract settings and costumes devised by the composer's grandsons, Wieland and Wolfgang.

Stuttgart.

After Munich, this capital of the southwestern state of Baden-Württemberg is the largest and most distinctive city of South Germany. Stuttgart is picturesquely built on hills overlooking the river Neckar. The people of *Schwaben* (Swabia, as this southwestern corner of Germany was formerly called) have the reputation of being similar to their neighbors, the Swiss, in the qualities of industry and frugality, and Stuttgart was a leader in the recovery of Germany's shattered cities. As early as 1946 its mayor was talking of making the Königstrasse, one of the main streets, as fine as the Bahnhofstrasse of Zürich, the opulent thoroughfare that runs from the city's railway station to the Zürich Lake. Today the mayor's dream has fully come true.

The young lady who represented the Stuttgart Internationes, an organization that facilitates German contacts for foreigners, certainly lived up to the Swabian reputation for diligent efficiency. I arrived in Stuttgart on a Friday morning, my stay limited until Sunday. Within that cramped space of time she set up for me an interview with the Baden-Württemberg Prime Minister Kiesinger, a visit to the headquarters of the big Daimler-Benz automobile company, an appointment with the office for investigating Nazi war crimes in nearby Ludwigsburg, and a talk with Giselher Wirsing, editor of *Christ und Welt,* one of the larger German weeklies, with Lutheran associations but mainly concerned with secular affairs. It was a dizzily exacting schedule, but it went off without a hitch. And in conclusion, she arranged for me on Saturday afternoon a visit to her hospitable family in Schwäbisch-Gmund, a town that had just celebrated with medieval pomp and ceremony the eight hundredth anniversary of its establishment. From Schwäbisch-Gmund it is possible to make an excursion to the site of the ancestral castle of the Hohenstaufen, most romantic of the dynasties of the medieval German Empire. Only a few stones remain of the castle, which was thoroughly destroyed during the peasant revolt in the sixteenth century. But its commanding location, with a far view over the rolling countryside, was worthy of an imperial family.

Prime Minister Kiesinger was as friendly and communicative as if he had been the governor of a midwestern state. He spoke of the old liberal tradition of the German Southwest, a region with a high proportion of small farmers (who now sometimes worked part time in factories) and hand workers. The state was becoming more industrialized, with big internationally known firms such as Daimler-Benz, one of the pioneers in the automobile industry, and Bosch, the maker of all kinds of electrical appliances, together with many medium-sized plants.

As chairman of the joint committee of the Bundestag and the Bundesrat, Mr. Kiesinger is a specialist in federal-state relationships. He believes that the new federal constitution has worked quite well, although he recognizes that the states must make some contribution to the ever growing federal budget needs. Before he left parliamentary life in Bonn and came to Stuttgart Mr. Kiesinger had been largely concerned with foreign affairs and represented Germany in many international meetings. He emphatically repudiated the idea that a close special association with France would, could, or should be a substitute for the alliance with the United States. To a question on this point he replied:

"Sheer folly. There is only one real guaranty of German freedom and that is the friendship and help of the United States in NATO. We don't want nuclear weapons. I should passionately oppose anything that would separate us from the United States."

Mr. Wirsing, the editor of *Christ und Welt,* was more critical, not to say skeptical, about the United States performance in Berlin and the protracted talks on this subject with the Soviet Union. He argued that it would be impossible merely to hold West Berlin indefinitely, because the significance of Berlin was its role as a symbol of German unity. He showed some anxiety as to whether there might be an anti-German bias among some of President Kennedy's advisers.

In these talks with the prime minister and the editor, as in other German contacts, one could sense two currents in German public opinion: the hope that American nuclear power would assure the existence in freedom of the Federal Republic and finally somehow make possible the unification of the whole country, and the fear that the two superpowers, the United States and the Soviet Union, would finally make a deal at Germany's expense.

South of Stuttgart lies one of Germany's most enchanting playgrounds, the Black Forest, so called because it is a region of dark pine-covered hills, interspersed with quaint old towns and villages, small lakes, and ruined castles. Here, as in southern Bavaria, there is still a peasant way of life that does not exist in the United States, and that is disappearing in Europe. The women wear old-fashioned colorful costumes on Sundays and holidays, and such handicrafts as making wood carvings and cuckoo clocks flourish when farm work is slack in the winter months. As everywhere in Germany, there are excellent trails laid out for the walker.

Frankfurt.

Frankfurt-on-the-Main (so designated to distinguish it from the city of similar name, Frankfurt-on-the-Oder, now a stagnant town in the Soviet Zone) is one of Germany's most historic cities. Here is the house where Goethe was born, destroyed by bombing but reconstructed with meticulous care, stone by stone, as a replica of the original. Not far from the Goethe House are the Rathaus and the Church of St. Paul, notable for the sessions of Germany's abortive liberal parliament in 1848. An old banking and commercial center, Frankfurt has always been characterized by a liberal atmosphere and did not take kindly to the substitution of Prussian rule for its old status as a free city. When I first saw Frankfurt after the war, in 1946, the city was a shambles. One symbol of its devastation which still remains is the ruined shell of the former opera house, on which one can still read the inscription, ironical against the background of destruction: *Zum Guten, Schönen, Treuen* ("To the Good, the True and the Beautiful").

Frankfurt has built a new opera house and shows few other signs of wartime destruction. Here, as in the Federal Republic in general, one is sometimes reminded of Remarque's novel of World War I, *"Im Westen nichts neues"* ("In the West nothing new"). An attempt to rename one of its main streets, the Kaiserstrasse, after Germany's first Social Democratic President, Friedrich Ebert, foundered on popular unwillingness to accept the change of a familiar name. Kaiserstrasse it remains, after a period of confusion when the hybrid "Kaiser Friedrich Ebertstrasse" was sometimes used.

The Kaiserstrasse leads from the big railway station to the Frankfurterhof, one of the most comfortable hotels in Germany, or in Europe, although at the time of my visit in 1962 the nocturnal quiet was disturbed by a terrific drilling and blasting operation in the immediate vicinity, designed to turn a waste area into a parking place. The city has retained its old banking specialty; the solid-looking buildings of the Bundesbank, the Deutsche Bank (largest of the private banks), and many similar institutions stand on the Taunus Anlage and other boulevards and streets. Such men as Karl Blessing, president of the Bundesbank, and Hermann Abs, the fabulous financier who heads the Deutsche Bank and is a director in many big industrial concerns, are extremely well versed in international as well as German finance and economics. They are able to give an inquiring visitor useful insights into the methods used to defend the purchasing power of the mark and into the techniques of co-operation between European central banks.

Frankfurt is also a literary and intellectual center. The old *Frankfurter Zeitung,* one of the best newspapers in Europe, was a casualty of the Nazi period. But its tradition is carried on to some extent by the *Frankfurter Allgemeine Zeitung,* which is, with *Die Welt* of Hamburg, one of the nearest German equivalents to *The New York Times.* Another newspaper, the *Frankfurter Rundschau,* is somewhat more to the left and has been a hot crusader against ex-Nazis in high places. Frankfurt is also the headquarters of some of the German publishing houses and intellectual magazines of limited circulation.

A short distance from Frankfurt is Bad Homburg, which, with its solidly built houses and carefully tended park, looks very much like the nineteenth-century German spas which attracted Turgenev and where he laid the scenes of some of his novels. A touch of

Old Russia is added by a miniature Orthodox chapel, built for the worship of the aristocratic and well-to-do Russians who frequented resorts like Bad Homburg before the Bolshevik Revolution wiped them out of social and economic existence. There is also a casino, with such games as roulette and chemin-de-fer as traps for the unwary visitor.

Frankfurt is located in Hesse, a new state created since the end of the war. Like Hamburg and Bremen, Hesse is a stronghold of the Social Democrats, who won an absolute majority in the local election in November, 1962, somewhat aided by the scandal about the methods employed in jailing the editors of *Der Spiegel*. Outstanding figure in the Hesse Social Democracy is Prime Minister Georg August Zinn. *Gewinn mit Zinn* ("Win with Zinn") has been an election slogan.

A visit to Mr. Zinn in his office in Wiesbaden, the pleasant Rhenish town which is the capital of Hesse, revealed why this very moderate Social Democrat has been able to gain a considerable amount of middle class support, while retaining the solid backing of his own party. He is the type of socialist who possesses most political appeal in the increasingly affluent society of the new Germany—not an ounce of revolutionary or Marxist dogmatism in his makeup.

Mr. Zinn talked in terms that would have been understandable to a progressive American state executive of any party: how to attract new industries to Hesse; encouraging village co-operatives (entirely voluntary) for better use of machinery; further improving the state educational system, already considered one of the best in Germany. Although city workers have usually furnished the bulk of the Social Democrat votes, Zinn's administration has made a successful bid for the votes of peasants, mostly small holders with twelve or fifteen acres. Competition has been started between villages as to which can provide the best local amenities. In an effort to raise country schooling to the city level, community schools, serving several villages, are being introduced, with bus transportation for the pupils.

What has won Zinn high marks in the esteem of many nonsocialists is his firm rejection of the idea of nationalizing any of Hesse's

big industrial plants, such as the Henschel machine works at Kassel
or the chemical plant at Höchst. Hesse is the one German state
which permits nationalization of industrial enterprises with compensation. But Zinn rejects the idea as unnecessary and undesirable. He remarked to me that the policies which had been carried
out in Hesse had helped to shape the Bad Godesberg program of
the Social Democratic Party, which discarded the last traces of
Marxism. And if one looks at the record of the Social Democrats
in power, of Zinn in Hesse, Brauer and Nevermann in Hamburg,
Kaisen in Bremen, Brandt in Berlin, it seems a very far cry to the
Communist Manifesto, the Gotha Program, and other classics in
the history of Marxism in Germany.

Outside the large cities there is a "green," rural Germany in the
farmsteads and villages that dot the landscape as seen from the air.
But this side of Germany has become politically and economically
less significant. The landowning nobility that played such a big role
in the history of Prussia has been wiped out, in some cases physically and altogether economically, because its former estates lie in
the Soviet Zone and in the area annexed by Poland and the Soviet
Union.

Western and southern Germany, in the Federal Republic, contains a much higher proportion of landowning medium and small
farmers and peasants. In these parts of Germany the aristocratic
landowners with prefixes of *von* and *zu* to their names have been
left undisturbed in their holdings. But they do not represent a
political and social force comparable with the Prussian Junkers.
In Germany, as in America and throughout the world, science and
machinery have made it increasingly hard for the small farmer to
make both ends meet. Since the end of the war about one million
peasants have left the land for the cities, where the industrial and
building boom provides plenty of jobs at higher earnings.

Farm output has held up extremely well. The Federal Republic
is about 75 per cent self-sufficient in foodstuffs, despite a population swollen by some 12 million expellees and refugees and a
standard of living that makes possible a richer and more varied
diet. The peasants who left the land were mostly marginal pro-

ducers who contributed little to the market. Farming has shared in the general reviving prosperity; the farms are larger and more consolidated; about a million tractors are now used in German fields. However, Germany cannot overcome the handicap that its soil is poorer than the more fertile sections of France and Italy. It cannot as yet compete on equal terms with specialized producers of dairy products such as the Danes, or of fruit and vegetables such as the Dutch and the Belgians.

German agriculture in the past has been protected by tariffs— free trading Economics Minister Erhard has encountered far more formidable resistance from agriculture than from industry in his constant effort to lower tariff barriers—and by subsidies. But the rules of the EEC forbid the indefinite maintenance of national subsidies. After a few years the principle of full competition within the Common Market will apply to agriculture as well as to industry. And Minister of Agriculture Werner Schwarz and the experts in his ministry are working on plans to make German farming able to meet this test. Specialization, mechanization, consolidation of land holdings which are sometimes held in separate strips, further elimination of the weaker, less economic "dwarf farms" figure in these plans.

A tour of Germany conveys the impression of a powerful economic machine operating in high gear, despite the handicap of overfull employment, and producing a constantly rising standard of living. The country has already left many prewar industrial records far behind; within a decade Germany may well have reached the point which America has reached today. Germany has always been physically a beautiful land, with its hills, mountains, and forests; with the majestic Rhine and its tributary streams, the Neckar, the Main, the Moselle, above which tower the remains of frowning old castles; and with its rich heritage of medieval art and architecture. Along with the old and picturesque there is now much building that is new and utilitarian.

And what one does not find in West Germany today may be as significant as what one finds. One does not find marching throngs shouting slogans, or hotheaded fanatics working out utopian schemes of well-being, or demagogues stirring up the masses with appeals to hate and vengeance. What one does find is some 55 million people busily at work and rapidly developing into one of the most prosperous national communities in Europe.

NOTES TO CHAPTER IX

1 This chapter is largely based on notes taken during a trip in the Federal Republic during June and July, 1962.

2 This is an almost untranslatable German word, with the general sense of pleasant, cosy, or comfortable.

CHAPTER X

The Spirit of the New Germany

FOR obvious reasons the inner spiritual forces of a country are harder to grasp than the trend of its politics or the growth of its industry and foreign trade. One is here dealing with intangibles and there are exceptions to almost every broad generalization. As an introduction to discussing German character, psychology, and way of life one may try two approaches: the reflection of German views, tastes, and preferences in public opinion polls and the observations on daily life and habits by an American woman, wife of a German-born American professor, who has lived in Germany for fairly long continuous stretches of time.

Public opinion soundings in the Federal Republic [1] indicate a quite consistently strong pro-Western attitude, which seems to furnish a solid backlog of popular support for the policy followed by the Adenauer administration and accepted, in recent years, by the opposition Social Democrats. So German response to the question as to whether their preference was for a Western, Eastern or neutral orientation in foreign policy in 1960 showed 64 per cent for the West, 22 per cent for neutralism. During the period 1952–60, those who favored an Eastern direction in foreign policy never rose above 2 per cent. This furnishes little support for the speculation, occasionally heard in Western countries, that West Germany might suddenly swing into the Soviet orbit.

To a question as to which of the great powers does everything in its power to avoid a new war, the reply was, regarding America, 44 per cent yes, 31 per cent no (in every public opinion poll there are, of course, a number who voice no opinion); as regards the

Soviet Union, 7 per cent yes, 68 per cent no. On responsibility for the breakdown of the Paris meeting of heads of government in May, 1960, 62 per cent blamed the Soviet Union, 4 per cent the United States. And 71 per cent of those questioned favored broadcasts to the peoples behind the Iron Curtain; 13 per cent were opposed.

The slogan "Yankee, go home" finds little echo in German public opinion. As of June, 1960, 67 per cent were for, 15 per cent against the presence of United States troops in Germany. There has not been time for full compilation of how Germans feel about the possible necessity of making a choice between the United States and France in national foreign policy. But on the basis of my own informal sampling of German public opinion, especially among politicians and intellectuals, I would not hesitate to say that the number of Germans who regard France as militarily a possible replacement for the United States is negligibly small.

On the necessity for German rearmament the vote was 63 per cent yes, 27 per cent no, unquestionably a shift in the positive direction from the state of public opinion when the new German Bundeswehr was in the stages of discussion and early formation. At the same time there was a majority against the use by Germans of nuclear weapons, 18 per cent for, 62 per cent against. Those questioned showed a slight majority for an army based on universal liability to service, as against a volunteer army.

By a narrow margin, 50 per cent to 42 per cent, Germans were in favor of keeping a national government rather than merging its functions in a European government. That such a large minority was prepared to merge German sovereignty in a new European state reveals how far the traditional German nationalism has receded. Three of the states which are nearest to France, Hesse, Rhein-Pfalz, and the Saar, registered majorities for a European government; Bavaria showed the strongest sentiment for retaining a German government.

As regards internal politics, the results of the public opinion polls indicate that the Germans, despite the complete restoration, in the Federal Republic, of personal and civil liberties and the rule of law, are still inclined to look on government administration as something on which they cannot exert much influence as citizens. A question as to the duties of a citizen elicited a high priority for acting responsibly in personal life, voting, and paying taxes. There was little affirmative response to such suggestions as participation in political discussion and, if necessary, criticizing the government. To a query whether politics is too difficult for the ordinary man to understand, 43 per cent agreed with the proposition, 33 per cent disagreed. Over half of those questioned believed they could do nothing to hinder the passing of a law disadvantageous to their interests by the Bundestag. Only 4 per cent had ever tried to influence the course of legislation, by letter writing, taking part in meetings, and the like. To the average German the government, although freely elected, is still regarded as "they" rather than "we."

In the matter of voting, party lines seem to be quite strictly drawn. Seventy-eight per cent know in advance how they will vote, 11 per cent are sometimes in doubt, 4 per cent usually in doubt. According to small majorities, German voters are apparently inclined to react negatively to election campaigning, becoming angry over what they consider some stupidity or false statement on the part of over-zealous party orators.

Foreign aid to poorer countries has become an issue, as Germany has been appropriating substantial sums for this purpose in recent years. The general principle is endorsed by a majority of more than two to one of those responding. Those in favor cite ethical reasons, winning friendship for Germany abroad, and checking communism. Opponents cite the undesirability of higher taxes, the need in Germany for more schools and hospitals, and Germany's obligation to look after the poor within its own frontiers.

A loosening of the patriarchal discipline of the old-fashioned German family is reflected in the fact that people of the older generation report the father as the maker of all important decisions in the life of the family. Those who belong to the present generation, on the other hand, report that such decisions are usually taken by both parents in consultation.

A poll taken in February, 1959, shows a majority in favor of competition, 53 to 15, the favorable vote being especially strong among the young and the well-to-do and in the cities. On the other hand, other tests indicate a clear majority for the welfare state. And in Germany one finds these two ideas, sometimes regarded as contradictory, practiced side by side. There is no more ardent advocate of competition than Economics Minister Ludwig Erhard; he often warns businessmen that if they don't compete, they have no very valid argument against socialism. At the same time the heritage of the war, the abnormally high proportion in the population of widows, orphans, and disabled persons, makes comprehensive measures of social relief morally and politically unavoidable.

Of the Germans reached in these interrogations 57 per cent read books, with novels, travel descriptions, and biographies most popular and little apparent taste for works on political theory. Austria and Italy are the countries preferred for vacation travel outside of Germany. In Austria there is the advantage of a common language, while sunny Italy has long exerted a magnetism for the Germans north of the Alps. Heidelberg, famed in song and story, is considered the university with the most prestige; Munich and Göttingen are tied for second place. Social Democrat Willy Brandt is individually the most popular political figure, even though in 1961 he fell considerably short of matching the vote for Adenauer's party in the national election. On the public opinion poll the genial, rotund Erhard outranks Adenauer in popularity and is far and away the most preferred candidate for the Adenauer succession.

A special survey carried out among students in universities and higher technical schools [2] gives some clues as to trends of thought and feeling among these presumptive leaders of German thought in the future. It is evident from this survey that German students are in several ways different from American. They are older, on balance, half of them between 18 and 22, the other half between 23 and 29; but only 4 per cent are married. The dormitory system in German and other European universities is almost unknown, and most students live in furnished rooms and are supported by their families. Automobiles are owned by 9 per cent.

The widespread impression of the present-day German students as a cool generation is supported by the fact that 60 per cent of those questioned subscribed to the proposition: "I have enough of political feelings and don't want to be concerned with the question of *Weltanschauung.*" Only 12 per cent took the more crusading viewpoint expressed in the following view: "Politics are too materialistic, everyone is out for money. What we lack are ideals for which one can be enthusiastic."

Yet 78 per cent, a substantial majority, expressed the belief that there are ideas worth dying for. The highest proportion, 35 per cent, listed as these ideas freedom, humanity, and human dignity. A proportion of 22 per cent mentioned the Christian religion. Only 6 per cent felt that Germany and the Fatherland are worth dying for—a mental attitude suggestive of a profound change in the contemporary German student generation. And the proved willingness of many students of the Free University in Berlin to risk death and imprisonment to rescue victims of Communist tyranny on the other side of the Wall shows that the German student, although much more down-to-earth, less addicted to dreams and utopian fantasies than his predecessors, can respond to a direct appeal to his sense of duty and humanity.

Although entrance to the university is open to anyone who has obtained his certificate of graduation from the Gymnasium, or classical high school, only 5 per cent of the students come from working-class homes, and 2 per cent from peasant families. The majority come from home backgrounds favorable to the more conservative parties, the CDU and the FDP, and it is not surprising to learn that students prefer the CDU to the Social Democrats by a majority of more than three to one. Adenauer's policies get a resounding, four-to-one vote of confidence, and among the students as among the CDU membership, Erhard is the favored candidate for the succession. There is one slight inconsistency. The students, by a slight majority, favor talks with the East in the hope of alleviating conditions in the Soviet Zone. Adenauer has always regarded this idea with deep distrust. Here, perhaps, the impulse of youth to strike out along a new line, to "do something," may explain the seeming inconsistency with general endorsement of Adenauer's policy.

An American woman who has resided in Germany for considerable periods three times in the last seven years offers the following observations on the "Americanization" of Germany and on general elements of change and continuity in German life:

"One must distinguish between Americanization and modernization, between specific American influences in Germany and the changes which have come about because Germany has become a very prosperous industrial society and for this reason is similar in many ways to America or to any other modern industrial state. The special American influence, in spite of the occupation, is not overwhelmingly significant. The teenagers go in for American jazz; American jazz performers and movie actors and actresses are widely known and admired; such American authors as Hemingway, Faulkner and Steinbeck are widely read; the children like to play cowboys and Indians. And there the list pretty much comes to an end.

"At the same time prosperity and industrialization, accompanied in Germany by a severe shortage of working hands, have replaced old German middle-class customs and habits with others more resembling America's. The most drastic social change is the lack of household help. This means that German men help much more in the household than they did in the past and also go in for 'do it yourself' projects, because hand workers have become as scarce as maids. So the old pattern of the patriarchal family has changed. Moreover, women have become much more independent, partly because of the responsibilities they had to carry during the war and the first postwar years, partly because many of them work and have their own incomes.

"The lack of domestic help and the growth of industry and incomes have created a boom in household appliances. All our friends now have refrigerators, which was by no means true seven years ago; washing machines are very common. Dishwashers and driers and deep freezes are just around the corner. The appearance of supermarkets, frozen foods, baby foods, and the like are all signs of households that depend less on human labor.

"Another field in which change is very evident is in education and bringing up of children. Freud has also come to Germany, and except for a few external manners, curtsies, and bows, German children are trained little more strictly than in the United States. Discipline in schools is sometimes easier than in many

American; of course this doesn't refer to America's problem of slum schools with considerable juvenile delinquency. Education has been considerably democratized, especially as it is not necessary to pay for study in the Gymnasium. Many children from working-class families now go to this secondary school. As a result there has been some dilution of standards; most German teachers with whom we have talked agree that the *Abitur,* the certificate of graduation from the Gymnasium, does not carry the same significance as in the past.

"Along with the adoption of some American habits, there remain certain differences between American and German ways of life. There is little contact between neighbors in Germany, and the American habit of helping out in crises, mutual baby-sitting, and so forth, is almost unknown in Germany, except perhaps in the villages. There is little sense of training school children for what is called in America life adjustment; German parents generally regard the school as simply an instrument for conveying education, not for training in citizenship.

"In spite of all the upheavals in German life, there is still a good deal of rank consciousness. Of course there is what sociologists call 'status seeking' in America; but in Germany people are more interested in family origins and in whether one has a *standesgemäss Beruf* ('a respectable occupation'). Social life is more formal; the use of the first name, even among friends, is unusual, and there is the distinction between the formal *Sie* and the seldom used, more intimate *du.*

"Television is almost as widely distributed in Germany as in America; the programs are usually of higher quality. The German fondness for good music remains; even medium-sized towns have their own opera companies, as well as their symphony orchestras."

German higher education is bursting at the seams because of the increased influx of students. There are plans to establish a number of new higher schools to relieve pressure on the eighteen universities, eight technical colleges, and five specialized high schools of university standing, in which over 200,000 students are now enrolled. New universities will soon open in Bremen, the Baltic port, and Bochum, in the Ruhr. But Professor Friedrich Edding of Frankfurt believes that the number of institutions of higher learning should be doubled, in order to take care of a corresponding increase in the number of students, which may be expected by 1980.

The number of German university and college students, in proportion to population, seems small by comparison with the United States. An American professor, lecturing in Germany and questioned about the position of the Negroes in the United States, replied that there are more Negroes in American colleges and universities than there are Germans. Technically correct, this answer, of course, overlooked the important question of comparative quality of education.

The German university is better understood if it is regarded as a combination of the last two years of an American university or college with two or three years of graduate school. The Gymnasium, the preparatory school before the university, carries the student much further than the American high school. The consensus of opinion in German academic circles is that it is more desirable to start new colleges and universities than to overtax the facilities of the existing ones.

German student life today seems to be more prosaic and matter-of-fact, less colorful than it was in the days somewhat romantically portrayed in *The Student Prince*. To the discontent of some ardent reformers, duelling fraternities have reappeared at some universities, but only in smaller towns; sentiment in the universities located in large cities, such as Hamburg, Frankfurt, and West Berlin, is against this custom. From top to bottom the German educational system has been purged of the excesses and absurdities of the Nazi period. Academic freedom is scrupulously observed; professors who were dismissed for racial or political reasons under Hitler have been compensated and invited, if they choose, to resume their chairs. The University of Freiburg, which became a center of neoclassical liberal economics as a result of the presence on the faculty of the late Rudolf Eucken, himself the son of a famous philosopher, has recently attracted to its staff an outstanding exponent of this viewpoint, Professor Friedrich A. Hayek, author of *The Road to Serfdom* and one of the founding fathers of the Mont Pelerin Society, an international organization of economists, political scientists, and others committed to the values—moral and political, as well as economic—of a free economy.

The removal of all obstacles to freedom does not mean that freedom is always exercised as vigorously and aggressively as it might be in some other countries. Except when aroused by some special challenge, like that of the West Berlin students in the face of the Wall or the Göttingen students when a well-known former Nazi was appointed minister of education in Lower Saxony (and quickly forced to resign by a storm of protest), German students are inclined to stick to their books and take little part in discussions of public affairs.

Although there has been some experimentation with parent-teacher associations in Germany, the idea does not seem to have caught on. Few parents showed much interest, and the school authorities in some cases were disposed to resent the association as an unnecessary intrusion into their domain.

Education under the German Constitution is a concern of the states. There is no federal Ministry of Education or federal legislation on school affairs. However, the state systems are uniform in principles, organization, and curricula, but with some variations of emphasis in line with local political and social circumstances. In most of the states, for instance, a four-year period of elementary schooling is followed by the separation of the more gifted children, who go to the Gymnasium, with its academic course pointing to the university, from those of less proved intellectual aptitude, who go to schools with more emphasis on vocational subjects. However, in three Social Democratic states, Hamburg, Bremen, and West Berlin, the point of separation is after six years of elementary schooling and there have been some experiments with a type of comprehensive school, offering differing curricula to a common body of pupils. This idea, however, has not met with much favor.

Religious teaching in the schools is general, the children being given Catholic or Protestant instruction according to the preference of their parents. Church influence on the schools is strongest in some of the more solidly Catholic areas, such as South Bavaria.

The framework of German cultural life has long been restored. Damaged or destroyed theaters, concert halls, and opera houses have been repaired or replaced with new ones. Music festivals, classical and modern, are frequent, some of the more famous being the Wagner Festival in Bayreuth, the Beethoven in Bonn, the Munich opera festival, and a series of concerts given over to modern experimental music in the small town of Donau-Eschingen, in southwest Germany. What is so far lacking, in literature, drama, films, and music, is any notable upsurge of creative genius. There is general agreement among Germans that cultural revival, in the sense of original creation, has lagged behind economic recovery.

This poverty in significant new works, so different from the atmosphere of the Weimar Republic, is especially marked in drama and films. It is a frequent German remark that two leading German dramatists are Friedrich Dürrenmatt and Max Frisch, both citizens of Switzerland. The noteworthy success in West Berlin of a German version of *My Fair Lady* was due not only to the catchy novelty of this adaptation of Shaw's work to the style of a musical revue, but also to the absence of serious competition. The German actress Maria Schell gave a fine performance in a moving film drama, *The Last Bridge,* which shows a German woman doctor, kidnapped by Yugoslav partisans, developing sympathy with their courage and devotion to their cause and finally dying in a skirmish as she cannot make up her mind whether to stay with the partisans or rejoin the forces of her own country. The Lutheran Church sponsored *Question 7,* a straightforward, realistic picture of a pastor's son in the Soviet Zone, torn between loyalty to his home and religious teachings and the seductive appeals of a teacher who is determined to win him over to serve the Communist cause. But films of significant form and content have been rare, partly because the German film industry has been going through a severe financial crisis.

The writer is not in a position to evaluate the modern German contribution to music, because of his subjectively negative reaction to modern musical forms of expression. But in this field the German pre-eminence, so marked during the eighteenth and nineteenth centuries, seems to have disappeared. It is easier to think of distinguished German opera and orchestra conductors (among whom

Herbert von Karajan has a claim to be considered the greatest in the world) than of outstanding contemporary composers.

Nor has this postwar era been one of great distinction in German literature. Most of the novels that have attracted widespread attention are experiments in surrealist and other unconventional forms of expression, with plots that are either subordinated to some ideological purpose or wildly improbable. Probably the most serious novelist of present-day Germany is Heinrich Böll, a Catholic with pacifist and socially radical overtones in his thinking. *Billiards at Half Past Nine,* the unrevealing title of one of his best-known works, deals with the problem of "inner emigration," experienced by Germans who were alienated by Nazism but would not or could not leave their country.

The novel is lit up by two dramatic episodes. The central figure, Robert Fähmel, an architect who escapes active service in the war by becoming a demolition expert, becomes so enraged by the contrast between the care for the preservation of historical monuments and the indifference to the slaughter of the human victims of the Nazis that he blows up a famous church, which has been built by his father. His mother makes an equally dramatic protest; she tries to thrust herself into a freight car filled with Jews bound for Auschwitz and is consigned to an asylum. The moral is obvious: Sanity is madness when the world is insane.

The characters in Böll's work are credible human beings, although manipulated to point morals. But in *The Tin Drum* by Günther Grass, a work that sold 150,000 copies in Germany and won prizes and aroused discussion throughout Europe, reality is completely superseded by fantasy. The story is built around a dwarf, Oskar, whose father is a grocer, who becomes a repulsive, slightly comic type of Nazi. The novel is full of grisly symbolism, the final touch being added when Soviet soldiers kill Oskar's father in the cellar of his grocery and a swarm of ants find their way around his body to a sack of sugar that has burst open. The influence of Melville's *Moby Dick* may be felt in the symbolism, sometimes of a revolting type, with which the novel is saturated.

Uwe Johnson, a young writer born in 1935 who moved from

the Soviet Zone to West Germany in 1960, is influenced in his writing by his psychological state of limbo between a Communist dictatorship which he rejects and a middle-class society which seems to him smug and purposeless. (This is not a unique state of mind among Germans who have left the East without accepting or approving the West.) Johnson's plots are negligible; what he offers is rather literary experimentation and general comment on life, with a rather strained effort to maintain a neutral position between East and West.

One may search modern German literature in vain for anything comparable with the restrained epic tragedy of the great postwar novel after the First World War, Remarque's *All Quiet on the Western Front*. There have been some novels about the decisive German defeat at Stalingrad, but these suggest descriptive journalism, rather than deeply felt imaginative literature. What is characteristic of German works of fiction in the postwar period is a sense of groping and experimentation, not one of artistic assurance and fulfillment. Böll, Grass, and Johnson belong to a loose association of writers known as Group 47, united by a strongly developed guilt complex about Nazism. This leads them to look beyond the executioners, the concentration camp guards, the obviously criminal types and seek to affix the brand of responsibility to the respectable conformists who looked the other way and did nothing to resist the triumph of evil.

Sometimes this leads Germany's vaguely leftist, anti-establishment, alienated intelligentsia into positions which are not logically very defensible. So, during the furore excited by the launching of legal proceedings against *Der Spiegel,* Group 47 put itself on record [3] in favor of the proposition that "the stealing of military secrets is a patriotic duty." If in the general public there is perhaps too much complacency about the Nazi past, reflected in very light sentences passed on individuals who were guilty of grave crimes against humanity, in the intelligentsia of the Group 47 way of thinking there is an opposite exaggeration, a sort of left-wing McCarthyism, which tends to confuse Nazism with conservatism and does not recognize the moral and practical difference between arming for wars of aggressive conquest and arming against a real and present threat, represented by the Soviet Union.

There are several causes for the alienation of a part of Germany's intellectuals, writers, professors, radio broadcasters from the political climate in Bonn. The early policy of the occupation powers gave leftists, sometimes Communists, a disproportionate influence in the newly licensed German press and radio. The outright Communists were eliminated; but many advocates of more or less radical social and economic change continued to raise their voices against what they regarded as too conservative attitudes in Bonn. To some extent this attitude is that of the "angry young men" (and some, like J. B. Priestley, not so young) in Great Britain: dissatisfaction with things as they are without any very clear-cut blueprint as to how the present order should be changed.

One cannot identify Germany's dissatisfied intellectuals with the Social Democratic Party, which to some of them looks like a stodgy annex to the establishment, since it abandoned nationalization of industry and opposition to Adenauer's foreign policy. One of the more extreme voices of discontent is that of Erich Kuby, a writer and broadcaster whose headquarters are in Munich. In talking with Kuby and reading the writings of those who more or less share his point of view one pieces together the following critical Credo: [4]

Too much clericalism and too much conformity.

No radical reorganization of values and social institutions, such as the moral collapse under Nazism demanded.

Resentment against the slogan under which Adenauer and the CDU swept to victory in 1957: *Keine Experimente* ("No Experiments").

Excessive materialism, insufficient attention to education and science.

Undue revival of nationalism; in this connection former Defense Minister Franz Josef Strauss is a favorite target for attack.

Neglect of opportunity to improve relations with Poland by recognizing the Oder-Neisse boundary and to ameliorate the condition of Germans in the Soviet Zone by a more flexible attitude toward the Ulbricht regime.

The sense of alienation is enhanced because Chancellor Adenauer, a man of a few simple, straightforward guiding principles and ideas, is not a sophisticated intellectual and has never favored intellectuals among his intimate advisers. Hence, among educated Germans of leftist leanings, it is almost instinctive to speak in deprecatory terms of "Chancellor Democracy," to ridicule the slogan "No Experiments." It may be that with the political passing of Adenauer this acute sense of alienation from the government, which sometimes leads to an attitude of almost nihilistic negativism, will abate.

During a conversation in Munich, Erich Kuby expressed the most pessimistic views about the possibility of maintaining the freedom of West Berlin, and he remarked that on a recent visit he got the impression of a dying city. Having just come from Berlin to Munich with a very different impression, I could not resist the temptation to suggest to Mr. Kuby that perhaps he got his impression from looking at East Berlin, not West Berlin.

Nationalist nihilistic negativism would be a fairly accurate formula for describing the editorial attitude of *Der Spiegel,* the weekly magazine which, by the prosecution of its editors, brought about the fall of Strauss and a more positive indication of the early retirement of Adenauer. Without being pro-Communist (the comments on conditions in the Soviet Zone have been severely negative), *Der Spiegel* has consistently poured cold water on all plans for the integration of the West, on Germany's American alliance, on NATO, on the development of the German armed forces.

A curious mixture, in style and format, of America's weekly news magazines and of publications specializing in alleged confidential gossip and scandal, *Der Spiegel* is one of the more widely read of the German magazines. It is the scourge and terror of Bonn officials and sometimes takes time out to present a full length candid—and seldom complimentary—sketch of some prominent beneficiary of the economic miracle.

A critical viewpoint more temperate and balanced than that of Erich Kuby and *Der Spiegel* is set forth in a public statement of eight more or less prominent Germans—professors, scientists, radio directors, and Protestant church leaders—published in the spring of 1962. This listed five proposals for reform, in the following order:

(1) Active foreign policy.
(2) Militarily effective, politically careful armament policy.
(3) Properly limited, but energetic measures for civilian defense.
(4) Uncompromising, planned policy in social affairs.
(5) Thoroughgoing school reform.

This manifesto of "The Eight" was greeted by Countess Marion Doenhoff in *Die Zeit* as a "lobby of reason," and it aroused considerable discussion. However, the influence of intellectual critics, whether of the moderate type of the eight signers of the manifesto or of the more radical nihilistic type represented by Erich Kuby and the writers of Group 47, should not be overestimated. They represent individual voices of protest, not a mass movement. To most Germans the advantages of the present order far outweigh the disadvantages. And, apart from *Der Spiegel*, which is probably read more for its scandals than for its ideas, the opponents of the German establishment do not reach a very wide audience. The mass circulation tabloids offer no serious criticism at all. Leading daily newspapers such as *Die Welt* and the *Frankfurter Allgemeine Zeitung*, follow a middle-of-the-road editorial policy, not endorsing Adenauer's course unreservedly but also not committing themselves to any principled opposition.

A German writer sympathetic with the alienated intellectuals remarked to me: "Surely something is wrong with a political and social order when so many educated individuals, writers, professors, spokesmen for churches, scientists find so much cause for criticism."

When I repeated this to an editor of more conservative views his comment was: "Yes, something *is* wrong—with the intellectuals."

It is not only on the left that one hears reproaches of Germany's affluent society. Religious leaders also sometimes express concern over what they regard as excessive materialism and indifference to spiritual and moral values. Octogenarian retired Lutheran Bishop of Berlin Otto Dibelius, known as a sturdy opponent of communism and finally barred altogether from the Soviet Zone, gave me a long lecture on the values of the simpler and sterner age in which he grew up, on the Prussian virtues which, as he felt, were now being eroded.

"My father," he said, "was a *Beamte,* a Prussian state official. We lived in a farmhouse and carried on a little farming on the side. There was no luxury in our home; I remember we drank skimmed milk because we had to sell the cream. But we read good books; my parents saw that we had a good education. State officials were paid very modestly. But there were two words that in my youthful days had a significance that has now been somewhat lost: *Stand* and *Pflicht.* The first meant a sense of belonging and vocation. My father was a poor man, by modern standards. But he had self-respect, and the respect of our neighbors because he was fulfilling his *Pflicht* ("duty") by serving something outside himself, the state.

"In its highest form this spirit, which made our old Prussian administration the envy of Europe for its incorruptibility, finds expression in the case of an old war veteran who said to Kaiser Wilhelm I: 'My three sons all died for Your Majesty.' And the Kaiser replied: 'No, not for me. For the state, for the Fatherland, of which I am only the first servant.'

"This spirit has very much evaporated today; men think more of purely selfish interests. But deep down in the human soul there is a sense of the need for dedication to something bigger than individual interest. Part of the strength of communism is that it professes to supply an answer to this need—a diabolically wrong answer, of course. But we in the West are still groping for this sense of something outside the self—call it duty or responsibility, as you like."

A prominent Protestant theologian, Helmut Thielicke, has been striking a similar note, perhaps in more modern terms than those of the venerable Bishop Dibelius, of the necessary connection between freedom and responsibility. In an address at Wiesbaden [5] he emphasized the necessity of not only being free "from something," but of being free "for something," and he illustrated this with the Parable of the Prodigal Son, who won freedom from the discipline of his father's home, only to fall under the domination of his own lusts and vices.

Before the war and the Soviet occupation, Germany was a predominantly Protestant country, with a substantial Catholic minority, especially strong in Bavaria and parts of the Rhineland. Now, because the population in the Soviet Zone is mostly Protestant, the balance between the two faiths is almost even. In Berlin the common threat of atheistic communism has led to closer Protestant-Catholic co-operation, in such matters as common religious radio programs directed toward the persecuted Christians in the East Zone. In the rest of the country there is still a sense of religious difference, and there is an attempt in the CDU, the first political party in German history in which Protestants and Catholics have formally co-operated, to preserve a fair proportion in the assignment of posts in the party and in the state service.

All traces of Nazi persecution of active Christians have, of course, long vanished; both large churches have re-established their organized activities, with a preference in leadership for those who showed the least disposition to conform during the Hitlerite period. But the religious revival which some Protestants and Catholics hoped for after the shattering experiences of the war does not seem to have occurred. The influence of a secular society, with its thousand distractions, television, radio, sports, various amusements and recreations, seems to have cut into the habit of regular churchgoing.

A study in the diocese of Fulda [6] revealed that only about one third of Catholic young men between the ages of nineteen and twenty-four went to mass regularly; the figures for younger and older Catholics were somewhat more favorable. Indifference to religion was especially marked among industrial workers. The situation is apparently no better with the Protestant churches. In the Protestant community, according to a study conducted by an editor of *Die Welt,* Bernt Conrad, "the great majority of the population belongs to the church only nominally; only four per cent attend church regularly. This is a shockingly small number. It supports the observation of Hanns Lilje, the leading bishop of the United Protestant Church, 'Germany has become a land for missionaries.' " [7]

The falling away from the churches has probably been even more marked in the Soviet Zone, under the various pressures employed by the Communist authorities. But here the faith of those who continue to adhere to religion is stronger, because of the element of moral courage involved in professing religious conviction.

Despite the talk of "clericalism" on the part of leftist intellectuals, themselves mostly atheists or agnostics, there is no serious evidence that church authorities, Catholic or Protestant, influence important government decisions. As a liberal Catholic publicist said to me:

"It is absurd to imagine that Cardinal Frings of Cologne tells Adenauer what to do. It rather works the other way; it is beneficial to Adenauer to have the support of Cardinal Frings and other prelates of the Catholic Church."

Religious teaching in the schools is not an innovation, but the continuation of an old German practice.

It is in the imaginative fields of literature and drama and music that the German achievement since the war has lagged behind that of the creative periods of the past. In history and journalism, in scientific and technical invention the lag is not so marked. There is probably no single editor in Germany today so outstanding as Theodor Wolff, editor of *Berliner Tageblatt* under the imperial regime and in the Weimar period. But newspapers such as *Die Welt* and *Frankfurter Allgemeine Zeitung* and magazines such as *Die Zeit* and *Christ und Welt* bring the Germans into close touch with what is going on in Washington and London and Paris, and also in Asia and Africa.

Professor Fritz Fischer of Hamburg University has brought out a work on the origins of World War I which makes out a rather worse case for the attitude of German civilian leaders, especially Chancellor Bethmann-Hollweg, toward annexations than had been generally accepted. This has aroused some critical comment and discussion, although with much less acrimony than would have been the case thirty years ago, when German historians were under the pressure of nationalist public opinion to present a united front against "the war-guilt lie."

Professor Hans Rothfels has devoted considerable research to a subject that should certainly be better known in Germany and abroad: the German opposition movement to Hitler. There are a number of interesting memoirs of things seen and experienced during the war and under the Soviet occupation. What is still lacking

is a massive examination, from a German source, of national socialism. The source material is there in such places as the office for
the study of war crimes in Ludwigsburg, the *Institut für Zeitge-
schichte* in Munich, and the voluminous records of trials of indicted
war criminals under the occupation and later in German courts.

Some day, no doubt, German historical scholarship will under-
take this task; some day there will be an adequate reflection in literature of the innumerable tragic personal dramas of Nazi rule and
Soviet invasion.

Critics of the present order in Germany are inclined to call it
"restorationist," using this word in a derogatory sense. And it is
true that in the spirit and institutions of the new Germany one finds
no big revolutionary changes. In view of what revolutionary change
has brought to Eastern Europe, not least to the sundered part of
Germany under Communist rule, many Germans probably feel this
is just as well.

Yet the German Federal Republic is not a carbon copy of any
German state that has existed before. To restore the Hohenzollerns
today would be as fantastic an idea as to restore the medieval
dynasty of the Hohenstaufen; the social groups with which the old
German Empire was bound up, notably the Prussian Junkers, are
"gone with the wind." Nor is the Federal Republic a restoration of
the Weimar Republic; the many differences will be discussed in a
later chapter. The contrast between present-day Germany and Nazi
Germany is as great as the contrast between the demonic adventurer Hitler and the conservative Catholic Adenauer.

Perhaps the nearest analogy to the spirit and purpose of the new
Germany is to imagine a bigger Switzerland or Netherlands, a country cured by the bitterest experience of the follies of military conquest and aggression, whose people's aim, so far as they have a common ideal—apart from their individual and family ambitions and
aspirations—is to be a prosperous member of a prospering united
European community. Not only is there no sign of a revival of
nazism in Germany, but nationalism is at its lowest ebb in almost
two centuries and there is an unprecedented willingness to make
large sacrifices of sovereignty for the sake of the European ideal.

To this general impression of a people that has had its fill of storm and stress, that wants to preserve the peaceful well-being it has won under such unfavorable circumstances by intelligently directed hard work, one reservation should be added. There will always seem to be something artificial and unfinished about the Federal Republic so long as a large part of Germany is isolated behind a wall of barbed wire. Saxony is one of the oldest German states. Dresden and Leipzig have been German cities much longer than Denver and San Francisco have belonged to the United States.

Should German reunion be achieved (and few Germans see how or when this will come about), a new chapter in German history will begin: the injection into the individualist, competitive society of the Federal Republic of a large body of Germans brought up under a completely different doctrine. Should Germany remain sundered, there will always remain in the hearts of the West Germans a nostalgic feeling for the lost lands and cities, for the seventeen million "separated brethren" in the Soviet domain.

Meanwhile, and barring some unpredictable international shock, the spirit of the new Germany remains eminently favorable to the maintenance of free parliamentary institutions, the rejection of extremist preachers of revolution, either from the right or from the left, and the maintenance of what Economics Minister Erhard calls "the social-minded market economy." This may be translated as a free competitive economy, modified by considerable social legislation.

NOTES TO CHAPTER X

1 The following public opinion polls may be found in *Umfragen, Band 3/4* of Divo-Institut, Frankfurt (Frankfurt: Europäische Verlag).

2 *Das geistige Bild der Studenten* (Bonn: Akademischer Verlag).

3 See *Time,* January 4, 1963.

4 A book entitled *Bestands-aufnahme: Eine deutsche Bilanz 1962* ("Balance Sheet: a German Balance of 1962") (Munich: Verlag Kurt Desch) contains many essays presenting the viewpoints of dissenting intellectuals.

5 Published in *Die Zeit,* October 19, 1962.

6 Published in *Die Welt,* January 11, 1963.

7 See *Meet Germany,* brochure published by Atlantik-Brücke, Hamburg, p. 91.

CHAPTER XI

Germany Rearmed

THE German military establishment during the last half century has oscillated between extremes of strength and weakness. The German Imperial Army, based on universal liability to service, was a formidable fighting machine. It took a world coalition more than four years of bitter struggle to bring Germany's defeat in the First World War. One of the most eloquent tributes to German fighting power was paid by one of Germany's greatest foemen, Winston Churchill, in the closing words of his memoirs of the First World War:

"For four years Germany fought and defied the five continents of the world by land and sea and air. The German armies upheld her tottering confederates, intervened in every theatre with success, stood everywhere on conquered territory and inflicted on their enemies more than twice the bloodshed they suffered themselves. To break their strength and science and curb their fury it was necessary to bring all the greatest nations of mankind into the field against them. Overwhelming populations, unlimited resources, measureless sacrifice, the sea blockade, could not prevail for fifty months. Small states were trampled down in the struggle; a mighty Empire was battered into unrecognizable fragments; and nearly twenty million men perished or shed their blood before the sword was wrested from that terrible hand. Surely, Germans, for history it is enough."

Unfortunately, and not least for Germany, it was not enough. After a period of enforced one-sided partial disarmament when the German Army, the *Reichwehr,* was a volunteer force limited to

100,000 men and denied tanks and airplanes, a new phase of intensive militarization set in after Adolf Hitler came into power in 1933. Another tremendous war ensued, after which Germany was bled white, much as France had been under Napoleon.

The first impulse of the victorious powers in 1945 was to disarm Germany completely, going to such extremes as disallowing pensions for wounded soldiers and their families and refusing peasants permits for guns to protect their crops from wild animals. At that time little or no distinction was made between the army, which had generally fought within the limits of civilized warfare, and the Nazi Party leadership, with its responsibility for genocidal atrocities.

At the same time, especially in the American Zone, there was a vast campaign of "re-education," designed to convince the Germans of the evils and errors of militarism. No such campaign was needed to create in the German postwar generation a profound aversion to warfare, which had brought terrific suffering and ended in such an unlimited national disaster. Indeed it required a good deal of political experience and of "counter re-education" to develop in Germany a public opinion willing to endorse the latest phase in Germany's checkered military history: limited rearmament within the framework of the Atlantic Alliance.

Soviet aggressive foreign policy after the end of the war was the strongest argument for the necessity of German participation in the defense of Western Europe. Stalin broke all his promises to permit free institutions in the territories occupied by the Red Army, including a considerable part of Germany. There were Soviet forward thrusts at various points, in the support of Communist rebellion in Greece, in the blockade of West Berlin, in the promotion of the invasion of South Korea.

All this led to a gradual revision of opinion in the West about the desirability and feasibility of keeping West Germany totally disarmed. The first breach in the maintenance of absolute disarmament was an agreement in 1950 to "a strengthening of the West German police, although only on a state, not on a federal basis."

Public opinion in Germany at this time was far from enthusiastic over the prospect of rearmament. A phrase often heard was *ohne mich* ("count me out"). Resentment against some Occupation measures and against what many Germans considered defamation of the German Army blended with war-weariness and cynicism to set up a roadblock against a return to arms. There was a strong antiwar tradition, verging on pacifism, in the powerful Social Democratic Party, which for some years fought all proposals for a German military contribution in the Bundestag, in the courts, in appeals to public opinion. Some Protestant church circles also opposed rearming. Martin Niemoeller, the former submarine commander who turned pastor after the First World War and was imprisoned for his outspoken criticism of Nazism, professed to see little difference between Soviet communism and capitalist democracy.

The leader of the Social Democratic Party at that time, Kurt Schumacher, a man of crippled body and fierce indomitable spirit, who had survived the ordeal of a Nazi concentration camp, opposed rearmament not on pacifist grounds, but because he considered the allied military forces in Germany as too limited. He wanted a forward strategy that would make possible, in his own words, "a military strategy on the Vistula and the Niemen." The fact that Schumacher was a native of East Prussia may have influenced his preference for an aggressive strategy that might save the eastern part of Germany from Communist rule. Speaking at Stuttgart on September 16, 1950, Schumacher said: [1]

"We are ready to bear arms once again if, with us, the Western allies take over the same risk and the same chance of warding off a Soviet attack, establishing themselves in the greatest possible strength on the Elbe."

Schumacher, however, spoke for himself, not for his party. Most Social Democrats (except for the Berlin group of the party, more militant because of the immediate Soviet threat) played up to the *ohne mich* elementary antimilitary feeling of many individual Germans. The Social Democratic attitude was also influenced by ideological suspicion of American capitalism and fear that rearming of West Germany would destroy the possibility of German reunion.

The outbreak of war in Korea in 1950 aroused fear that the fighting might spread to Europe and speeded up the search for a formula that would provide for a German contribution to European defense. Adenauer's position was willingness to co-operate in the buildup of a European army, but opposition to a German national military establishment. The chancellor believed that a national army might place too heavy a strain on Germany's still young free institutions. Moreover, Germany, standing alone, was no match for the enormous Soviet empire. Its only chance was to become a member of a larger American-European alliance.

A committee of senior German officers, among whom Generals Hans Speidel and Adolf Heusinger were most prominent, in October, 1950 worked out plans for a German armed force of 500,000 and they laid down certain prerequisites for German rearming. These included full equality of rights for the new German formations, and naturally a scrapping of all Allied regulations designed to enforce disarmament.

As already described in Chapter III, German rearmament was considerably delayed by the long wrangle over a French plan for a close integration of the armed forces of six continental powers (France, Germany, Italy, the Netherlands, Belgium, and Luxembourg), which the French Chamber of Deputies finally refused to ratify. By taking up and dusting off the almost forgotten Brussels Treaty, an alliance of Great Britain, France, Italy, and the Benelux powers directed against Germany, and admitting Germany as a member, the long-sought formula was reached. As from May, 1955, Germany was free to raise its own armed forces, committed to NATO. The German government renounced the right to manufacture nuclear, chemical, and biological weapons.

The military buildup was still to be achieved. During the years of wrangling over the implementation of the finally abortive project for a closely integrated European Defense Community, the Adenauer administration had scrupulously refrained from adopting any measures of recruiting and training, confining itself to conferences and drawing up provisional memoranda and blueprints. Nor had there been any attempts to form illegal military units, such as occurred after the First World War. For the first ten years after the surrender, Germany, for the first time in its history, had been completely without its own armed forces. The creation of the

Bundeswehr, as the new military force was called, had to start from scratch.

There were many obstacles to be surmounted and these explain why the raising of a military establishment of 500,000 men proceeded slowly and had not been completed by the autumn of 1962, when Adenauer told the Bundestag that 380,000 men were in service. Two of these obstacles were the low German birth rate in the war and postwar years, reducing the number of available recruits, and the economic boom, which discouraged seeking a military career. The ten-year gap during a period of rapid changes in weaponry and tactics imposed obvious disadvantages, and for a time public opinion was not enthusiastic; in the beginning there were cases when soldiers in uniform were attacked or insulted.

This attitude changed noticeably after the ruthless Soviet suppression of the Hungarian people's revolt in October-November, 1956. Here was a vivid demonstration, almost on Germany's border, of the unrealism of clinging to an *ohne mich* position. And considering the strong initial opposition to rearming, the morale of Germany's new soldiers has been surprisingly good. The law of military service provides generous exemption for conscientious objectors, on nonreligious as well as religious grounds. But less than 1 per cent of those called for service have tried to take advantage of this exemption.

A captain in the Bundeswehr, son of a high government official, wrote home that his regiment, largely composed of Ruhr miners, left nothing to be desired in spirit and discipline. In the time of the Weimar Republic such a regiment would have contained a fair proportion of Communists.

In the early phase of rearmament much time was spent on matters of organization and administration. It was necessary to create an officers corps that was professionally competent and also free from active former Nazis. A screening commission was set up to examine the records of former officers, especially in the higher ranks. There was general agreement that the new German armed forces should be organized along democratic lines, with elimination of unnecessary privileges and distinctions for officers and harsh and brutal methods in discipline. At first this led to some differences of opinion as to how democratic an army could be without suffering in military efficiency. This problem seems to have been solved along common-sense lines, with the aid of the German instinct to get a job done well. The goosestep and other frills of formal parade training were dropped; attention was concentrated on developing physical fitness and mastering the use of new complicated weapons.

For political considerations, the period of service was first set at the unrealistically short term of twelve months. After the election of 1961 this was raised to eighteen months. One difficulty that has loomed large from the beginning has been the shortage of suitable training areas. The best of the old imperial maneuver fields, such as Grafenwöhr, in North Bavaria, have been pre-empted by American and other foreign troops stationed in Germany. And the Federal Republic is a crowded country, where alienation of land for military training purposes excites protests from the states and the municipalities.

Space limitations and a cloudy climate have handicapped air force development. A modern jet fighter can fly from one end of the Federal Republic to another within an hour. With a view to avoiding incidents aircraft are forbidden to fly within fifty miles of the eastern frontier. This difficulty has been met in part by sending between 1,000 and 2,000 German pilots to the United States for instruction. German military units have also been stationed in France and in South Wales, where a hostile demonstration, organized by Communist sympathizers from outside, did not seem to stir up unfriendly feeling among the local inhabitants.

The complete cessation of military exercises and studies left Germany behind in knowledge of the new weapons, nuclear and conventional, which had developed in this period. However, the Germans have absorbed the new military technique fairly rapidly, as might be expected from an industrially and technically minded people.

Troop indoctrination presented some new challenges. A purely nationalist approach was no longer suitable. Yet there were soldierly values in the old Prussian and German traditions which were worth conserving. So a compromise was struck, with examples from German history back to Frederick the Great mixed with explanations of Germany's new role as a partner in NATO. A school for "internal leadership training" attended by officers and noncommissioned officers, from generals to sergeants, was set up at Koblenz. Here there are courses and lectures, given by senior officers and also by civilians—industrialists, educators, and clergymen. An American military observer remarked that a German recruit, after three months of basic training, could give a better account of what he was prepared to fight for than an American in similar circumstances. Of course the danger of Communist conquest and domination is much more real to the German, if only because of the experiences of his friends and relatives in the Soviet Zone.

The former head of this leadership school, now commandant of the Staff College in Hamburg, General Ulrich de Mezière, talked with me at length about methods of cultivating morale and general strategic problems. I had met General de Mezière earlier in the plain building on the Ermekailstrasse in Bonn, clearly converted from other uses, which houses the Ministry of Defense. Here he had been active in the inner circle of military planners. The name sounded unusual for a German, and the General's slender build and delicate features also suggested French descent. He proved to be a descendant of one of the French Huguenot families which had found asylum and a new homeland in Prussia after Louis XIV revoked the Edict of Nantes which had guaranteed the toleration of Huguenots.

The Staff College gives a two-year course of training to some two hundred officers, mostly captains and majors, of the army, navy and air force, all men of war experience. It is here that new German staff officers are trained, with courses in military history and organization, administration, finance, law, elementary science, economics, and geography.

"Every army," said General de Mezière, "needs a hierarchy of command and certain military virtues that are good for all time, courage, obedience, fidelity, comradeship. At the same time, in training citizen-soldiers, we must take account of Germany's changed international position. We can think of effective defense only in terms of our alliance. We must carry a heavy moral burden, until the memory of national socialism is outlived. As a borderland of communism we must be prepared to meet this doctrine ideologically, as well as on the field of battle. We try to study Communist psychology and methods, to show the soldier what he must defend, that he has a cause worth giving his life for. We stress still more the positive sides of a free society, of the rule of law.

"As for our strictly military training, our object is to make this hard, purposeful, realistic, with a good deal of outdoor living in near-campaign conditions and emphasis on modern technical weapons."

In response to the number one military question today, whether the American, German, and other NATO forces in Germany could withstand a Soviet invasion, General de Mezière offered the following opinion:

"These forces would be adequate for defense with non-nuclear weapons against the twenty-two Soviet divisions in the Soviet Zone of Occupation. But if there would be a big, all-out invasion, with large reinforcements from Russia, nuclear weapons would be required to stem the attack. It is sometimes suggested that the Soviet Union might start an offensive with conventional weapons, hoping that the West would refrain from using its nuclear power. I do not share this view. I believe a Soviet attack designed to overrun all Germany would be delivered with all available weapons. To act otherwise would be to leave the initiative to the West, to give America a chance to get in a devastating first strike. This is a risk I don't believe Soviet strategists would take."

From the beginning of Germany's new military buildup, the United States Army has played a considerable role as coach and purveyor of war matériel, of which Germany was quite destitute after the end of the war and the decade of full disarmament. A large American military mission in Bonn has maintained close liaison with German ground, air, and sea forces. And as the Bundeswehr became more advanced in development, there have been a number of joint maneuvers of German with American and other NATO forces, British, French, Danish, Dutch, and Belgian.

A substantial initial American grubstake for the new German military establishment was the transfer of about a billion dollars worth of tanks, airplanes, and other weapons from American stocks. Later Germany's improving financial position made this kind of subsidization unnecessary. By 1962 German purchases of United States arms had exceeded $2 billion and furnished a substantial favorable item in the American balance of payments. Recent purchases of American equipment in 1962 included 1,700 medium tanks, 2,100 personnel carrier vehicles, and a considerable number of portable bridges.

I saw American-German co-operation in action in 1959 at Fürstenfeldbruck, an air base located about 12 miles west of Munich. At that time (later the base was turned over entirely to the Germans) there was a group of some 40 American officers and 50 or 60 enlisted men at the base under the command of Col. W. J. Choninski of Austin, Texas, a veteran professional aviator who had remained in the Air Force after serving as a combat pilot during the Second World War.

In charge of 185 German air cadets, mostly in their early twenties, was Col. Dietrich Hrabak, a native of Leipzig, now in the Soviet Zone, who had flown more than 800 combat missions on the Russian front during the war. Choninski and Hrabak might have clashed in the skies in those days. But, as often happens when old soldiers meet after having fought on opposite sides, they became very good friends during their association at Fürstenfeldbruck. Hrabak expressed the view that his cadets were as good as the German pilots who flew in the last war. Choninski testified that the accident rate was not higher than would have been normal at an American air base.

More recently, in the summer of 1962, I saw another example of the Bundeswehr in training at Schöngau, in the foothills of the Bavarian Alps, southwest of Munich, where a parachutist and air transport school was located. The men here, like those in the mountain division, also stationed in South Bavaria, were an elite, all volunteers and accepted after especially strict examination of their physical and psychological qualifications. The son of Prime Minister Kiesinger of Württemberg-Baden wanted to become a parachutist, but was rejected because he was too tall.

Schöngau turns out every year 2,800 qualified parachutists and

2,200 members of the air transport corps. In the absence of the commanding general, Lieutenant Colonels Paul and Hornung were in charge of operations. Both were veterans of Luftwaffe operations in Africa, Greece, Crete, and on the Eastern Front, and they wore appropriate ribbons. Both conveyed the impression of being commanders who, on the basis of their personalities and war records, would have no difficulty in inspiring respect and quick and ready obedience from the young recruits.

One of the more striking exercises, going on continuously throughout the day, was a practice jump from a forty-foot tower.

"Are you happy?" the instructor would shout to the student.

"Ja," came the reply.

"Do you want to jump?"

"Jawohl."

"Then, go!" And the soldier would leap from the top of the tower, being pulled up with a jerk after a ten-foot drop, then sliding along a steel cable to land several hundred feet beyond.

In Schöngau one could also leap from aircraft; some of the more advanced students were competing for a chance to take part in an international parachute-jumping competition that was to be held in Orange, Massachusetts. The cadets here are all volunteers, sent from their units for three weeks training, following which they receive the parachutist's insignia. To complete their training they must jump twenty or thirty times from the tower and five times from airplanes, one of these jumps being at night. The competitive sporting element in parachute jumping, with the objective of landing as closely as possible to a circle marked on the ground, makes it especially popular.

The spirit of co-operation in NATO is maintained at this base; American, French, and Danish parachutists have attended the school, and six West Point cadets were expected at the time of my visit. The air transport students are taught how to load and unload aircraft at maximum speed, and the school varies outdoor training with classroom courses in tactics, logistics, air traffic control, and other subjects. One took away from this installation the impression that such characteristic German traits as physical fitness, fondness for outdoor life, ready acceptance of discipline, and pride in achievement would outweigh, in the end, the disadvantages which have already been listed as facing the Bundeswehr.

Another of these disadvantages is the composition of the new officer corps. Senior officers, between the ranks of colonel and captain, are apt to be a little overage, if they are veterans of the last war, or somewhat inexperienced, if they entered the service after 1955. Pay of officers is low, compared with what industrial executives or university professors receive. The scale starts at 500 marks a month for a lieutenant and reaches a top limit of 3,000 marks for four-star General Friedrich Foertsch, who, as inspector-general, is the highest officer of the new German Army.

The goal of the Army, the most important of the three services, is 12 divisions, three Panzer (armored), seven Panzer-Grenadier (armored-infantry), one airborne, and one mountain. Nearly all these divisions have now been committed to NATO (March, 1963), but some are under full strength and the quality of their preparation varies. The difference between the Panzer and the Panzer-Grenadier divisions is that the former consist of two brigades of armor and one of infantry, while this proportion is reversed in the Grenadier. Perhaps the greatest potential military responsibility is placed on the four German divisions—the 1st, 3d, 6th, and 11th, with corps headquarters at Münster—which, with the British Army of the Rhine and some Belgian and Dutch units, constitute the defensive force for the North German plain which presents the fewest natural obstacles to a Soviet sweep to the West. This is because the British forces leave much to be desired, in numbers (about 50,000) and in modernization of arms.

The most impressive shield for Germany and West Europe at the present time is the superbly equipped American Seventh Army, with headquarters in Heidelberg, under the command of Gen. Paul Lamar Freeman, a veteran of the Korean War. This force is composed of about 250,000 combat troops, organized in six divisions, and covers the southern and southwestern areas of the Federal Republic. In this Army, with a strength varying from 250,000 to 300,000 (it was reinforced at the time of the Berlin Wall crisis) are about a quarter of United States Army personnel, about two thirds of American forces stationed abroad. Its "armored cavalry" units are on constant patrol along the zonal border, making any intrusion from the Soviet Zone impossible without provoking a head-on collision.

General Freeman, with whom I talked in Heidelberg in July, 1962, took an optimistic view of the military situation. He characterized the Bundeswehr as "a magnificent army, built from scratch, capable and enthusiastic, meeting its NATO obligations." He was sure that, given the American forces ready for instant commitment, the Soviet Union could not hope to engage in any piecemeal aggression in Germany without touching off a general war which, in the General's opinion, it would be sure to lose.

Not all military observers are as sanguine as General Freeman. His predecessor in command, General Bruce Clark, in a NATO publication expressed the belief that 30 effective divisions, with reserve support, would be necessary to stem the shock of a potential Soviet attack. At the present time, according to General Clark, "NATO has on the central European front (mainly in Germany) 23 divisions in varying stages of combat readiness." And the secret NATO report which led to the prosecution of *Der Spiegel* gave a very reserved estimate of the present military capabilities of the Bundeswehr.

The principal German military effort has gone into the development of ground forces. The Air Force, not yet built up to planned capacity, is supposed to include 1,300 jet fighter-bombers; so far the American Star F-84's and F-104's are the types in general use. The Air Force is assigned only tactical tasks in NATO and is equipped only with fighters, light bombers, close support planes, reconnaissance and transport aircraft. Nike missiles are available for air defense. About 80,000 of the 100,000 men planned for air service were available in 1962.

The new German Navy, with a personnel strength of 25,000 not fully reached in 1962, is strictly defensive in function and is designed for coast defense and for guarding egress from the Baltic Sea into the Atlantic through the narrow strait between Denmark and the Scandinavian peninsula. The naval force is composed of submarines, destroyers, minelayers, minesweepers, corvettes, and fast patrol boats.

Although the new German military establishment owes much to American advice and aid, German commanders have displayed initiative in organization, strategy, and tactics. Gen. Victor L. Haugen, head of the United States Military Mission in Bonn in the summer of 1962, noted as a specific German contribution the self-sufficient equipment of the brigade, designed to enable this smaller unit to fight on in isolation if necessary. The Germans have also carefully appraised the tactics of dispersion which would be necessary in the event of the use of nuclear weapons.

The individual most closely associated with the rearming of Germany is Franz Josef Strauss, the bulky, highly intelligent, immensely energetic defense minister from 1956 until the end of 1962, when he stubbed his political toe badly over the *Der Spiegel* affair. Strauss's successor, the former prime minister of Schleswig-Holstein, Kai-Uwe von Hassel won in his former post the reputation of an efficient, conservative, coolheaded administrator. Von Hassel has not been in office long enough to create a clear image of his own outlook on military affairs.

Before Germany regained its sovereignty and its right to rearm, Strauss was pointed out as a rising young politician who would probably be minister of defense. At first this post was given to Theodor Blank, a Catholic trade unionist, whom Adenauer may have selected as the last man whose personality would suggest a revival of militarism. But the well-intentioned Blank was not a very forceful or effective administrator and rearmament moved faster after Strauss, who had been filling in as minister for Nuclear Affairs, took over the Defense Ministry.

By 1963 German expenditure on defense, negligible in the first years of rearming, had reached the figure of $4.5 billion, about one third of the federal government budget. One of the thorniest problems, and one which exists on a European as well as a German scale, was whether and how German soldiers should be equipped with nuclear weapons. More than once in conversations with me Strauss has emphasized the moral and military importance of giving the German armed forces full equality with other allies in NATO. He snorted with contempt at a propaganda campaign against nuclear weapons for Germany which the Social Democrats once mounted under the slogan *Gegen den Atom Tod.*

"Of course we are all against nuclear death!" thundered Strauss, whose voice, in moments of excitement, matches his burly Bavarian frame. "We are against death by conventional weapons. We are against death in general. But should we try to fight tanks with bows and arrows? That would be the situation if the enemy has nuclear weapons and we do not."

The minister was inclined to be all the more insistent on making nuclear firepower available to German troops because he considers 500,000 the top figure for the German armed forces, for reasons of population, economics, finance, and space. He set forth his views on the role of nuclear and conventional weapons in Europe's defense with considerable frankness in an interview published in the newspaper *Bonner Rundschau* of June 27, 1962:

"Since 1956 the Federal Government has stood for a strengthening of conventional arms on the middle European front. It has asked for this strengthening, both in a modernizing of existing weapons and in an increase in the quantity of these weapons. It goes without saying that deterrence based exclusively on nuclear weapons is not credible in the case of border clashes and military probing actions.

"On the other hand Western Europe can no longer be defended exclusively by conventional weapons. A defense based only on non-nuclear weapons has no deterrent effect on an adversary who possesses nuclear weapons and proclaims with conviction that he will use these weapons in a serious crisis. Between these two extremes must lie the limit to which it is sensible to build up and expand conventional weapons on the middle European front.

"It is obvious that on this middle European front there cannot be a division of labor between nations which possess only conventional and nations which possess only nuclear arms. . . . The German Federal Government sees the solution not in national (nuclear weapons) systems, but either in a European system, fully coordinated with NATO, or in nuclear partnership between NATO and Washington, in which the final decision remains with the

American president, but a right of consultation must be assured to the NATO partners."

Strauss was here touching on one of the most sensitive and difficult of international issues, and one which is by no means restricted to American-German relations. As Europe has become stronger, more prosperous, more united, Europeans have become increasingly restive over their complete dependence on American nuclear power. General de Gaulle has sought a way out by trying to make France an independent nuclear power in its own right. Some phrases in the speeches which de Gaulle delivered during his triumphal tour of Germany in September, 1962 and some clauses in the Franco-German treaty which was signed in Paris in January, 1963 might be interpreted as hinting at possible Franco-German co-operation in the development of a nuclear deterrent, although there has been no official confirmation of this. And certainly few Germans are so unrealistic as to take French military power, nuclear and other, as any substitute for American.

However, Germany, because it is on the frontier of Soviet military power, because it has seen a considerable part of its territory annexed and a larger part permanently occupied by Soviet troops and organized as a Communist dictatorship, is almost abnormally sensitive to any hint of a possible faltering in American purpose. An intimation of a deal with Khrushchev on West Berlin, a hint that a Soviet military thrust into Germany might be met not by instant nuclear retaliation, but by a pause and a period of negotiation sends shivers down many German spines. This sort of thing conjures up dire visions of the Red Army marching into Hamburg (almost within artillery range of the Soviet Zone border) and holding this big city as a pawn during a subsequent period of talks.

Perhaps the only way to calm and silence these exaggerated apprehensions is to give the Germans more power and responsibility for their own defense. One move in this direction would be to place directly in the hands of the Bundeswehr the smaller tactical weapons which could not be used to mount an offensive (impossible, in any case, because of the close logistical tie-in of the German forces with the whole NATO system), but would constitute a warning against any aggressive move by the Russians or their German satellites. The present arrangement is that the Germans have been instructed in the use of these tactical weapons, while the warheads remain under American lock and key. Whether this would get the weapons into German hands fast enough in the atmosphere of split-second crisis that might be expected in the event of a big Soviet offensive is perhaps questionable.

To reconcile the American conviction, forcefully stated by Defense Secretary McNamara, that small nuclear weapons systems are useless, or worse, with the desire in European countries for more share and voice in their own defense may be as difficult as squaring the circle. But it seems safe to predict that unless a solution is found, this question will come up again and again in and outside of NATO meetings.

The viewpoint of Strauss about the desirability of a European nuclear deterrent, with German participation, is by no means universally shared in Germany. Hamburg Senator Helmut Schmidt, expert on defense for the Social Democratic Party, stated an opposing view, sometimes taking issue directly with Strauss, then still in office, in two issues of *Die Zeit*.[2]

In Schmidt's view, the United States and the Soviet Union are rapidly approaching, if they have not yet reached, a state of nuclear stalemate, when each side can retaliate for a first-strike nuclear onslaught by the other with an overwhelmingly devastating blow of its own. In this situation a resort to the more awesome big nuclear bombs is the equivalent of mutual suicide. Even the smaller tactical nuclear weapons are not required so much for actual use—for a war begun with tactical atomic weapons could quickly escalate into conflict with the use of the bigger, more destructive bombs and missiles—as to insure that the opponent does not use them.

In these circumstances of absolute or near-absolute mutual deterrence the principal danger to Germany and to Europe lies in a Soviet attack with conventional forces. This can and should be stopped not by touching off a nuclear holocaust that would involve the United States, the Soviet Union, and Europe itself in common destruction, but by building up Europe's non-nuclear armaments to deterrent defensive strength. Or, to quote Mr. Schmidt's line of argument in his own words:

"The view (of Defense Minister Strauss) that also a little war in Europe must be made impossible is correct; but in the future an aggressor can no longer be frightened out of a 'little war' by nuclear bombs, but only if the defender maintains enough weapons for the little war to make the attack seem hopeless. . . .

"From this standpoint the prolongation of the German term of service was right; the reintroduction of conscription in England is necessary; the concentration of the military budget of England and France on conventional striking power is vitally important.

"What NATO needs in Europe are more soldiers, better equipped soldiers, more tanks, better tanks, more tactical aircraft for air defense, more short-range rockets, standardization of equipment and reserve organization. . . .

"What the NATO in Europe absolutely does not need are additional nuclear weapons. . . .

"All theories of the inevitability of nuclear defense are untrustworthy, because their realization would annihilate large parts of Europe, especially Germany."

As a remedy for the dependence of Europe on American nuclear power, which he accepts as necessary, Mr. Schmidt proposes more sharing of American plans with its allies, a bigger role for the NATO Council, hitherto a rather insignificant organization, a European as head of the NATO forces in Europe. He dismisses General de Gaulle's projected French national nuclear striking force with the disparaging comment:

"The fifty vulnerable Mirage bombers which are supposed to embody France's pretensions to be a nuclear world power in 1965 are senseless, from the nuclear strategic standpoint, in the event of war; scarcely one of them would be able to strike a target on Soviet soil."

Mr. Schmidt argues his viewpoint, which is close to that of American Defense Secretary McNamara, clearly and cogently. But General de Gaulle and Germans who think along the lines of Defense Minister Strauss might reply that the possession of nuclear weapons, which everyone hopes will never be used, is calculated to strengthen Europe's independent position at the bargaining table and its sense of independence vis-à-vis America.

From the time when it was first proposed, German rearmament has excited exaggerated hopes and exaggerated fears, some of the latter genuine, some hypocritical. Optimists imagined a new German military force thrown into the scales on the Western side equivalent to what Germany represented in 1913 or 1939. Pessimists foresaw hobnailed German soldiers marching through Europe's capitals as conquerors again.

Neither of these developments occurred, or could have occurred, and for the same reason. The Federal Republic, despite its consolidation under free institutions, despite its spectacular economic recovery, is militarily much weaker than the German states of the past. It has lost almost half the territory and some seventeen million inhabitants of prewar Germany; war losses are reflected in a low birth rate; the gap of enforced total disarmament for ten years is a serious handicap in an era of rapid changes in military technique.

One look at the map, showing the contrast between the expanse of the Soviet empire and the small speck represented by the Federal Republic, is a sufficient answer to the suggestion that the Soviet Union has anything to fear from present-day Germany. The cracked record of Soviet and satellite propaganda about the alleged war danger from "revenge-hungry Bonn militarists" does not harmonize with Khrushchev's frequent boast of how few nuclear missiles would be needed to wipe West Germany off the face of the earth. With its narrow frontiers, its dense population, and its many urban industrial centers, the Federal Republic is peculiarly vulnerable to air and missile attack. It would be sheer suicide for a country in such a position to start a war.

Even if one could imagine a German government obsessed with suicidal mania, as Hitler was in his last days, the means to launch a serious offensive toward the East are nonexistent. The new German Bundeswehr is firmly enmeshed in the web of NATO command, supply, and munitions arrangements. Most of Germany's bases are located outside Germany, in other NATO countries. No heavy artillery is manufactured in Germany. Jet fighters are being partially produced and assembled in German factories, but in an interlocking program with the participation of Belgium, the Netherlands, and Italy. Germany is a partner, not a monopolist, in two important military research projects, one with Great Britain on a plane capable of a vertical take-off, and one with France on a "European tank" which will mount a British gun.

German warships are fitted with radar from the Netherlands, guns from France, torpedoes and tubes from Great Britain, and light antiaircraft guns from Sweden. Machine pistols for the German Army are made, of all places, in Israel. The NATO command system reflects this thorough intermixture of national contributions in the buildup of German and other NATO forces.

Germany alone has no national army. All its forces are committed to the NATO command at SHAPE, outside Paris, where American Gen. Lyman Lemnitzer replaced American Gen. Lauris Norstad as commander in 1962. Lemnitzer's deputy is a Briton; the over-all command in central Europe is in the hands of a French general; and German Gen. Hans Speidel is in command of ground forces in central Europe. With this kind of setup it would be physically impossible for Germany to wage an independent war.

And this is just what Chancellor Adenauer always wanted, a German armed force that would be part of a larger military alliance of the free peoples of Western Europe and North America. Old men are sometimes obsessed with nostalgia for a national power and glory that belong to the past. It is a credit to the vision and insight of Germany's octogenarian chancellor that he accepted so quickly and followed through so logically the proposition that the price, for Germany, of independence and freedom was association in a larger political, economic, and military community.

If the significance of Germany's re-emergence as a military power should not be exaggerated, it also should not be dismissed as negligible. Many early obstacles to rearming, psychological and material, have been wholly or partially overcome. The Bundeswehr is the largest military force on the frontier of international communism, and the most effective, after the United States Seventh Army. It is an earnest, hardworking organization, its leaders intent on detecting and ironing out weak spots in training and equipment.

The morale is good, because there are no subversive groups with any following on the right or on the left, and Germans are now generally agreed on the necessity of making their contribution to defense against the very real and present threat of communism. If NATO has not achieved a satisfactory ratio of ground forces against the Red Army, it is easy to recognize how much worse the situation would be if there were no West Germans in uniform.

Germany, like Sweden, like France, has outlived its era as a military conquering power. But the new German armed forces fulfill creditably a most necessary function as part of the NATO shield. Now, as in the Middle Ages, history and geography have imposed on Germany the role of holding the eastern march of Western civilization against a modern danger comparable with the Hungarians in the tenth century and the Mongols in the thirteenth.

There were two further developments in Germany's posture as a NATO ally during the first months of 1963. There was a NATO decision in May to send a German corps into the northeast corner of the Federal Republic, in the area around Hamburg, Celle, and Wolfsburg, thereby making it possible for the British troops to shorten their lines and prepare a more convincing posture of counterattack. Another German corps was to move into the region along the northern flank of the United States Seventh Army, with the same purpose of making possible more consolidated defense lines.

Germany was also concerned with the United States' proposal to create an integrated deterrent force of missile-carrying merchant ships with mixed crews. The German reaction to this plan was more favorable than the British or French because it carried the implication of German participation in nuclear powers and re-sponsibilities. However, the military value of this scheme seemed questionable and its political value was much diminished because of the United States' retention of the ultimate power of decision. If the United States, in the last analysis, is to have the power of deciding when nuclear weapons are to be used, separate European nuclear forces seem superfluous. The only value of an independent European nuclear deterrent force would seem to be as a warning to the Soviet Union that, if America should flinch from risking nuclear devastation to save Europe, there would be enough modern destructive weapons in European hands to be used as a last resort.

This is the basis of General de Gaulle's insistence on an independent French nuclear striking force.

NOTES TO CHAPTER XI

1 For Schumacher's views see *Germany Reports* (Bonn: Federal Press and Information Office, 1953), p. 292.

2 See copies of *Die Zeit* for August 24 and 31.

CHAPTER XII

Is Nazism Outlived?

THIS question assumes special importance because of a more or less systematic campaign, designed to convince Americans that Nazism is a real and dangerous force in Germany today; that Hitlerism was not a horrible aberration, but a typical manifestation of German character; that most Germans today are Nazis at heart. Regardless of the motives of this campaign, which will be discussed later, the charges of Nazi survival and revival should be carefully examined. For they have a bearing on the reliability of the Federal Republic as an ally in the defensive front against totalitarian communism. Among various charges against the new Germany the following are perhaps most frequently heard:

(1) Nazism continues to flourish through clandestine groups and parties.

(2) Many ex-Nazis are to be found in important public positions.

(3) The German courts turn a blind eye to past Nazi crimes and present Nazi activities and many judges and prosecutors have Nazi records. The truth about Nazi crimes is not taught in German schools.

(4) The Germans, on their historical record, are a peculiarly and uniquely militaristic people, who may be expected to launch a war of aggression at the first opportunity.

(5) There is no real democracy in the Federal Republic.

How far do these statements correspond with present German realities?

(1) That Nazism today represents any danger to existing free

institutions in the Federal Republic is unqualifiedly false. This is a conviction based on ten trips to Germany since the end of the war, on talks with hundreds of Germans, from old friends to casual acquaintances, and on the study of much documentary material on the subject. Incidentally, I have yet to meet a single German, including those who are strongly opposed, for various reasons, to the Adenauer administration, who believes in a menace of reviving nazism. The eclipse of Nazi sympathies is most vividly demonstrated by the results of national elections.

In the first Bundestag, elected in 1949, there were four representatives of the Socialist Reich Party, a neo-Nazi political group subsequently outlawed as subversive. In three subsequent elections not one representative of a pro-Nazi group was chosen. This is surely an emphatic "No" postwar plebiscite on Hitler and his ideas.

In a large number of contacts with Germans, often in the informal atmosphere of mountain hikes, I met here and there middle-aged people who maintained that Hitler had done some good things, such as eliminating unemployment, building auto highways, creating among Germans more sense of national solidarity and social equality. I never met one who defended the genocidal measures that marked the climax of the persecution of the Jews. And for the great majority the war bombings and the misery of the first postwar years far outweighed what were considered Hitler's positive accomplishments in the first years of his rule.

What seemed especially significant was that I never met any young person, of the generation that has come to maturity since the end of the war, who showed any sympathy with Hitler's fantastic racist theories or even much trace of old-fashioned German nationalism. United Europe had replaced Fatherland as the goal of the future.

Of course, in a nation of 56 million people some Nazi sympathizers undoubtedly remain. Especially in drunken brawls pro-Nazi and anti-Semitic views are sometimes expressed. But if one considers that Germany for twelve years was subjected to Nazi domination through the combined totalitarian weapons of terror and propaganda, the surprising thing is not that such manifestations sometimes occur, but that they are so rare. There is no personality of any stature in present-day Germany who seems cast for the role of a Führer, who goes about the country stirring up throngs with rabble-rousing oratory. The few would-be imitators of Hitler have been pitiful fiascoes, so far as arousing popular response was concerned.

In the years before Hitler took over power *Der Stürmer* and other violently anti-Semitic publications were hawked on the street corners of Berlin and other large cities. Such anti-Semitism as exists in Germany now is a hole-and-corner affair, expressed in gibe and innuendo, not in open blasts of hatemongering. The daubing of swastikas on a Cologne synagogue in December, 1959, which touched off similar acts of vandalism in other towns, met prompt and universal condemnation, from Chancellor Adenauer and from national and local representative bodies, and it was followed by the prompt arrest, trial, and punishment of the offenders. The tiny German Reich Party, of which the daubers were members, expelled them and expressed disapproval of anti-Semitism. One may be skeptical of the sincerity of this statement. Yet it is significant that even a small extremist group found it expedient to issue such a repudiation.

Hendrik G. Van Dam, president of the Central Committee of Jews in Germany, whom I visited in Düsseldorf in the summer of 1962, declared that the Jewish community had nothing to complain of in the attitude of the Federal Government or of the three large parties, the CDU, the Social Democrats, and the Free Democrats. As regards the German public, he appraised its attitude as follows: The majority are indifferent, unconscious of any "Jewish problem." At one extreme he noted some covert anti-Semitism. At the other there is an idealistic minority of young people who make pilgrimages to the grave of Anne Frank, the German-Dutch Jewish girl who perished in the Belsen concentration camp and whose posthumously published diary excited a wave of sympathy throughout the world. Almost a million copies of the diary were sold in Germany, and a play based on Anne Frank's life with her family while in hiding, up to the time they were betrayed and discovered, was widely presented.

The Jewish community in Germany now is only a shadow of its former size and activity. It numbers about 30,000, compared with 600,000 in pre-Hitler times. A high proportion of these are elderly or middle-aged persons, living on pensions or restitution payments. There is no political discrimination against Jews. Three, Jacob Altmayer, Jeannette Wolff, and Peter Blockstein, have been elected to the Bundestag. Another, Herbert Weichmann, is minister of finance in the state of Hamburg. Dr. Katz was vice-president of the Supreme Court and several Jews have held important posts in the municipal administration of West Berlin. The former prominence of Jews in trade and finance, in literature and the arts has disappeared; most of the present Jewish residents of Germany are beyond the age of active careers.

Obviously the mad crimes of the Nazis could not be atoned for by anything a German government might do. But the Adenauer administration, with the full agreement of the Social Democrats, has carried out a generous reparation and restitution policy for the benefit of the survivors. German payments to Jewish victims of Nazi persecution amount roughly to $4.5 billion, including about $1 billion, paid as a kind of collective indemnity to the state of Israel. This payment took the form mainly of providing machinery and equipment for Israel's industrial development. Every Jew who returned to Germany was given a sum of 5,000 marks, over and above the amount of restitution to which he was entitled. Professors dismissed on racial grounds were invited to resume their posts in German universities.

This factual record shows the absurdity of the allegation that Nazi influences have affected the policies of the Federal Government. Indeed this policy, in every important aspect, is a precise reversal of Hitler's. Hitler stood for the totalitarian method of governing by a combination of unlimited propaganda with unlimited terrorism. Adenauer has maintained free elections, freedom of the press, habeas corpus, the rule of law. Hitler exploited crackpot theories of a superior "Nordic" race for brutal German domination over supposedly inferior peoples. The ruling party in the Federal Republic upholds Christian principles and has done everything in its power to promote European co-operation and unity on the basis of full equality of peoples. German universities now welcome large numbers of students from Asian and African nations which Hitler denigrated as racially inferior.

Nazi Germany regarded as desirable autarchy, maximum economic self-sufficiency, overwhelming German military might. The Germany of Adenauer and Erhard has been a pacemaker in breaking down trade barriers, restoring freely convertible exchange, substituting interdependence for autarchy. And German rearmament, as was shown in the preceding chapter, is so closely tied in with that of America and other NATO countries that a resumption of an aggressive German military policy would be impossible.

Unfortunately there is one part of Germany where the Nazi spirit and methods still survive. This is the "German Democratic Republic." The brutal young Vopos (People's Police), who have stained the Berlin Wall deep with blood, carry on the traditions of Hitler's SA and SS and represent the same combination of fanatics and thugs. Although Nazism is a German responsibility, the Germans are not to be blamed for what goes on in the area of Soviet occupation. Ulbricht's system would vanish very quickly if it were not propped up by Soviet tanks.

(2) While the charge of Nazi influence on government policies is quite false, it is true that a number of former members of the Nazi Party have been and are in the German government service. It could hardly be otherwise. The Nazi system was so comprehensive in its organization that Nazi Party membership, for many Germans, was a condition of employment. It would have been impossible to recruit an adequate civil service exclusively from the small minority who carried their resistance to the point of emigrating abroad or getting into concentration camps.

Two things might have reasonably been expected of a government based on strongly anti-Nazi principles. The first and most important was to tolerate no infiltration of unreconstructed ex-Nazis into positions where they could dictate or seriously influence government policy. The second was to bar from public office men who were gravely compromised by their activities under Hitler.

The first of these tests has been passed satisfactorily; on the second some reservations are in order. The only serious attempt at infiltration of which there is any convincing evidence occurred in 1952 under the leadership of Werner Naumann, a former secretary of state in the Goebbels Ministry of Propaganda. Living under assumed names, he evaded denazification procedures and became the moving spirit in a group of hard-core ex-Nazis, operating in Hamburg and Düsseldorf. Their purpose was to elect and organize a pro-Nazi group of Bundestag deputies which could hold the balance of power between the CDU and the Social Democrats and finally emerge as an independent party.[1] Whether this design could have met any success is uncertain, because it was promptly broken up by the British high commissioner at that time, Sir Ivone Kirkpatrick. This incident, of course, antedated the restoration of German sovereignty in 1955. Since that time German parliamentary institutions have been tested and consolidated and there is no case where a hidden Nazi hand may be detected in legislation or administrative action.

On the other hand, there have been some appointments to public office that have been unfortunate, others that have been questionable. For some years Theodor Oberländer, a former ardent Nazi, was a member of the cabinet as minister for refugees. He had rendered considerable political service to the Adenauer administration by mustering the support of large numbers of refugees, the most embittered and potentially explosive element in the population. He was an industrious, efficient minister.

Ugly charges got about that he had been in Lvov, in Eastern Poland, in the first weeks of the German-Soviet War, when Ukrainian forces, operating with the Germans, committed a pogrom against the Jewish population of the city. Oberländer voiced a blanket denial of any wrongdoing and it was never proved that he was personally involved in the pogrom. Still, most German liberals felt better when he resigned from the cabinet in 1960.

A favorite target for those who like to point to alleged Nazi influence in high places is Dr. Hans Globke, secretary of state in the chancellor's office and a trusted confidant of Adenauer for important state transactions. Globke was never a Nazi Party member. He was an official in the Ministry of the Interior who stayed in his post and acquired unenviable notoriety by preparing an explanatory commentary on the racial laws promulgated at a Nazi conference in Nürnberg. Globke's defense, as set forth in one of his rare personal interviews (he is the *éminence grise* type of confidential adviser who appears as seldom as possible in the public eye) in *Die Zeit* is that he was a double agent during the Hitler period, who remained in the Ministry at the request of high Catholic authorities, ecclesiastical and lay. In his position he was able to give advance information of impending Nazi moves and thereby to save many from death or concentration camps. In order to keep the confidence of the regime he had, of course, to give an appearance of willing co-operation and sometimes to lend his name to unsavory actions. The former Berlin Cardinal Konrad von Preysing, a vigorous foe of Nazism, offered this appraisal of Globke:[2]

"Dr. Hans Globke has been personally known to me for many years. He has always correctly appraised the dangers and errors of National Socialism. Over and above his fundamental opposition, he has always sought to obstruct or render impossible unlawful actions and acts of injustice and violence on the part of the Nazis, to the fullest extent possible to him within the scope of his activities. He disclosed to me and to my fellow-workers plans and decisions made by the Ministry and certain proposed bills of a highly confidential nature. . . . He rendered highly valuable assistance in our relief work for the persecuted Jews and half-Jews by giving timely warnings."

So Globke emerges with a good character certificate, although a double agent cannot always work with immaculate kid gloves, and must accept a bad public reputation as part of his job.

People joined the Nazi Party with the most varying degrees of dedication, from fanatical faith in Hitler and his ideas to mere opportunism. Sometimes there are varying episodes in the life of the same individual. As a young law student the present foreign minister, Gerhard Schroeder, joined the Nazi Party as a condition of continuing his profession in 1933. Later, however, he married a "non-Aryan" wife, which entailed his prompt expulsion.

Some unsuitable appointments have been made in the judicial system. There was a stir, in Germany and abroad, in the summer of 1962 when the public prosecutor (*Bundesanwalt*) attached to the Federal Supreme Court in Karlsruhe, Wolfgang Immerwahr [3] Fränkel, was exposed as responsible for many death sentences for minor offenses when he was serving as assistant in the office of public prosecutor in the Reichsgericht ("Supreme Court") in Leipzig in the Hitler period. The evidence came from files which had fallen into the hands of the authorities in the Soviet Zone.

This was not a morally unimpeachable source. The courts in the Soviet Zone operate on much the same principle as Nazi courts. However, the evidence that Fränkel had repeatedly demanded the death sentence when the prosecution would have been content with lighter penalties was sufficiently convincing to lead to his suspension. And the Fränkel case led to much discussion as to how such scandals are to be avoided in the future. According to a statement which I received from the Ministry of Justice in Bonn, some 200 out of a total number of 11,600 judges and 2,200 prosecutors were adversely affected by the periodic exposures from the Soviet Zone.

There have been a number of obstacles to a thorough screening of all applicants for judicial office. Records are often lacking in the Federal Republic and are produced in the Soviet Zone, for propaganda purposes, after appointments have been made. A judge, under German law, may only be removed from office if it can be proved that he *deliberately* rendered unjust verdicts. It is notoriously difficult to establish legal proof of motivation and state of mind. Moreover, the laws of the Nazi period, especially after the outbreak of the war, were often so ruthless that a judge could maintain that he was merely following the letter of the law if he passed a harsh sentence for violation of the blackout or some other military regulation or for some minor offense by a Pole or other member of a nationality considered inferior by the Nazis.

In recognition of the fact that some judges and prosecutors, on their past records, were unsuitable for their offices, the Bundestag passed a law permitting judicial officials who had served in criminal cases during the war years to retire on pension before the regular retirement age. About 150 took advantage of this possibility; 18 obstinately held out and may be dealt with by special legislation.

One reason for the tarnished record of some German judges and prosecutors in the Hitler era is the prevalence in modern German legal studies of a theory known as *Rechtpositivismus,* which may be summed up in the aphorism: *Gesetz ist Gesetz* ("Law is law"). In other words, no matter how savage, how contrary to higher morality a piece of legislation may be, the judge is under no obligation except to enforce it. It was the application of this theory, plus a normal share of human weakness and opportunism, that created a situation which elicited an eloquent expression of repentance on behalf of the legal profession by Attorney General Max Güde: [4]

"We jurists, lawyers, and judges, more than any others, must assume our share of the guilt. We cannot avoid admitting our special responsibility and our special failure—our responsibility because the upholding of the law was entrusted especially to us—our special guilt because we were not strong enough and above all not brave enough to fight for the law as we should have, even at the risk of our lives. Our guilt is that while justice was murdered we survived."

Another factor that has led, in some cases, to the reappearance in the public service of seriously compromised former Nazis is a German version of the "old school tie" spirit. Men who worked together in some government department under Hitler sometimes form little cliques to promote each other's rehabilitation and advancement. A scientist of personally strong liberal sympathies remarked in this connection: "They are just trying to protect their jobs, not to perpetuate Hitlerism."

Personal interest, not a desire to undermine free institutions, is behind most of the cases of ultimately exposed prominent ex-Nazis. The war ended in an atmosphere of chaotic collapse; records and documents were lost or destroyed in air raids. It was not difficult for a local Nazi chieftain who would have been notorious in one region to start life somewhere else under an assumed name. So there have been and no doubt will be revelations of unjust judges in the service of the Federal Republic, of police chiefs in West German cities who were implicated in atrocities in the East, of physicians who took part in cruel experiments on human beings. The problem of tracking down every guilty person is probably, by its nature, insoluble. But the danger of any concerted move for the restoration of Nazism steadily declines with every year that relegates the Hitler tyranny more and more to the realm of the past.

(3) However, it would be a mistake to imagine that Nazi criminals get off scot-free or that German children grow up without any knowledge of Hitler's crimes. Almost all the more notorious former Nazis live abroad—in Argentina, like Adolf Eichmann, in Spain, in Egypt, and other Arab countries. This is the surest sign that they would not be welcome or free from the danger of prosecution in the Federal Republic.

In the first years after the end of the war the punishment of alleged war crimes was reserved to the Allied occupation powers. These trials led to 5,000 convictions and about 800 death sentences, of which a considerable number were commuted. After the restoration of German sovereignty, the German courts took over. Up to 1962 there had been over 30,000 prosecutions for such crimes as brutality in concentration camps and participation in massacres of civilians. Over 5,000 sentences of conviction were imposed. Some of these sentences seem light in proportion to the gravity of the offenses. This must be attributed to a general German psychological impulse, after all the country lived through, to pass a sponge of oblivion over what now seems an increasingly unreal and remote past.

A central office representing the state ministries of justice was set up in Ludwigsburg, near Stuttgart, in 1958 for the purpose of collecting evidence about Nazi crimes committed outside of Germany, especially in Poland, the Baltic States and the Soviet Union. Some of the difficulties in the way of the work of this office are thus described by the chief prosecutor, Erwin Schüle: [5]

"The Nationalist Socialist leaders had given top secret protection to all of their extermination orders and the persons involved in the execution of these crimes had been sworn to utmost secrecy. Only this fact explains how it had been possible that the large majority of the German population had remained unaware of the proportions of the crimes that had been committed in the occupied territories. . . . Moreover the entire evidence material which had fallen into the hands of the Allies had been taken to the archives of the various Allied countries, for purposes of historical research, after the completion of the Nürnberg trials. . . .

"Among other things, the investigations of the Ludwigsburg Center brought to light the fact that in the spring of 1945 the Gestapo had distributed among its members a large number of forged identity cards. With the help of these documents many individuals involved in crimes managed to disappear unnoticed and to assume new identities within the Federal Republic or to escape to foreign countries. This explains why neither the Allies nor the German law enforcement authorities had been able to ascertain the whereabouts of Eichmann and to institute legal proceedings against him."

Despite the handicaps which made its start rather slow, the Ludwigsburg Center has initiated about 900 cases against major war criminals, as individuals and in groups. More than half of these have been turned over to the courts and prosecuting authorities of the various states for further action. A spokesman for the Center, with whom I talked in 1962, said its policy was to prosecute the "higher-ups" rather than the rank and file. He estimated that the total number of the *Einsatzkommandos* which carried out the work of extermination was not over 5,000. The attitudes of those who have been brought to trial varied. Some showed signs of remorse; others took the familiar position that they were merely obeying orders.

The Eichmann trial was fully publicized in Germany and the general reaction, especially among the youth, was that he got what he deserved. It may seem strange that a creed which commanded absolute obedience for twelve years should have left so few visible traces of survival, that there should be little sign of anti-Semitism after the unremitting Nazi propaganda. An explanation was suggested by Mgr. Erich Klausener, whose father, a prominent Catholic layman, was murdered by the Nazis in the purge of June 30, 1934.

"Nazism," Monsignor Klausener said to me in his West Berlin office, "was no real philosophy, capable of surviving a crushing defeat. It was a crazy compound of racist and extreme nationalist ideas which could not convince any rational human being. Communism, on the other hand, is more subtle, better grounded philosophically, and not restricted in appeal to any nation or ethnic group. Therefore it is a more formidable enemy."

The Jewish victims of Hitler's genocidal frenzy were not slaughtered in mob outbreaks, with extensive participation. They were rounded up and sent to death camps, the location and very existence of which were kept secret. The responsibility of the large minority of the German people who voted for Hitler in the last free election was in entrusting power to a paranoid demagogue. This responsibility was heavy, and has been heavily atoned for. But the number of Germans who, as individuals, were directly concerned with the extermination of the Jews is very small.

It is not true, as is sometimes alleged, that Nazi influence is potent in German schools or that German children are not told of the evil features of the Nazi period. Education, under the German Constitution, is a subject reserved for the states. However, there is a central council of state ministries of education in Bonn, and its rulings prescribe that at suitable ages, students receive full information, with appropriate reading matter, about Nazi policies of violence and cruelty and also about the heroism of those Germans who took part in the resistance movement, which reached its climax on July 20, 1944, when only an accidental shift of movement saved Hitler from being killed by the time bomb which Count Stauffenberg had deposited in his headquarters.

The whole German resistance movement, too little regarded and understood in the West, was one of the noblest of tragic failures, led by men ranging in background from aristocrats to Social Democrats, of uncommon highmindedness, dedication, and moral and physical courage. In retrospect it is all the more tragic because, even had it been successful in killing Hitler and seizing power at the center, the probabilities are that the United States, where Roosevelt was obsessed with the "unconditional surrender" psychosis, would not have seized the opportunity to keep communism out of central Europe by concluding a fair peace based on the proper German ethnic frontier, which would have been that of 1937.

Had the overthrow of Hitler, while German armies were still on foreign soil, been followed by the imposition of a ruthless peace and the annexation of historic German territory, a new "stab in the back" legend [6] would have arisen, and Nazism, in retrospect, might have been mourned and regretted, as it certainly is not today. Apart from all such hypothetical considerations, the men of the German

Resistance deserve the honor that is always due those who sacrifice their lives in a good cause against overwhelming odds.[7] Maj. Gen. Henning von Tresckow, one of the military conspirators, composed a suitable epitaph for the movement when he wrote, just before he took his own life after the failure of the plot became clear:

"Now the whole world will fall upon us and load us with abuse. But I am still firmly convinced that we did right. I consider Hitler to be not only the archenemy of Germany, but of the world. When I appear before God's Judgment Seat in a few hours' time to account for my actions and omissions, I believe I can stand up with a good conscience for what I have done in the battle against Hitler. Just as God once promised Abraham that he would not destroy Sodom if ten just men could be found there, so I hope that for our sake God will not destroy Germany."

The men of the Resistance have given the forces of freedom in Germany its indispensable legacy of heroes, martyrs, and idealists. They did what they could to save their country's honor.

Films of Nazi brutalities have been widely shown in German schools, and the interest of the children is kept alive by discussions and questionnaires. One of the most authentic German liberals, in the best sense of that somewhat ambiguous word, is Mrs. Annadore Leber, widow of a Social Democrat who was executed as one of the participants in the anti-Hitler plot. Mrs. Leber is the last person who would be "soft" on any survivals of Nazism in the schools. She assured me in Berlin in 1962 that very good progress, more than was recognized abroad, had been made in eliminating the last vestiges of Nazi and extreme nationalist viewpoints in schoolbooks.

It could not be stated with certainty that every school in Germany gives equal attention to the Nazi phase in German history. Local conditions, the sentiments of the parents, the personality of the teacher enter into the situation. There is a difference of opinion among educators as to the proper age when children should be told of acts of revolting cruelty and brutality. But on the broad question of whether there are serious pro-Nazi influences in the German schools one may quote the testimony of an expert, Dr. Benjamin Fine, former education editor of *The New York Times,* who wrote, after returning from a survey of German schools in 1961:

"Hitler and his philosophy are dead, so far as German youth are concerned. Perhaps some traces of his influence still linger in neo-Nazi circles; but this is little more than the 'lunatic fringe' you could find in any country. Films showing Hitler and his followers are met with laughter or scorn. Schools stress the evils that Hitler and the Nazi regime did and the destruction they caused to Germany."

(4) The image of the Germans as incurable militarists in every epoch of history does not square with the facts of history. For centuries the division of Germany into a multitude of states, some microscopically small, encouraged and invited the aggressions and intrigues of stronger neighbors. During the Thirty Years' War (1618–48), French and Swedes and Spaniards and foreign mercenaries fought over German territory and France and Sweden emerged from this conflict with annexations at the expense of Germany.

Louis XIV launched repeated invasions of Germany. At that time, in the late seventeenth and early eighteenth centuries, France was the strongest European continental power and its ambitions were opposed by a defensive coalition of England and various European powers. The same pattern was repeated at the time of Napoleon, a century later. Many of the names of streets that radiate from the glorious Arc de Triomphe in Paris commemorate battles that were fought far outside France's frontiers, Wagram, Friedland, Jena. Indeed for a time Napoleon was almost successful in deploying the German states as his military auxiliaries.

France never fully recovered from Napoleon's bloodletting, and Germany's rapid industrial development in the second half of the nineteenth century helped to swing the balance of power in its favor. However, the Franco-Prussian War, in which a united Germany avenged Jena, Auerstadt, and Austerlitz, was not an instance of unmitigated German aggression. It was France that declared war on Prussia, not the other way around, and on a pretext that would now seem so frivolous as to be almost incredible: an alleged insult to the French ambassador. If Bismarck set a trap for Napoleon III, the French emperor rushed into it with a blind overconfidence of victory that was not justified by the course of the war.

There has been a tendency to forget the verdict of the cooler and more impartial investigations of the causes of the First World War because of Adolf Hitler's unmistakable responsibility for the Second. Yet the opinion expressed by the American historical scholar, Prof. Sidney B. Fay, at the end of his monumental analysis of this subject [8] is worth remembering:

"Germany did not plot a European war, did not want one and made genuine, although too belated efforts to avert one. She was the victim of her alliance with Austria and of her own folly. . . . It was the hasty Russian general mobilization, assented to on July 29 and ordered on July 30, while Germany was still trying to bring Austria to accept mediation proposals, that finally rendered the European war inevitable."

Hitler's responsibility for the Second World War was clear and unmistakable. It is, however, highly doubtful whether the German people desired this war. One of Hitler's favorite oratorical poses was that of the old front-line soldier who hated war because he knew its horrors too well. Foreign observers in Germany are in general agreement that neither the crushing of Poland nor the swift and inexpensive victory over France unloosed any visible enthusiasm among German civilians.

In any case, the crushing nature of the final German defeat (about one German out of three between the ages of twenty and forty is estimated to have lost his life) was calculated to extinguish forever any spark of militarism, if one understands by that word glorification or lighthearted acceptance of war. It was far easier to keep the Germans disarmed after 1945 than to induce them to take up arms ten years later.

(5) There remains, finally, the charge, voiced by some German left-wingers and foreign critics of the new Germany, that Adenauer's regime is not truly democratic. Certainly respect for strong personal leadership and also for party discipline [9] is stronger in Germany than in some other countries. There is less practice in public discussion of political affairs, although this situation is changing under the influence of American and British models of foreign affairs discussion groups and radio and television symposiums.

But when one considers the vacuum left by twelve years of totalitarian rule, the current degree of revival of free institutions is, on balance, highly encouraging. Elections are free, the press is free, speech is free. If Adenauer has run his administration with a rather high hand, he has also had to submit at regular intervals to the judgment of the people at the polls. And, especially in recent years, his personality and his policies have often been sharply criticized in the press.

And the Germans do not vote like passive robots. In the early summer of 1961 all signs pointed to a repetition of the election result of 1957, when the CDU won an absolute majority in the Bundestag. Then, on August 13, the Berlin Wall went up. Adenauer's reaction seemed a little cold, lacking in sympathy and imagination. I was in Germany at that time and one could almost feel marginal and undecided votes dropping away from the old Chancellor. When the ballots were counted, Adenauer received a plurality, not a majority. It would be impossible to prove the point; but it seems quite probable that the Wall and its aftermath caused a swing of perhaps 5 per cent of the voters away from the CDU to the other parties.

The actual character of the new Germany that has arisen from the ashes of Hitler's fantasy of a European empire, dominated by the Nordic race, has been blurred, obscured, and distorted by much biased misrepresentation in books, films, and radio propaganda, misrepresentation that at times, both in the United States and Great Britain, has suggested the proportions of an organized campaign. In this anti-German campaign, which was especially marked in the United States in 1961 and 1962, one may distinguish several motives and psychological factors:

The most obvious beneficiary of distrust between the United States, the other Western powers, and the German Federal Republic is the Kremlin. In postwar Europe free Germany has been the keenest Soviet disappointment and the biggest Soviet stumbling block. In contrast to the situation in France and Italy, there is not a single Communist in the Bundestag. West Germany's economic revival has raised the standard of living to a point where Communist efforts to stir up class hatred and split society as a prelude to a Communist takeover have little prospect of success, especially as the object lesson of the squalid poverty of the DDR is always before the eyes of the Germans.

So it is no accident that Soviet propaganda, in diplomatic notes, in radio propaganda, and in the many less direct channels at its disposition, repeats the familiar themes of "Adenauer's Nazi generals" and "the revenge-hungry Bonn militarists," with all the continuous emphasis of a high-powered advertising agency trying to make popular a new brand of soap or cigarettes.

A second element in creating an anti-German mood, more important in England than in the United States, is the bitterness of doctrinaire Socialists over Germany's striking revival on the basis of private enterprise and a free economy. This revival forced the German Social Democrats to scrap their Marxist principles and was a potent object lesson in discrediting socialism as a theory all over the world.

It was inevitable that the barbarous crimes of the Nazis should leave a legacy of deep and bitter hatred with those who felt identified by faith and blood, sometimes by closer ties of kinship and friendship, with the victims of these crimes. It is a testimony to human capacity for generosity and fairmindedness that from the first bleak days of the occupation, many Jews, both Americans and German refugees, drew a clear distinction between Nazi fanatics and the German people as a whole and were quick to recognize the moral as well as the material achievements of the new Germany. But there remains a hard core of irreconcilables, convinced that nothing good can come out of Germany. From this source comes much of the driving force behind the anti-German campaign and much of its audience.

Another element in this campaign has been crude commercialism. One successful anti-German book or film inspires imitators. In at least one case a book that was, in substance, reasonably objective, was built up into a lurid diatribe against an imaginary neo-Nazi danger by misleading advertising, designed to attract anti-German readers.

Not all Americans have awakened to the tremendous change in the international balance of power since the end of the Second World War. Without this recognition, a suggestion that Germany might "try it again" does not fall flat from its inherent absurdity and impossibility.

Nor are the motivations and political implications of the "Hate Germany" drive always clearly understood. It was regrettable and pathetic to see among the signers of a tribute to a book which is a malicious and fantastic misrepresentation of what has happened in West Germany since the end of the war the name of a venerable religious publicist, long known as a staunch anti-Communist. He apparently did not realize that there is no better way to play the Communist game than to libel the country that has become a key position in the European anti-Communist front.

Of course it would be an exaggeration to say that no traces remain of a creed and a system that dominated Germany for twelve years. But what is important is not the occasional act of hoodlumism or vandalism, the anti-Semitic outburst in a tavern brawl, the foolish speech at a rally of war veterans. It is the broad trend of German political and social life. This trend, for a variety of reasons indicated in earlier chapters, is unmistakably away from, not toward, any revival of Nazism in its original form or in any camouflaged version.

NOTES TO CHAPTER XII

1 See Terence Prittie, *Germany Divided* (Boston: Little Brown & Co., 1960), pp. 322–327.

2 Cited in Christopher Emmet and Norbert Muhlen, *The Vanishing Swastika* (Chicago: Henry Regnery Co., 1961), pp. 33 ff.

3 Fränkel's middle name, Immerwahr ("Ever True") became the subject of a good many gibes, because he had clearly been somewhat less than candid in describing his past record.

4 Cited in *Die Zeit* of February 12, 1962.

5 See article by Erwin Schüle in *Meet Germany*, published by Atlantik-Brücke, Hamburg, pp. 35, 36.

6 After the First World War there was a persistent legend in German nationalist circles that the victorious German army had been the victim of a *Dolchstoss* ("stab in the back") by treacherous and defeatist forces in the rear. This despite the fact that on September 29, 1918 the German Supreme Command had insisted on an immediate armistice to avoid a military catastrophe. See Erich Eyck, *A History of*

the Weimar Republic (Cambridge, Mass.: Harvard University Press, 1962), p. 32.

7 The fullest account of the German Resistance is to be found in Hans Rothfels, *The German Opposition to Hitler* (Chicago: Henry Regnery Co., 1962).

8 See Sidney B. Fay, *The Origins of the World War,* 2d ed. (New York: The Macmillan Co., 1961), pp. 552, 554.

9 In Great Britain, also, it is most unusual for a Conservative or for a Labour member of Parliament to vote in opposition to his party.

CHAPTER XIII

"Bonn Is Not Weimar"

THIS is the title of an extremely penetrating and objective interpretation, by a foreigner, of the spirit and significance of the new Germany.[1] It sums up an important political truth. As shown in the preceding chapter, there is no element of similarity between Hitler's madly fantastic Third Reich and Konrad Adenauer's eminently sane and sober Federal Republic. And there are a number of reasons why the sad story of the breakdown of the attempt to create free representative institutions in Germany under the Weimar Republic is not likely to be repeated.

By the spring of 1963 eighteen years, almost the span of a generation, had elapsed since Germany's unconditional surrender. A similar time measurement from the First World War Armistice of November 11, 1918 would bring Germany to 1936, with Hitler firmly entrenched in power and the Weimar Constitution a forgotten scrap of paper. The Federal Republic in 1963 is very much a going concern, with no internal threat to its stability of any consequence. And it is no accident that Adenauer succeeded where the statesmen of Weimar, from Ebert to Brüning, failed. There are several reasons why German development after two great wars followed such contrasted lines.

First and most obvious, the reaction to defeat after 1918 and after 1945 was profoundly different. This is because the circumstances accompanying defeat were so different. The armistice imposed on Germany by Marshal Foch was signed when German troops were still deep in French territory, when the Germans everywhere, in the East and in the West, were in foreign lands.

The German people generally, and especially the poorer classes in the towns, were suffering severely from lack of food,[2] the consequence of a stringent blockade. But, except for a brief interlude of Russian invasion of East Prussia in the first weeks of the war, the soil of the Fatherland was untouched. Germany's cities were not bombed.

This situation of surrender at a time when the military situation outwardly still seemed favorable made it easy for extreme nationalists to create a legend that the German Army had never been defeated at all, but betrayed, "stabbed in the back" by cowardly civilians at home, Socialists, Jews, pacifists, whatever target prejudice might suggest. It is a matter of historical record that Hindenberg and Ludendorff, the supreme commanders in the field, had demanded of the home government an armistice as the only alternative to military disaster. But this fact did not stop the flow of nationalist oratory, which became one of Adolf Hitler's propaganda trump cards. Among a considerable proportion of the German population there was a fierce emotional rejection of the Treaty of Versailles and a determination to repudiate its hateful provisions at the earliest opportunity.[3]

Germany in 1945 was not like Germany in 1918. Its big cities were a shambles from air bombing. Foreign troops had poured into the country and occupied every square foot of its territory. If there had been any voices of nationalist defiance, these would have been silenced under a military rule that, in its first years, was stern in the West as in the East. But there were no such voices. The fantasy of a Hitlerian Third Reich, to last for a thousand years, had gone up in smoke, along with the remains of Hitler himself in the bunker where *der Führer* shot himself as the Soviet troops battered their way into his capital. Never was an ideology that had seemed all-powerful in its time of triumph outlived so quickly. This was partly because Nazism was rooted in fanatical devotion to a single personality, partly because it had brought to Germany far and away the greatest national disaster since the Thirty Years' War.

In the years after the First World War Germany swarmed with irregular fighting forces, so-called free corps, which moved in to suppress Communist and other left-wing riots and attempts to seize power in Berlin, Bavaria, and the Ruhr. Some of these irregular paramilitary forces continued to exist, in defiance of the disarmament provisions of the Treaty of Versailles, and out of their members came many recruits for the Nazi movement.

But after 1945 there were neither revolutionary disturbances nor bands of unreconciled nationalists. This is partly explained, of course, by the fact of military occupation. But those who had predicted that occupation authorities would be harassed by underground resistance, sabotage, guerrilla activity, were proved wrong. In the United States Zone, and probably also in the other three areas of occupation, there was not one case when a soldier lost his life as a result of political resistance.

Germany's will to fight had been completely crushed. There was no instance of secret arming, so popular in the twenties. It took considerable pressure to push through a moderate, strictly defensive military establishment against the skeptical *ohne uns* attitude which was widespread in the younger generation.

Antidemocratic trends appeared in the wake of defeat in the First World War, slackened as economic well-being improved from 1925 until 1929, and sprang up again with irresistible force after the world economic depression hit Germany at full blast in 1929. Such trends have played practically no role in the Federal Republic.

The word "democracy" calls for definition, since Communist-ruled states have tried to appropriate it for their own purposes. The administration in the Soviet Zone calls itself the German Democratic Republic, although not one of the basic principles of Western democracy is practiced or respected there. These principles are freedom of the ballot, of religion, speech and press, of movement across frontiers, of security of person and property against arbitrary arrest and confiscation, of trade-union organization. All these liberties were guaranteed by the Weimar Constitution, all were denied under Hitler and are still denied in the Soviet Zone, where Hitlerite methods still prevail.

From the beginning the German Republic established under the Weimar Constitution was caught in a crossfire of attack by extremists of right and left. Liberalism was a word of hatred and contempt in both extremist camps. The fanatical nationalists, who finally, in the great majority, accepted Hitler's leadership, wanted to create a militarist state along racist lines that would restore German strength and unity at home and make possible in time revenge for Versailles. The German Communists, composed of left-wing Social Democrats and other radicals, looked to Moscow for inspiration and set as their goal a Soviet Germany, with ruthless liquidation of classes and individuals that would not fit into this new order.

Much of the German youth in the twenties and early thirties was caught up in this struggle of conflicting ideologies. Young men of the middle class put on the brown shirts of Hitler's SA (Sturm-Abteilungen). Many young workers joined the Communist organization, Rotfront, and bloody clashes between these groups were frequent until Hitler's assumption of power restricted the violence to one side and suppressed all open opposition.

The appeals of the middle-of-the-road political groups, Social Democrats, Catholics, liberals, for reason and moderation—making haste slowly—fell on deaf years in a time of widespread unemployment and misery. The doom of the first German experiment in republicanism was perhaps pronounced when, in the election of July 31, 1932, the Nazis and the Communists together polled more votes than all the other parties. The cause of freedom is in a hopeless plight when the majority of voters, in a free election, deliberately cast their votes for parties that reject freedom in principle.

Of all this ferment of extremism there has been no repetition in Germany since 1945. Nazism is thoroughly discredited by its heritage of material ruin and international moral obloquy. To the generation that is coming of age it is an increasingly vague memory. The attempts to promote Hitler-type movements have ended in pitiful fiascoes.

Communism, for the average German, has been equally discredited for different reasons. Three developments have pulled the rug from under any popular pro-Communist sentiment in West Germany. First, while invading troops of any nationality inevitably commit some excesses, the orgy of murder, looting, and rape that marked the capture by the Red Army of Budapest, Vienna, Berlin, and smaller German towns was exceptional in savagery. This will not be forgotten within the memory of this generation. Not for nothing was it said that Stalin incurred two disadvantages by the incursion of his troops into Central Europe. The Red Army had seen Europe, and Europe had seen the Red Army.

Second, the West Germans know what communism is in practice. There is hardly a family in the Federal Republic that does not have friends or relatives in the Soviet Zone. A nonpolitical letter from such a friend or relative, giving a matter-of-fact account of everyday hardships and deprivations, is far more convincing to the average German than any amount of theoretical argument about the merits and defects of capitalism, socialism, and communism. West Germans have received very few letters giving them the impression that communism had created, or was likely to create a better life than they are enjoying. Shock and horror at the shootings and killings along the Berlin Wall have intensified this impression.

Third, all Germany's territorial grievances, after the Second World War, are in the East. No German today thinks of reclaiming Alsace-Lorraine. With the return of the Saar to German sovereignty the western frontier of the German Federal Republic is satisfactorily set. The Treaty of Versailles was bitterly resented because it assigned to Poland former German territory where there was a more or less numerous German minority. But Versailles was a model of moderation compared with the *de facto* peace settlement imposed by Stalin and upheld by Khrushchev. This assigned to Poland big areas which had been thoroughly German in nationality and culture for centuries, and to the Soviet Union such a historically German city as Königsberg, home of the greatest German philosopher, Immanuel Kant.

Moreover, the Soviet Union has imposed on its zone of occupation an alien, heartily detested dictatorship which could not survive without Soviet military backing. The withdrawal of American, British, and French troops from the Federal Republic would gravely compromise its international security, but would be no threat to its internal stability. The presence of these troops has not changed a vote in German elections. The withdrawal of Soviet troops would be a death sentence for the Ulbricht regime.

So in the Federal Republic there are no roots from which neo-Nazism or communism may be expected to spring. Another sign that Bonn is not Weimar is the vigor with which the government has moved, under the law, to eliminate parties which are considered committed to violent subversion. The Supreme Court has forbidden the functioning of the Communist Party and of the Socialist Reich Party, a neo-Nazi group. Neither of these organizations had much popular support while they were allowed to exist. But both were nipped in the bud before they could do any mischief.

Too often, in a commendable attempt to uphold the principle of liberty, the Weimar authorities gave unlimited latitude to the sworn enemies of liberty. It is interesting to speculate on how the course of German and world history might have been altered if Hitler had been deported to his native Austria as an undesirable alien after serving his term of fortress imprisonment for his attempt to seize power by violence in Munich in November, 1923. The penalty would scarcely have seemed excessive for an attempt at armed revolt. And without Hitler's charismatic personality, his movement, then very much in embryo, might have dissolved and disappeared, along with many other extremist groups.

The sentiment of the youth that has grown up in the shadow of the greatest debacle in German history is not that of the turbulent younger generation that dreamed of far-reaching social changes in the sorry gray aftermath of 1918. Not for the present German youth is the flamboyant oratory of *völkische* [4] rabble rousers, nor the apocalyptic appeal of a Karl Liebknecht or a Rosa Luxemburg for social revolution that would eliminate war and inaugurate a world-wide triumph for communism.

German youth today is distinctly allergic to all utopian visions, to all big projects of social regeneration. It is concerned with every-day tasks and amusements, with studies conceived as the prelude to a career, with sports, camping and boating, cars and motorcycles, with making both ends meet during student days. Later comes concern with marriage, jobs, careers. Among many young

Germans there is a positive aversion to politics. A student whom I met in Bonn offered this explanation:

"If we were in anti-Nazi parties before Hitler took over we were likely to be persecuted under the Nazis. If we were identified in any way, however slightly, with the Nazis we could be 'denazified' under the occupation, barred from desirable employment. Why should we stick our necks out again by taking any controversial stand? We are content to study and work and lead our personal lives."

There is now much skepticism about all ideologies, right-wing or left-wing. There were some student riots in Pasing, a district of Munich, in the summer of 1962. But these were completely non-political and started because the police were accused of being too rough in compelling strolling musicians to move on. One of the few cases when there was political motivation behind a student demonstration occurred in the University of Göttingen, in the state of Lower Saxony, in 1955. A conservative local government had appointed as minister of education a man named Schlüter, who had published writings that tried to make out a case for the Third Reich. So strong were the manifestations of protest, led by Göttingen students and spreading to other localities, that Schlüter was soon forced to resign. And this happened in a German state where, in some country districts, there had been feeble attempts to revive Nazi sympathies, where the Socialist Reich Party, forbidden by the Supreme Court, had found most of its supporters.

The following general diagnosis of the profound contrast between present-day Germany and Germany after the First World War seems sound and convincing: [5]

"The great and probably the decisive contrast with the period between 1918 and 1933 lies in the fact that today there are no living alternatives to the idea of a democratic society, with parliamentary institutions. Democracy and parliamentarism, if not accepted as positive ideals of the whole people, are at least accepted as facts."

The economic climate of Bonn is not that of Weimar. To be sure, both the lost wars, for Germany, were paid for by a ravaging inflation, which robbed savings of most of their value and made it necessary to start from scratch with a brand-new currency. But after a few years of comparative prosperity in the late twenties, when the Hitler movement seemed to be but a minor nuisance, Germany succumbed to the world-wide depression that began in 1929. Millions of people became permanently unemployed. The well-meaning, unimaginative chancellor, Heinrich Brüning, aggravated the situation by pursuing a policy of ruthless deflation. Stagnation beset almost every branch of industry.

The Nazi vote in elections and the figures of unemployment mounted in parallel columns. There was also a marked rise, on a smaller scale, in the following of the Communists. Hope and confidence in the future evaporated as year after year dragged on with no improvement. Taking as a slogan the title of a popular novel, *Volk ohne Raum,* many Germans began to pity themselves as a "people without room," compelled to expand by force or to stagnate in hopeless poverty.

What has happened in the Federal Republic is a striking contrast, and has, incidentally, knocked into a cocked hat the whole "people without room," "have-not nations" legend. Starting under far less favorable conditions, with almost half of Germany's prewar area lopped off, with a legacy of widespread war destruction, the Federal Republic staged an economic recovery (described in an earlier chapter) which is one of the wonders of the postwar world. Here was the most convincing proof that a high standard of living depends not on space, or physical possession of vast natural resources, or overseas imperial possessions, but on intelligently directed hard work. If there were any doubt of the truth of this proposition one need only look at Switzerland, a landlocked country without colonies or natural resources which still maintains one of the highest living standards in Europe.

It has already been pointed out that overfull employment brings its own troubles, among which the most dangerous is perhaps the threat of creeping inflation. But whatever may be the latent dangers and inconveniences of overfull employment, it does not, like mass unemployment, carry a menace of turning to the desperate remedies of revolution. Chubby, round-faced Economics Minister Erhard, who looks like an Oriental figure of the god of wealth, has confounded Karl Marx. He has proved that a predominantly private enterprise system can provide work for all, with a rising standard of living. One can scarcely imagine a more effective damper for extremist theories, whether of Fascist or Communist origin.

A severe economic depression is a test of stability which Germany's free institutions have not yet been compelled to face. But of this there seems little prospect. The permanent German boom could abate considerably without causing serious unemployment. Such developments as the advance toward a tariff-free European Economic Community and the provision of equipment for economically backward areas of the world open up new prospects for German industrial and commercial energy.

Although Germany, except in the Soviet Zone, did not experience a planned social revolution, there have been social changes since the end of the Second World War that improve the prospect of stability for a republican parliamentary order of things. The Hohenzollern dynasty and the lesser royalties in the smaller German states were swept away by the tide of defeat in 1918. But the former governing class, the landed aristocracy, the bureaucracy, survived with little change and its members, in the majority, were contemptuous, if not actively hostile in their attitude toward the Weimar Republic.

Now the old Prussian Junker class, with its virtues and its faults, has gone. Some of its individual members continue to serve the government in various capacities, but Prussia itself has disappeared from the map; its territory is mostly in the Soviet Zone; the landed estates which furnished a social and economic base of power have been confiscated. Neither Adenauer nor any of his likely successors is a member of this class. The Federal Republic does not have to face the nostalgic inner resistance of a large class of officeholders, government officials, judges, and army officers who look instinctively to a past which seems to them far superior to the present.

And the disappearance of the old Prussian landed aristocracy as a solid cohesive force is not the only social change that makes the political outlook for Germany's second republican experiment more favorable. There is now less direct individual management on an old-fashioned paternalistic basis in industry; there are more new men in this field, and much of the management is in the hands of impersonal boards.

The universities have become less exclusive and less glamorous. Any German youth who can show an *Abitur,* may attend a university. The natural result is that these famous institutions are bursting at the seams with the inflow of new students. The makeup of the student body is more heterogeneous; student life has become more businesslike, less colorful and glamorous, and the atmosphere in academic circles is, in the main, less conservative than it was before the war.

The Germans did not regain free institutions by popular uprising; it seems to require the shock of complete military defeat to overthrow a totalitarian regime. But, in distinct contrast to the Weimar period, a political system based on free elections and the rule of law has had time to strike deep roots without being blighted and withered by extralegal extremist opposition. Perhaps democracy in present-day Germany has won by default, for lack of any practicable alternative. But the important thing is that, as of 1963, it has won, with no visible challenger on the horizon.

One of the unfortunate decisions of the founding fathers of the Weimar Republic was the institution of a strict system of proportional representation for national and local elections. Whatever may be said in theory for proportional representation, it does not make for efficient and responsible working of a parliamentary system. Especially in time of storm and stress, PR makes for the proliferation of small parties which would be unrepresented under a system like the American or British, where the candidate with a plurality is elected. Some of these little parties in Germany were of the freak or crackpot variety and helped to discredit the whole idea of parliamentary government, which had been accompanied by many brakes and restraints under the old imperial system.

In the German parliaments after 1918 there were regularly half a dozen parties of some size, plus up to a dozen little splinter groups. There was no clear mandate for any individual political leader, and the formation of a cabinet, as in France before de Gaulle, involved complicated and sometimes undignified bargaining, or *Kuhhandel* ("cattle trading"), as the Germans contemptuously called it. Frequent changes of administration gave occasion for hostile propaganda to associate democratic parliamentarism with weakness and instability. These charges were more effective because the Germans, on balance, give a higher priority than some other peoples to order and efficiency, as compared with full liberty. Many Germans would rather be well governed than directly self-governed.

Moreover, voting under the Weimar Constitution was not for individual candidates, which would have given the voter more sense of identification with his representative, but for party lists. The rule was: one member in the Reichstag for every 60,000 votes cast. The Bonn Constitution retains an element of proportional representation, but with some healthy modifications. One of the most important of these denies representation in the Bundestag to any party that does not poll five per cent of the total vote or elect three candidates in constituencies. This excludes splinter parties with a negligible vote scattered over the whole country.

Another important new provision of the present constitution makes it impossible to vote a chancellor out of office unless there is a majority for a successor. This rules out the irresponsible negativism which formerly made it possible to pull down a government without agreement as to what should take its place.

Still a third important change is the right of the Supreme Court to declare parties which aim at the violent subversion of the constitutional order illegal. This is a corrective to the unlimited liberty to agitate against free institutions which prevailed under the Weimar Constitution and which enabled Hitler, in the end, to substitute dictatorship for democracy while observing formally constitutional rules. These constitutional changes, combined with the profound alteration in Germany's international position and psychology since the Weimar Republic, explain why the new Germany up to 1963 knew only one chancellor, Konrad Adenauer, whereas between the end of the First World War and the coming into power of Adolf Hitler there were a score of shifts of administration during the fifteen years of the troubled existence of the Republic.

Some Germans believe that Adenauer has dominated the political stage too much and too long. But for a physically and emotionally exhausted people which craved nothing so much as peace and stability, order, and normal living conditions, Adenauer's firm, fatherly, authoritarian hand at the helm of the ship of state was probably much more suitable political therapy than a succession of interparty and intraparty bickerings, with frequent changes of leadership.

Again in contrast to the Weimar period, the trend of German politics now is toward fewer and larger parties. The splinter groups have faded out. Of the three parties represented in the Bundestag the smallest, the Free Democrats, must struggle and maneuver desperately to avoid being squeezed out of existence by its bigger rivals, the CDU and the Social Democrats. Should these two large parties agree on changing the electoral law to eliminate the present element of proportional representation, the Free Democrats might go the way of other small political groupings with are unable to elect any deputies under the present method. And the differences between the CDU and the Social Democrats are much more marginal, more capable of being settled by compromise than the fierce feuds that were fought out against a background of riots and street fighting in the uneasy period between the end of the First World War and the coming to power of Hitler. Again in contrast to that earlier period, Germany today is one of the calmest, most orderly countries in Europe.

New Germany has been called a land without dreams. Perhaps this is a slight exaggeration. The European idea has taken considerable hold on the imagination of young Germans; it is still too soon to say how this may be affected by de Gaulle's move to exclude Great Britain from Europe. There is almost a cult of internationalism, of desire to travel and study in foreign countries. But it is true that Germany, by and large, has forsworn big ideological dreams of all kinds, Marxist, nationalist, racist. The emphasis now is on personal happiness, not on sacrifice for some extrapersonal loyalty, but on enjoying what the affluent society has to offer.

Austria is a German-speaking country and its economic recovery success story is a fairly close replica of Germany's. During a visit to Austria in 1961 I was told of an incident that symbolizes what has happened to "proletarian class consciousness," and this certainly applies to Germany as much as to Austria. Left-wing socialists in a Vienna suburb had renamed a street in honor of Karl Liebknecht, the German revolutionary, who perished in street fighting in Berlin in January, 1919. Now the great problem of the residents on the Karl Liebknechtstrasse is to find some means of easing the pressure of new automobiles, which block both entrances to the street. This reflects the new world of working-class prosperity which Karl Liebknecht, with his Marxist faith, could never have imagined.

There is, perhaps, something a little flat in a "land without dreams," especially if that land, as in the case of Germany, contains so many monuments to ideals of the past, to the medieval Empire, the Church, the free cities, the Reformation, and the Renaissance, in its castles on the Rhine and Danube, its cathedrals and monasteries and steepled Protestant churches, and its town halls, that date far back into the Middle Ages and suggest Hans Sachs and the guilds of old Nürnberg.

The transformation of a war-ruined country into a bigger prosperous equivalent of Switzerland or the Netherlands (an impression that is likely to strike the traveler in present-day Germany) is inevitably somewhat prosaic. Concentration on economic development may account for the fact that the recent German contribution to literature, music, and drama is not as impressive as it was in some of the more creative periods of the past.

But there is the authority of Dr. Samuel Johnson for the proposition that there are few ways in which a man may be so innocently occupied as in making money. It is better for Germany, and for the world, that the younger German generation should be without utopian visions than that it should be obsessed by a dream based on false premises and certain to turn into a nightmare. And, after the necessary underpinning of political stability in freedom and assurance against poverty is built, as a generation comes to maturity free from the inhibitions of the Nazi period and from the effects of the years of collapse and hunger, Germany may be expected to regain its old prominence in the world of cultural creative achievement.

Meanwhile it is no small achievement that the German Federal

Republic seems to have succeeded where the Weimar Republic failed, in bringing ordered freedom to the German people and establishing for Germany close ties with Western Europe and America.

NOTES TO CHAPTER XIII

1 The book is by Fritz René Alleman, *Bonn ist nicht Weimar* (Cologne-Berlin: Kiepenhauer and Witsch, 1956). The author is a Swiss journalist and publicist of many years of experience in Germany. Unfortunately the work is unavailable in an English translation.

2 Many of the disturbances in the months after the end of the war were prompted by hunger, rather than by any clear political objective.

3 It would be accurate to say that practically no Germans, however much opposed to the imperial regime with its militarist tradition, accepted the Treaty of Versailles with wholehearted approval. However, there was a line of division between those who hoped that in time it would be possible to obtain by peaceful negotiation the abolition or alleviation of its more oppressive provisions and an irreconcilable nationalist group that stood for root-and-branch rejection.

4 *Völkische* is an almost untranslatable German word with a connotation of racism and extreme nationalism.

5 Alleman, *op. cit.*, p. 428.

CHAPTER XIV

America and Germany: Allies for Peace

"In a larger sense the United States is here on this continent to stay. So long as our presence is desired and required, our forces and commitments will remain. For your safety is our safety, your liberty is our liberty, and any attack on your soil is an attack on our own. Out of necessity as well as sentiment, in our approach to peace as well as war, our fortunes are one."

PRESIDENT JOHN F. KENNEDY,
speaking at Cologne on June 23, 1963

THE United States and Germany, politically aloof from each other until 1917, enemies in the two great wars of this century, have become partners for peace. Both are members of the NATO alliance, which came into existence to thwart the expansionist drive of Soviet communism. Twice, at the time of the Soviet blockade of West Berlin and during a period of high tension as a result of more recent Soviet threats to West Berlin, the significance of American willingness to risk armed conflict to maintain its treaty obligations has been put to the test.

The only solid cement for an alliance is mutual self-interest. And this exists today between the United States and Germany. American public opinion has generally accepted the proposition that Europe outside the Iron Curtain must be saved from Communist domination. And a glance at the map shows that the key to Europe, geographically and militarily, is the German Federal Republic. Support of Germany's independence is not a sentimental luxury, but an imperative necessity of United States foreign policy.

Recognition of this fact is implicit in the stationing on German soil of about one quarter of America's ground forces, including some of its best-equipped divisions.

At the same time Germany, as almost all Germans realize, is dependent for its security and freedom on the American military guaranty. There is no longer, as there was before the war, a military equilibrium between Germany and the Soviet Union. It is conceivable that a united Europe might create such an equilibrium; but this is an uncertain and, in any case, a very long-term prospect. So, despite occasional German grumbling and voicing of grievances, some justified, others imaginary or exaggerated, the maintenance of a close Washington-Bonn understanding is of vital concern to Germany. This is recognized by the opposition Social Democrats as much as by Adenauer's CDU. Indeed, of the two parties, the Social Democrats approve with fewer reservations the foreign and defense policies of the Kennedy Administration.

Mutual national interest is the basic foundation of an alliance. But historical memories and friendly personal relations help to strengthen America's ties with Great Britain and France. With Germany friendly ties are just beginning to form, after the blight of the Hitler period. The two wars, neither fought on American soil, have not left any especially bitter memories in the United States. Curiously enough, in both conflicts American soldiers came to Europe to fight for France against Germany and in many cases, ended by liking the Germans and cherishing a much cooler feeling toward the French. This was partly because American troops in Germany held for a time the privileged position of occupiers, and partly because Germany, as a more mechanized and modernized country, was easier for Americans to become adapted to.

However, Americans, with few exceptions, have not developed the sense of intimacy, of being almost at home, which a considerable number of Americans feel in England and a smaller number in France. The many elements of the United States inheritance from Britain are too obvious to require emphasis. The Lafayette tradition has not lost all its potency and is kept alive by French skill and address in various forms of cultural propaganda.

From the American Revolution until the First World War political contacts between the United States and Germany were very slight. Germany was a land power with almost exclusively European interests. A latecomer in the colonial field, it acquired some of the less desirable parts of Africa and a modest concession area in China. The United States, following the principles of Washington's Farewell Address and the Monroe Doctrine, limited its political interests to the Western hemisphere until it acquired the Philippines, almost accidentally, after a war with Spain which was touched off in Cuba. With Germany there was no occasion either for conflict or for co-operation.

The American image of Germany was shaped by nonpolitical influences. Baron von Steuben, veteran of the wars of Frederick the Great, supplied a badly needed element of drill, training, and organization to Washington's troops and took his place in the pantheon of foreign friends of the American Revolution, which also includes Lafayette and Kosciusko. Some of the American colonists, especially in Pennsylvania, were members of pacifist German sects.

In the nineteenth century there was a substantial migration to America, from Germany as from other European countries. Some cities in the Midwest, especially Milwaukee, St. Louis, and Cincinnati, took on a considerable German coloration and substantial numbers of Germans settled on the land in Minnesota, Wisconsin, Iowa, and Nebraska. They generally conveyed the impression of being energetic, hardworking, frugal people who helped to develop the United States and benefited themselves in the process.

A political element was injected into this German immigration after the attempt to create a unified Germany with liberal parliamentary institutions in 1848 fizzled out in failure and disillusionment. Among the Germans who quit the Fatherland for political reasons at this time a number became active supporters of Lincoln and fought in the Union armies in the Civil War. Prominent among these was Carl Schurz (1829–1906), soldier, politician, publicist, and author. Schurz started his political career as a Republican, but took a critical independent line on such issues as corruption and hard treatment of the defeated South. Schurz revisited Germany and was received by Bismarck. He told the Iron Chancellor that the American soldier, while less rigorously drilled, would excel the Prussian in resourcefulness and initiative.

In the first half of the nineteenth century the German image in American eyes was that of a nation of poets and thinkers, philosophers and dreamers, a little impractical, but on balance amiable. (The figure of Professor Bhaer, in Louisa M. Alcott's popular stories, was a good embodiment of this conception.) The Germany of that time, broken up into many states, posed no aggressive threat to America.

American reaction to the Franco-Prussian War was limited to intellectual circles and was, in the main, pro-German. The defeat of France was regarded as retribution for the many invasions of Germany by Louis XIV and Napoleon. However, the much more powerful Germany which emerged from this war and the unification of Germans in one state was regarded with mixed feelings. There were, with some exceptions, unfavorable impressions of Kaiser Wilhelm II, with his rare genius for tactless and intemperate speech, and a stereotype developed of the monocled, arrogant, saber-rattling Prussian officer; both the virtues and the faults of the German Junker class were alien to America, with its leveling democratic tradition. At the same time the prestige of the German universities was high; a Ph.D. degree from Berlin, Heidelberg, or Göttingen was a prized asset in American academic life. And German music was a most influential cultural ambassador. At the turn of the century German music was overwhelmingly predominant on American programs, and most conductors of leading orchestras were of German or Austrian origin.

This somewhat mixed image of Germany shifted to a hostile caricature of a nation of villains after the United States entered the First World War. From the beginning American public opinion, apart from German-American and Irish-American pockets of dissent, had been for the most part on the side of the Allies. Apart from the still debatable and debated question of degrees of war responsibility, Great Britain enjoyed a triple advantage in the contest for American public opinion: a common language, a broadly similar political and moral outlook, and superior advantages in communication, thanks to its mastery of the sea and control of other communications. Especially in the region between the Alleghenies and the Rockies there was a fairly strong survival of the old American instinct to "keep out of European wars." But the German declaration of unlimited submarine warfare on January 31, 1917 and the interception and publication of the Zimmermann Note, suggesting to Mexico alliance with Germany and the prospect of recovering California, New Mexico and Arizona, brought majority support for the declaration of war which Congress voted, at President Wilson's request, on April 6, 1917.

Wilson was eager to give the war the character of a crusade against militarism and autocracy,[1] for self-determination (a tricky word which he employed with too few reservations), for a just peace and a League of Nations that would be an instrument of preventing war in the future. These lofty aims were understood and shared by a number of young intellectuals, in Great Britain as well as in the United States. But the American masses, subjected for the first time to the operation of a modern apparatus of war propaganda, responded to more primitive slogans. There was a vociferous pastor who liked to intone: "And I say God damn the Kaiser! And I'm not swearing either!" There were so-called four-minute men, mobile orators who sold Liberty Bonds to an accompaniment of such outbursts as "I'd compare those Huns to snakes, only it would be insulting the snakes."

The word "Hun," first employed in reference to Germans by the Kaiser, in a heated exhortation to German troops who were proceeding to China to help put down the Boxer Rebellion, and quickly applied to the Germans by Allied propaganda, came into general circulation in the United States. A German-born American scholar of strongly anti-Nazi views, looking back at this period remarked a little resignedly: "War propaganda convinced many Americans that Imperial Germany was what Hitler's Germany later became."

Most of this rather synthetic extreme anti-German emotionalism faded away as the war became a memory of the past. It was replaced by fear of the new threat of Soviet communism and by disappointment with the results of the war, which had been oversold as a crusade of good against evil. Some of Wilson's more principled sympathizers were shocked by the divergence between the

President's Fourteen Points and the actual provisions of the Treaty of Versailles. This was one of two main factors (the other, and stronger, was desire to return to America's old position of disengagement in regard to Europe) which influenced the rejection by the Senate of United States participation in the League of Nations.

The decision of the British and French governments to stop payments on their war debts to America after the financial crisis of 1929–33 had led to a suspension of payments of German reparations, and this strengthened the American mood of rather acid disillusionment with what was increasingly regarded as a mistaken intervention in the First World War. An impressive testimonial to the strength and depth of this disillusionment was the elaborate neutrality legislation of the thirties, designed to insure American nonparticipation in any war not caused by direct foreign attack.

American public opinion sympathized with the Weimar Republic in its effort to give Germany a democratic form of government. So there was a reaction of shock and disappointment when Hitler took over power in March, 1933. If some voices were raised in defense of Hitler as a man who brought unity to a disintegrating people and overcame unemployment, these became fainter as the excesses of the Nazi regime at home and its bellicose attitude in foreign affairs became increasingly clear.

Hitler found practically no intellectual defenders in America. At this time Americans who thought of themselves as liberals in many cases maintained a double standard of morals. Justified indignation over offenses against liberty and humanity on the part of Hitler, Mussolini, and lesser dictators was illogically combined with an almost fanatical determination to think, hear, and speak no evil of Josef Stalin's totalitarian rule, then engaged in the perpetration of some of its bloodiest crimes, from the crushing of peasant resistance to collective farming by starvation and mass deportation to the purge of large numbers of veteran Communists.

While Germany under Hitler rapidly lost the credit it had gained under republican institutions, there was no general American desire to rush into a second crusade. United States involvement in the Second World War followed a slow and tortuous course and might have been delayed much longer if the issue had not been abruptly settled by the Japanese attack on Pearl Harbor and Hitler's declaration of war.

This time, during and after the war, American propaganda was more sophisticated. There was less talk of "Huns," unworthy to be called snakes. But the psychology of the ruling group was more vindictive, less farsighted than Wilson's had been. The worst injustices of the Treaty of Versailles were mild compared with the political ferocity and economic insanity of the Morgenthau Plan. There was no recognition by President Roosevelt and his advisers of the existence, under the forced suppression of a totalitarian state, of "another Germany," capable of providing the leadership that would make Germany a partner in the postwar task of assuring the freedom and economic well-being of Europe.

Overtures from leaders of the German underground movement that was to give such a heroic demonstration of its seriousness of purpose on July 20, 1944 were systematically rebuffed. The rational goal of a peace of self-determination with a non-Nazi Germany never seems to have been considered.

Two other failings of American policy makers in the war and early occupation years may also be noted. There was an obstinate refusal to recognize the distinction, familiar to all students of totalitarian states, between a minority of hard-core fanatics, another minority of dedicated opponents, and a majority, disapproving of much of what was going on but lacking the impulse to be heroes and martyrs. Equally obstinate was the refusal to face the facts about the nature and aspirations of Soviet communism, to recognize the danger of permitting another totalitarian tyranny to inherit the power position of the one which was being destroyed. Hence golden political opportunities, such as the seizure of Berlin before the Russians could reach the German capital, were missed.

Against this background it is easy to understand the excesses and mistakes of the first phase of occupation, described in Chapter II. These were gradually stopped and corrected. But the building of new bridges of understanding between the United States and Germany has proceeded rather slowly and has lagged behind the forging of the political and military alliance.

There has been much less contact between Americans and Germans than one might imagine from the unprecedented number of Americans who have been living in Germany for the last two decades as soldiers, diplomats, civilian officials, businessmen, and tourists, with or without a special interest in some aspects of German life. For the majority of Americans resident in Germany live in segregated communities, where special schools, amusement, and social facilities create little replicas of American life. There is little social contact with the Germans.

Even when there has been a frank exchange of views, the result is sometimes a blank wall of mutual noncomprehension. The American often thinks only of what the Germans, under Hitler's rule, inflicted on other peoples; the German is more likely to be mainly concerned with what he or his friends and relatives suffered in bombing raids, or at the hands of the Russians, Poles, and Czechs after the tide turned against the Third Reich. The cruelties that occurred during the Soviet invasion of Germany and the expulsion of Germans from Czechoslovakia and from lands east of the Oder-Neisse frontier line have been little noticed in reports available to Americans, but are very real to most Germans.

And there was an element of naïveté in the expectation of some Americans in the first phase of occupation that individual Germans would feel a deep sense of individual guilt for the concentration camps and other brutalities of the Nazi regime. The German reaction could probably be summed up in one question: Suppose we had known about these things, what could we, as unarmed individuals, have done against a state with unlimited military and police power? To take an analogous situation, the Russian people, as individuals, can scarcely be held responsible for the huge network of slave labor camps under Stalin.

Undoubtedly some Germans go too far in attempts at total self-exculpation. They forget that the Second World War, unlike the First, was the sole responsibility of a German government which had come into power with the enthusiastic support of about half the German people and no effective opposition from the other half. This government soon made itself irremovable—except through a successful conspiracy—by familiar totalitarian methods. If there had been no September 1, 1939, and no June 22, 1941, (the dates of Hitler's invasions of Poland and the Soviet Union) there would, in all probability, have been no unnatural partition of Germany, no streams of pitiable refugees, driven from their homes in historic German land, no offensive Soviet war memorials in Berlin. It is surely now time to recognize that grave mistakes were committed by the governments of the Western powers, both in the political conduct of the war and in the first years of occupation. But these mistakes should not, as sometimes happens, obliterate from the German consciousness recognition that Adolf Hitler was the principal architect of the 1945 debacle and all the national humiliation and individual suffering associated with this debacle.

I once discussed with Frau Annadore Leber [2] a book about the occupation of Germany published by an American author. This work contained some well-justified social and economic criticisms, but suffered from exaggeration, overstatement, and a failure to recognize that the Germans had been in any degree responsible for the hardships they suffered under foreign occupation.

Frau Leber shook her head. "This could be a useful book for Americans," she said, "if it could show them where their policies were mistaken and unsound. But for Germans it is psychologically a bad book, feeding their self pity and making them forget Hitler's primary responsibility."

As it happens, the book sold negligibly in America, but quite well in Germany, indicating that people are more inclined to read what they want to hear than what might be good for them.

The time has long passed when there were any artificial barriers to communication between Americans and Germans. Indeed, the two-way flow of professors and students made possible by the Fulbright programs and by similar grants from the German authorities for the promotion of educational contacts has far exceeded anything of the kind in the past. This has helped to destroy misconceptions on both sides. German visiting students are often impressed by the library and research facilities of the leading American universities and by the larger opportunities for personal contact with professors.

American scholars who give lectures in Bonn, Heidelberg, Hamburg, and other German universities may find some difficulty in adjusting to living conditions in a country where housing is scarce and expensive and household labor-saving devices are not yet as plentiful as in America. (A former advantage of living in Germany, efficient and inexpensive household help, has been vanishing with the overfull employment.) But at least these visiting American professors are not likely to take away an impression of modern German youth as indoctrinated with Nazism.

Chancellor Adenauer has always received a warm welcome when he has appeared at American universities to receive honorary degrees. In fact the venerable Chancellor is probably more universally admired abroad than he is in Germany. His big constructive conceptions in foreign affairs stand out more clearly abroad, while the finesses and tricks in German domestic policy which create some unpopularity at home are little noticed or considered.

Mayor Willy Brandt of West Berlin won an impressive personal success when he delivered two talks on the situation of West Berlin at Harvard, not an institution known for pro-Germanism. The largest auditorium available to the university was filled to the last seat and the number turned away exceeded those admitted. Brandt received repeated standing ovations. No doubt his record as a Social Democrat appealed to some who might have considered the Bonn Government too conservative. And the cause of West Berlin is so clearly rooted in justice and freedom that only the most embittered anti-German could refuse sympathy.

It is difficult to generalize about the American attitude toward Germany today, because there are several currents of public opinion, and these do not all run in the same direction. Of course it is only a minority that is much concerned with the subject, one way or the other.[3]

Undoubtedly, as sensible and realistic Germans recognize, the legacy of Nazism is deep suspicion, merging in some cases into downright aversion on the part of those groups in the American population which feel closely identified with the victims of Hitler's savage racial policy. This is a burden which only time will lighten, although many American Jews have been ready to recognize the profound change which has come over Germany under Adenauer and to acknowledge the constructive achievements of the Federal Republic.[4]

Americans of Polish and Czech extraction are affected by the same considerations. Although most Polish-Americans are strongly anti-Communist, they are, for the most part, inclined to endorse and defend Poland's claim to the Oder-Neisse frontier.

Professors in eastern universities and colleges and people in intellectual professions generally have been somewhat allergic to the Federal Republic. Here, again, it is partly the bad public relations heritage of Nazism that has to be overcome and outlived. Some sociological research on the subject indicates that, of all groups in American society, the intellectuals are most consistently left of center in their views. In this connection it was perhaps noteworthy that a number of college and university polls in 1962 revealed a majority among students for Nixon, among professors for Kennedy. This is not unnatural, because professors often came to maturity in the bleak days of economic depression, when economic radicalism and a one-sided moral indignation against Nazism and fascism (to the exclusion of communism) was fashionable on college campuses. The students, on the other hand, have known only the affluent society.

So there are some forces, affecting public opinion, that are cool, if not antagonistic to the Federal Republic. There are also favorable forces. Among these one may note the American "founding fathers" of the Bonn Republic, men who played important formative roles during the time when Germany was regaining self-government and sovereignty. Prominent figures in this group are former head of Military Government Lucius D. Clay, former High Commissioner John J. McCloy, former Secretary of State Dean G. Acheson, and James B. Conant, first United States ambassador to the Federal Republic.

Conant, although an amateur in diplomacy, won immediate respect in Germany as a distinguished scientist and former president of Harvard University. He carried away a very favorable impression of the new Germany and, with his wife, has delivered many addresses destroying the silly myth that the Federal Republic is run by secret Nazis pulling strings in the background.

All these men feel, with justice, that they contributed appreciably to the rebirth of Germany in freedom and have taken a favorable attitude toward the foreign and domestic policies of the Adenauer Administration. General Clay, especially, enjoys high prestige in Germany.

Quite naturally the land of the "economic miracle" enjoys the esteem of American businessmen. Apart from the growing volume of profitable trade and investment in Germany and the good effect created in financial circles by the resumption of payments of principal and interest on debts virtually repudiated by the Nazi regime, the German economic recovery is a most impressive pragmatic argument for what most businessmen believe in, reliance on competitive private enterprise. The very characteristics of the Federal Republic which excite distrust, if not aversion, in the left-wing intellectual— the tax system more favorable to savings and investment, the membership of many businessmen in the parliamentary group of the governing party, the infrequency of strikes—appeal to the conservative industrialist.

So the state of American public opinion toward Germany is somewhat divided.[5] The influences hostile to Germany have maintained the upper hand in the character of certain books and films. However, the United States government under three administrations has stood by its treaty obligations to defend West Berlin and to recognize only the government of the Federal Republic as representative of Germany.

Official American-German relations since the establishment of the Federal Republic fall into three periods: from the founding of the Republic to its acquisition of sovereign status; from this development until the end of the Eisenhower Administration, and from 1961 until the present time. Of these three stages the second was the calmest and least troubled.

During the time when John Foster Dulles was Secretary of State there was hardly a breath of disagreement between Washington and Bonn. This was partly due to the warmly congenial personal relationship that developed between Dulles and Adenauer. Both were elderly men of conservative outlook; both shared the conviction of a common American-German purpose in fighting communism. And especially in his first years in office, Mr. Dulles found in Bonn a refreshing atmosphere of agreement, after the difficulties and procrastinations which he encountered in Paris on the issue of including Germany in the future project of European defense. There was never any occasion for Mr. Dulles to warn of a possible "agonizing reappraisal" of American-German relations. The United States ambassadors in Bonn, James B. Conant, David Bruce, and Walter Dowling, were all favorably impressed by Adenauer's personality and unswerving devotion to the Western orientation of German foreign policy. The first German ambassador in Washington, Heinz Krekeler, was an unassuming engineer with considerable background of experience in IG Farben, Germany's big chemical concern. In a quiet way he rebuilt many bridges to the American world of business and finance.

It was hardly to be expected that the warm personal relation between Adenauer and Dulles would carry over to a young President with a somewhat different outlook on politics and world affairs. And certain new problems, on which American and German views diverged to some extent, began to appear on the horizon. Among these were the extent and character of aid to underdeveloped countries, the method of conducting negotiations with the Soviet Union on Berlin, and the character of military co-operation between the two countries. Germany is also at least indirectly concerned with the vexing reappraisal of United States policy toward Europe which has been made necessary by General de Gaulle's rejection of British membership in the European Economic Community and his insistence on possessing a national nuclear deterrent.

A clash of personalities, in which there were probably mistakes on both sides, between German Ambassador Grewe and some high officials in the State Department precipitated a tempest in a teapot in the spring of 1962. To keep alive the talks between Washington and Moscow on the Berlin issue was a task of no small difficulty, especially as there was extremely little the United States could honorably concede. The problem was further complicated because the opinions of Bonn and London (which sometimes differed) were sought at all stages of the discussion. Early in 1962 the United States representatives conceived the idea that a thirteen-power highway authority, charged with general supervision over routes of access to Berlin, might smooth the way to agreement. In addition to the four powers directly involved in the Berlin situation, this authority was to include representatives of the Federal Republic, of the "German Democratic Republic," of the municipalities of East and West Berlin, and of some representatives of NATO and of the Soviet bloc.

This scheme was viewed rather distrustfully in Bonn as implying some recognition of the Ulbricht regime and also as weakening the principle of four-power responsibility for maintaining unhampered access to Berlin. Tension was created when Washington abruptly demanded a German comment on the plan within a very short time limit, and it was aggravated when the contents of the project, hitherto kept secret, leaked out in Bonn. This was followed by an intemperately worded note from Washington, accusing the Federal Government of "a breach of confidence," although the precise circumstances of the leak were never clearly established.

The tone of this note, and especially the use of the expression, "breach of confidence," angered Adenauer so much when it came to his knowledge that he was dissuaded with some difficulty from declaring the communication unacceptable. It required some expert diplomatic footwork on the part of Ambassador Dowling in Bonn, and later of Secretary Rusk during a visit to the German capital, to soothe the Chancellor's offended dignity and restore relations to a more normal temperature.

Meanwhile personal relations between Grewe and some of the officials with whom he dealt in Washington steadily worsened. Before his appointment as Ambassador to the United States, Grewe had been the legal expert of the Ministry of Foreign Affairs; he had resigned his chair as professor of international law in the University of Freiburg to enter the diplomatic service. With this background he was naturally very sensitive to fine points of law, and perhaps unconsciously developed the habit of returning "position papers" submitted by the State Department annotated with critical reservations and objections, such as he might have noted on the term papers of his students. Matters finally reached such a pass that Adenauer decided Grewe's usefulness in Washington was ended and replaced him with Hans Heinrich von Knappstein, a former liberal journalist who had served with the German observer delegation at the United Nations.[6] Grewe received another important appointment as German ambassador to NATO.

This end of his mission was unfortunate, because Dr. Grewe was a man of exceptional ability and knowledge of international affairs, devoted to his country and to the cause of the Western alliance. It may be, however, that he was somewhat miscast as a diplomat. At least this was the judgment of one observer who had an inside view of the passing storm:

"Dr. Grewe is a very able public servant. But he did not seem to grasp the point that the function of an ambassador is to conciliate differences, not exacerbate them. If an ambassador must report his own government's disagreement with the government to which he is accredited, his normal procedure is to take the line: 'I presented your position as well as I could; my government, however, is unable to agree.' But in situations of this kind Grewe was apt to take an 'I told you so' attitude that ruffled feathers instead of smoothing them down."

The American-German alliance is unbalanced in the sense that Germany is obviously the weaker partner; and this leads to psychological dangers on each side. There is a German tendency, which Washington sometimes finds irritating, to ask over and over again for assurances and reassurances on points where the American attitude, in Washington's judgment, has been made abundantly clear. On the American side there is a temptation to override German objections too brusquely, to take rather lightly the natural sensitiveness in Bonn to such a vital German interest as avoiding any appearance of accepting or sanctioning the partition of Germany.

A somewhat sour joke, long current in Bonn, is that the United States, Great Britain, and France would like to see a German army strong enough to cope with the Soviet Union, but too weak to resist tiny Luxembourg. Like most political jokes, this contains an element of obvious exaggeration. Yet in British and to a less degree in American thinking about Germany there is an element of schizophrenia that may lead to trouble if it is not recognized and cured.

There is a desire, perhaps unconscious, to have one's cake and eat it too, to expect Germany to take the risks of an ally while being subject to the restraints of a protectorate. Here is perhaps the basic issue not only in American-German, but in Western-German relations. Is the German Federal Republic a full-fledged ally of America, Great Britain, and France, sharing equally in the rights, risks, and responsibilities of the NATO association? Formally the answer is certainly yes.

The German Federal Republic has cast in its lot with the West, has resisted the temptation to experiment with neutralism and seek to play East against West, and has built up from scratch what is now probably the strongest armed force on the European continent, apart from the United States Seventh Army in Germany. Although France, once the strongest opponent of German rearming, has now become a staunch supporter of this move, thinking in Great Britain and in the United States has not always kept pace with the transformation of Germany from a defeated enemy into a valued ally. Especially in Great Britain, one finds in some circles of public opinion (not in the British government) a positively morbid obsession with the idea that the threat to peace comes not from the Soviet Union, but from Germany.

The baiting of Germany is notably popular among left-wing Labourites, who, along with incurable softness in regard to the aims of the Soviet Union, are unable to forgive Germany for a brilliant economic recovery achieved by a conspicuous disregard of such Socialist dogmas as nationalization and economic planning. An example of expressed anti-Germanism on the part of a man who will presumably become prime minister of Great Britain if the Labour Party wins the next election is this statement made in a parliamentary debate early in 1963 by Mr. Harold Wilson:

"We are completely, utterly, and unequivocally opposed, now and in all circumstances, to any suggestion that Germany, West Germany or East Germany, directly or indirectly, should have a finger on the nuclear trigger or any responsibility, direct or indirect, for deciding that nuclear weapons are to be used."

Since the German Federal Republic is a member of NATO and is particularly entitled to a consultative voice on the use of nuclear weapons because of its common frontier with the Communist world,

Mr. Wilson's statement, to put it mildly, did not reveal a very high level of statesmanship. It was quite as divisive and disruptive as any of General de Gaulle's pronouncements. An ally not treated as an ally may not remain in that position, and the defense of Europe against communism, surely a common interest of the United States and Great Britain, would be impossible without German co-operation.

Among appeasers and unilateral disarmers in all Western countries there is a kind of distrust of Germany as the country where, as a result of Soviet pressure, war might break out. American public opinion is more conditioned to the view of Germany as an ally than is British. But here, too, books and movies that keep alive the horrors of the Nazi period keep alive a certain amount of distrust. One prominent political personality gave circulation to a story that West Germans make pilgrimages to the bunker where Hitler perished, apparently oblivious of the fact that this bunker is in East Berlin and hence out of bounds to West Germans since the erection of the Berlin Wall.

President Kennedy has repeatedly reassured Chancellor Adenauer as to the firmness of the United States position on West Berlin. But some of his replies in an interview granted to Khrushchev's son-in-law Aleksei Adzhubei, the editor of *Izvestia,* were not calculated to excite enthusiasm in Bonn and West Berlin. For instance, the President conceded to the Soviet Government a permanent veto on the unification of Germany when he said: "We recognize that today the Soviet Union does not intend to permit reunification, and that, as long as the Soviet Union has that policy, Germany will not be reunited."

Of course it may be said that this is merely realism, since the United States obviously has no intention of going to war to enforce German reunification. But the subject is so sensitive in Germany that a blunt statement of this kind is in the nature of shock treatment. The President also said: "I would be extremely unwilling to see West Germany acquire a nuclear capacity of its own."

If Great Britain possesses that capacity and France is working to achieve it, why should Germany, if it is a full treaty partner and ally, be excluded from the company of nuclear powers?

Proverbially anyone who tries to sit between two stools gets a hard fall between them. The idea of treating the German Federal Republic not as an equal ally, but as an auxiliary protectorate with second-rate military status becomes less feasible with every year as German economic strength, political stability, and national self-confidence become stronger.

Symptomatic of the basic unity of German public opinion on foreign affairs was the general agreement between spokesmen for the three leading parties in a Bundestag debate early in December, 1961. Christian Democrats, Social Democrats, and Free Democrats took the same position in supporting the maintenance of allied garrisons and the security of West Berlin's communications and against recognition of the Ulbricht regime in the Soviet Zone. They were equally categorical in rejecting the idea of severing West Berlin's ties with the Federal Republic.

Should there be any attempt to force on the Federal Republic any plan for a settlement with the Soviet Union that would suggest a Munich for the Western position, the consequences for America's policy of holding the front in Europe would be disastrous. So long as West Germany is treated as an ally, its bond of interdependence with America and the West is unbreakable. Give the Germans a feeling that they have been let down and all sorts of wild schemes for dealing separately with Moscow might gain a popular response. And the heart would go out of Germany's essential co-operation in NATO.

As the American international balance of payments worsened in the late fifties and early sixties, there was a disposition in Washington to look critically at comparative German expenditures in such fields as military appropriations and aid to underdeveloped countries. Germany has tried to meet these criticisms by repaying a good deal of its debt to America ahead of time, thereby relieving the strain on the dollar, by placing sizable orders for arms in the United States, and by increasing its outlay on foreign aid to about $750 million annually.

Probably the biggest issue between America and Germany, and indeed, between America and Europe, concerns the organization, control, and direction of nuclear weapons. The American view, which is probably sound from a strictly technical military standpoint, is that the United States, with a stock of atomic weapons sufficient to destroy the Soviet Union several times over, should be the nuclear arsenal of the alliance. Therefore European national nuclear weapons systems are superfluous and may be positively harmful, insofar as they may increase the danger of war by accident or may be a provocation to Soviet attack. In any event such systems are likely to be too weak to possess any decisive influence, even as deterrents. European military resources, in the American view, could be most profitably devoted to building up conventional forces to counter any Soviet attempt to commit aggression without resort to atomic weapons.

But there are political and psychological reasons which make many Europeans, of whom General de Gaulle is the powerful and articulate spokesman, unwilling to accept this division of military labor. No matter how formidable the United States nuclear arsenal may be, or how impressive is the demonstration of American good faith in stationing such a large contingent of its military forces in Germany, the front-line area of Europe's defense, a nagging suspicion persists in Paris and Bonn and London that, confronted with the grim threat of Soviet nuclear devastation of America's large cities, some future American government might resort to appeasement and isolationism, leaving Europe in the lurch.

The fears and objections which a purely national build-up of nuclear weapons would arouse are generally recognized in Germany, and few Germans desire this. What almost all Germans would like, however, is a more effective voice in deciding when, where, and how nuclear weapons should be used. It is widely believed that the NATO Council and its standing military committee are shadowy organizations without real consultative functions. Most German Social Democrats would be content with an expansion of the power and authority of these NATO bodies.

Some Germans would go further. They would like to see Germany as a partner in a European deterrent which, in a desperate emergency, could be used independently of the United States. Just whose finger would press the button in such an arrangement has never been very clearly spelled out. The proposals which American diplomat Livingston Merchant took to various European capitals in February-March, 1963, providing for a "European deterrent" based on a system of mixed crews and missiles on surface ships, and with an American veto, definitely did not satisfy the European desire for a last-resort form of nuclear security. Such an arrangement seemed militarily useless because of its extreme vulnerability to Soviet air attack, and little seems likely to come of it.

An American-German agreement that would strengthen the defense of Europe might take the form of a concession by each country to the viewpoint of the other. Germany could accelerate the build-up of its present establishment to and perhaps beyond the agreed maximum figures of 500,000 men in the three branches of the service. The United States, at the same time, might make tactical nuclear weapons available, without restriction, to the Bundeswehr. There is a good deal of truth in the saying attributed to plain-speaking former Defense Minister Strauss that when there is a tactical weapon in the knapsack of every West German soldier, the danger of Soviet aggression will be ended.

The often expressed American fear of the proliferation of nuclear weapons seems beside the point, because it is based on the false assumption that it is within the power of the United States, or the Soviet Union, or both together, to prevent other powers which possess the necessary resources and scientific capability from joining the nuclear club. This is simply not true. The United States cannot prevent General de Gaulle from creating his independent nuclear striking force. Nikita Khrushchev cannot stop Communist China from developing a nuclear weapons system. Since the United States cannot, except by waging a preventive war, divert the rulers of an enemy power, Red China, from developing nuclear weapons, it is hard to understand why there should be so much fear of sharing nuclear weapons with friendly allied powers.

The rift which opened in the Atlantic Alliance when General de Gaulle vetoed British membership in the European Economic Community finds Germany somewhere in the middle, unwilling to make a choice between America and France, anxious to retain both the American alliance and the advantages of the Common Market and the reconciliation with France. There are divergences of emphasis in German public opinion, in the German Government itself.

Chancellor Adenauer, who has sometimes displayed a little suspicion of British firmness in facing up to the Soviet Union, attaches a higher priority to a close special understanding with France than his most probable successor, Economics Minister Erhard. Erhard, a convinced free trader, was shocked and disappointed by the rejection of Great Britain. But the probability is that the German Government, under Adenauer and after Adenauer, will cling to the American alliance while retaining the advantages of the European Economic Community and the close contacts with France which Adenauer has hailed as marking the end of "four centuries of conflict." It seems likely that German pressure for some kind of economic association of Great Britain with continental Europe and for lowering the external tariff wall around the EEC will be stepped up after Adenauer quits the political scene.

Whatever flaws and fissions the strong-willed insistence of General de Gaulle on French independence in national defense may introduce into the structure of the Atlantic Alliance, it is interesting and significant that for the first time in history, the United States, Great Britain, France, and Germany are allies in a common cause.

It is interesting, if perhaps futile, to reflect how the course of history might have been changed—probably for the better—if there had been a three-power understanding among the United States, Great Britain, and Germany about 1900, when German foreign policy was fluid and Great Britain had not allied herself with France. The basis of such an understanding might have been maintenance of the British Empire and of the United States' paramount position in the Western hemisphere, and recognition for Germany and its ally Austria of a field of industrial and commercial expansion in the Near and Middle East. Any such possibility, if it ever really existed, has long been outpaced by the movement of events.

In very changed circumstances America and Germany find themselves on the same side in international politics. And friendship and understanding between the two peoples should be advanced by the disappearance in Germany of some things that were alien to United States experience and sympathy. Gone forever is the aristocratic pomp and splendor of the German Empire. Prussia, with standards far removed from those in America, has disappeared from the map of Europe, and the Prussian influence on German life and character has much diminished. German everyday life has in many ways become Americanized, partly because of the effects of occupation and travel interchange, partly because industrialism is producing similar effects in many countries.

Blue jeans are now accepted dress for German young women. "OK" is often heard in the midst of a conversation in German. Turn on the radio in a German hotel and one is more apt to get jazz than Beethoven. The cult of Coca Cola and of the snack bar has made a considerable advance. The reserve of peasant maids that lent ease and leisure to German middle-class life has almost disappeared because of overfull employment. Consequently the German household, except in the case of the very well-to-do, is like the American, on a "do-it-yourself" basis.

Similar changes may be noted in other European countries. Moreover, the Germans since the end of the war have become more malleable, more open to foreign influence. One meets a surprising number of young German diplomats who have American and British wives. A German journalist offered this footnote on the element of more or less conscious imitation of American ways:

"Germans have always imitated what seemed to them the leading foreign power. When France occupied that position, in the seventeenth and eighteenth centuries, every little German prince wanted to build his miniature Versailles. It was the fashion in the nineteenth century to adopt British manners. Now it is the turn of America."

In the nineteenth century, when Anglo-German relations were at their best—as the two countries still looked on France as a common enemy—the British novelist Edward Bulwer-Lytton dedicated one of his works to "the great German people." More recently General de Gaulle used this expression in addressing cheering throngs in Hamburg, Munich, and other German cities. Perhaps the time has not come when all Americans can associate themselves wholeheartedly with this tribute, although the quality of greatness is surely not lacking in a people that produced Goethe and Schiller,

Beethoven and Wagner, Ranke and Mommsen, Planck and Helm-holtz—and the heroes and martyrs of the conspiracy against Hitler.

However, the prospect for increasing friendship and mutual understanding between America and Germany is favorable. The expansion and the continuing threat of Soviet communism has produced one good effect: there is no longer the possibility of fratricidal war among the Euro-American heirs of the Judeo-Christian and Greco-Roman spiritual and cultural heritage. There will never again be a third American-German war, as there will be no more Anglo-German or Franco-German conflicts.

One may hope that, as American-German contacts multiply, in letters and arts, in scholarship and sport, in business and military training, both nations will become pillars of the great Euro-American community of free peoples which, despite all difficulties and setbacks, seems to be an achievement marked out for the twentieth century.

NOTES TO CHAPTER XIV

1 This was easier because the Tsarist Empire, most autocratic of the main powers involved in the war, collapsed on March 12, 1917.

2 See page 253 for characterization of Frau Leber.

3 German-born professor of history at Brown University, Klaus Epstein, contributed a very fair estimate of pro- and anti-German influences on American public opinion to a supplement of the German magazine, *Parlament,* of November 21, 1962.

4 A very thoughtful, objective appraisal of Adenauer's achievement in giving a pro-Western orientation to German foreign policy may be found in Hans Kohn, *The Mind of Germany* (New York: Charles Scribner's Sons, 1960), pp. 343–354.

5 A study conducted by the Survey Research Center of the University of Michigan on the attitude of Americans toward West Germany in May-June, 1962 showed that favorable reactions toward West Germany exceeded unfavorable by four to one. Three out of five questioned believe that Germany can be relied on if the United States gets into trouble with the Soviet Union; one out of six expresses a contrary opinion. About two thirds favored a unified Germany, four times the proportion who believe that Germany should be kept divided; 69 per cent are in favor of trying to keep East Germany from taking West Berlin, as against 6 per cent who would acquiesce. By and large this

survey is more optimistic about United States feeling toward Germany than are the impressions of Professor Epstein.

6 There is no direct German representation in the United Nations because of the division of the country. The Soviet Union would veto the admission of the Federal Republic unless the "German Democratic Republic" were also admitted; and this, of course, would be entirely contrary to the policy of Bonn and the Western Allies.

Bibliography

The following list of books falls far short of being a complete bibliography on the German Federal Republic. It includes the works which I found most helpful for reference and information and which in some cases give more expanded treatment to the subjects I have discussed in preceding chapters.

ALLEMAN, FRITZ RENÉ, *Bonn ist nicht Weimar* (Cologne-Berlin: Kiepenheuer and Witsch, 1956).

ALTMANN, RÜDIGER, *Das Erbe Adenauers* (Stuttgart: Seewald, 1960).

Bestands-aufnahme: Eine deutsche Bilanz 1962 (Munich: Kurt Desch).

BULLOCK, ALAN, *Hitler: A Study in Tyranny* (New York: Harper & Row, Publishers, 1952).

CHURCHILL, WINSTON, *Triumph and Tragedy* (Boston: Houghton Mifflin Company, 1953).

CLAY, LUCIUS D., *Decision in Germany* (Garden City, N.Y.: Doubleday & Company, Inc., 1950).

DAVIDSON, EUGENE, *The Death and Life of Germany* (New York: Alfred A. Knopf, Inc., 1959).

Divo-Institut, *Umfragen, Band 3/4* (Frankfurt: Europäische Verlag).

DULLES, ALLEN WELSH, *Germany's Underground* (New York: The Macmillan Co., 1947).

EPSTEIN, KLAUS, *Matthias Erzberger and the Dilemma of German Democracy* (Princeton, N.J.: Princeton University Press, 1959).

ERHARD, LUDWIG, *Prosperity Through Competition* (New York: Frederick A. Praeger, Inc., 1958).

300 / BIBLIOGRAPHY

ERHARD, LUDWIG, *Deutsche Wirtschaftspolitik* (Düsseldorf: Econ Verlag, 1962).

EYCK, ERICH, *A History of the Weimar Republic* (Cambridge, Mass.: Harvard University Press, 1962).

FLENLEY, RALPH, *Modern German History* (New York: E. P. Dutton & Co., Inc., 1959).

FREUND, GERALD, *Germany Between Two Worlds* (New York: Harcourt, Brace & World, Inc., 1961).

Das geistige Bild der Studenten (Bonn: Akademischer Verlag).

Germany Reports (Bonn: Press and Information Department of the Federal Government, 1953).

GISEVIUS, HANS B. *To The Bitter End* (Boston: Houghton Mifflin Company, 1947).

GREWE, WILHELM G., *Deutsche Aussenpolitik der Nachkriegszeit* (Stuttgart: Deutsche Verlag).

HANKEY, MAURICE PASCAL ALERS, *Politics, Trials and Errors* (Oxford: Pen-In-Hand, 1950).

HEIDENHEIMER, ARNOLD J., *Adenauer and the CDU* (The Hague: Martinus Nijhoff, 1960).

HILGER, GUSTAV, AND MEYER, ALFRED G., *The Incompatible Allies* (New York: The Macmillan Co., 1953).

HORNE, ALISTAIR, *Return to Power* (New York: Frederick A. Praeger, Inc., 1956).

HUBERTUS, PRINZ ZU LOEWENSTEIN, AND VON ZÜHLSDORFF, VOLKMAR, *Verteidigung des Westens* (Bonn: Atheneum Verlag).

KOHN, HANS, *The Mind of Germany* (New York: Charles Scribner's Sons, 1960).

LEONHARD, WOLFGANG, *Child of the Revolution* (Chicago: Henry Regnery Co., 1958).

MANN, GOLO, *Deutsche Geschichte des neunzehnten und zwanzigsten Jahrhunderts* (Frankfurt: S. Fischer, 1958).

MEISSNER, BORIS, *Russland, die Westmächte und Deutschland* (Hamburg: H. H. Nölke Verlag).

MOESSINGER, MARIO, *Zweifel an Europa* (Stuttgart: Seewald, 1961).

MORGENTHAU, HENRY, *Germany Is Our Problem* (New York: Harper & Row, Publishers, 1945).

NETTL, J. P. *The Eastern Zone and Soviet Policy in Germany, 1945–50* (London: Oxford University Press, 1951).

PRITTIE, TERENCE, *Germany Divided* (Boston: Little, Brown & Co., 1960).

ROBSON, CHARLES A., ed., *Berlin: Pivot of German Destiny* (Chapel Hill, N. C.: University of North Carolina Press, 1960).

ROTHFELS, HANS, *The German Opposition to Hitler* (Chicago: Henry Regnery Co., 1948).

SBZ von A-Z (Bonn: Deutsche Bundes-Verlag).

SOLBERG, RICHARD W., *God and Caesar in East Germany* (New York: The Macmillan Co., 1961).

STAHL, WALTER, ed., *Education for Democracy in West Germany* (New York: Frederick A. Praeger, Inc., 1961).

STOLPER, WOLFGANG F., *The Structure of the East German Economy* (Cambridge, Mass.: Harvard University Press, 1960).

ZINK, HAROLD, *The United States in Germany, 1944–1955* (New York: D. Van Nostrand Co., Inc., 1957).

BIBLIOGRAPHY 312

Index

Acheson, Dean G., 284
Adenauer, Konrad ("Der Alte"), 56, 88, 93–108, 270–71, 283
  Berlin policy, 95
  criticisms of regime, 212–13, 214, 255–56
  and domestic politics, 96–98
  election as Chancellor, 58, 96
  foreign policy, 96
  personality and leadership characterized, 101–8
  retirement and question of successor, 98, 106, 112–27
  See also Federal Republic, West Germany
Adzhubei, Aleksei, 290
Alden, Robert, quoted, 139
Altmayer, Jacob, 244
American Committee for Liberation, 190
Anti-Semitism, 24, 243–44, 258
Association of Free Jurists, 135
Atlantic Bridge, 188
Augstein, Rudolf, 97
Automobile industry, 75, 80–83

Bad Godesberg, 181
Bad Homburg, 195–96
Balance of payments:
  United States, 291
  West Germany, 74–75, 92
Bavaria, 57, 188
Bayreuth, 191–92
Beitz, Berthold, quoted, 88–89
Berlin, 33–34, 156–78
  Adenauer policy on, 95

  in an all-German peace settlement, 171–73, 177
  East and West compared, 159
  election of 1946, 132–33
  housing and construction in, 138
  See also East Berlin, West Berlin
Berlin wall (1961), 55, 96, 130, 137, 145, 150, 158
  construction, 175–76
  effect of, 167–68
  escapes, 163–64
Bernstein, Bernard, quoted, 39
Billiards at Half Past Nine (book), 210
Birrenbach, Kurt, 87, 110
  quoted, 89
Blank, Theodore, 232
Blockstein, Peter, 244
Blumenfeld, Erik, 187
Böll, Heinrich, 210
Bonn, 58, 95
  description, 179–82
Brandenburg Gate (West Berlin), 160
Brandt, Willy, 58, 97, 107, 158, 168, 203, 283
  characterization of, 119–21
  quoted, 167–68
Brauer, Max, 77, 185
Brenner, Otto, 90
Brentano, Heinrich von, 114, 117
Bruce, David, 286
Brussels Treaty, 223
Bucher, Ewald, 123–24
Bulganin, Nikolai, 149
Bundesrat (Federal Republic), 55

Bundestag (Federal Republic), 55, 96
  Social Democrats in, 119
Byrnes, James F., 50–51

Chemical industry, 76, 86
Child of the Revolution (book), 183
Choninski, Col. W. J., 228
Christ und Welt (periodical), 192, 217
Christian Democratic Union Party (CDU), 57, 58, 65, 97, 99, 100, 104
  characterization of, 110–11
  effect of Berlin wall on votes, 256
  present status, 118–19
Churchill, Winston, 61, 130
  quoted, 79, 220
Clark, Gen. Bruce, 231
Clay, Gen. Lucius, 43, 51, 53, 54, 60–61, 72, 83, 176, 284, 285
Coal, 83, 85
Coal and Steel Community, 61
Cologne, description, 182–84
Communism in West Germany to-day, 263–65
Communist Party:
  in East Germany, 132
  in West Berlin, 56, 158
  in West Germany, 57–58, 124
Conant, James B., 284, 286
Conrad, Bernt, quoted, 216
Construction industry, 78
Cost of living, 73
  East and West Germany compared, 138
Council of Europe, 63
Currency, 52, 75, 92

Democracy, definition, 262
Democratic Republic (DDR), 129–45
  foreign relations and diplomatic recognition, 150–51
  formation and developments in, 134–36
  See also East Germany
Denazification, 38–43
Dibelius, Bishop Otto, 214–15
Dillon, Douglas C., 174

Doenhoff, Marion, 188, 214
Dowling, Walter, 286, 287
Dufhues, Josef Hermann, 113
  characterization of, 116–17
Dulles, Allen W., 43
Dulles, John Foster, 285–86
Düsseldorf, 85
  description, 184–85

East Berlin:
  contrast with life in West Berlin, 159, 160
  postwar reconstruction, 158–59
  revolt (1953), 129–30, 135
  See also Berlin, Berlin wall, West Berlin
East Germany:
  borders, 130–31, 135, 138
  collectivization and co-operatives, 135, 136–37
  education and schools in, 135, 136
  food shortages in, 136–37
  migrations from, 130, 135, 136, 161–63
  People's Police (*Volkspolizei*), 142, 159, 245
  political parties in, 132–33
  religion in, 135–44, 216
  See also Democratic Republic
Economic development:
  Germany, Marshall Plan, 74, 79
  West Germany, 68–92
Eden, Anthony, 147
Education:
  in East Germany, 135, 136
  in West Germany, 203–4, 205–8, 269
    Nazism in curriculum, 252, 253–4
Eichmann, Adolf, 251
Eisenhower, Dwight D., 174
  quoted, 105, 131
Eisler, Gerhart, 39
Erhard, Ludwig, 57, 71, 72, 88, 94, 99, 106, 203, 219, 267
  as Chancellor-Elect, 125–26
  characterization of, 112–13
  quoted, 68, 71, 88
Erler, Fritz, 100
  characterization of, 121–22

Essen, 78, 83
Etzel, Fritz, 98–99
Eucken, Rudolf, 72, 207
European Defense Community, 62, 64, 223
European Economic Community (EEC), 61, 91, 185, 269
European Payments Union (EPU), 74

Fay, Sidney B., quoted, 255
Federal Republic (*Bundesrepublik*):
  aid to West Berlin, 165, 166
  Chancellor, successors to Adenauer, 112–27; *see also* Adenauer, Konrad
  comparison with Weimar Republic, 260–73
  constitution, legislature, and courts, 55–56, 270
  criticisms of, as non-democratic, 212–13, 224, 255–56
  elections:
    1949, 57
    1953, 59
    1957, 96
    1961, 112
  foreign policy and relations, 200
    France, 293–94
    United Kingdom, 289–90
    United States, 274–96 *passim;* summary, 285–88
  and high commissioners, 59–67
  payment of foreign debts, 64
  political parties in, 109–27
  pro-Western attitude, 200–1
  Spiegel affair, *Der,* 97–98
  See also Adenauer, Konrad; West Germany
Federation of Trade Unions, 89, 90
Fine, Benjamin, quoted, 254
Fischer, Fritz, 217
Foertsch, Gen. Friedrich, 230
France, relations with West Germany, 66, 94–95, 234, 293–94
Fränkel, Wolfgang I., 248
Frankfurt-on-Main, 33
  description, 194–96
Frankfurter Allgemeine Zeitung (newspaper), 195, 214, 217

Free Democratic Party (FDP), 57, 58, 65, 97, 109
  characteristics of, 123–34
Free Europe Committee, 190
"Free German Youth," 143
Freeman, Gen. Paul L., 230–31
Friedrich, Otto, 87
Fürstenfeldbruck, 228
Furtwängler, Wilhelm, 40

Garmisch-Partenkirchen, 191
Gaulle, Charles de, 62, 66, 94–95, 234, 236, 286
German Party, 57–58
German Peace Union Party, 58
Germans as militarists, 254–55
Germany:
  annexation of territory by Poland and Soviet Union, 152–53
  anti-German campaign, 256–58
  comparison, after World War I and today, 261–66
  denazification after World War II, 38–43
  division of, 128–54
  economic recovery after World War II, 51–52
    Long Term Program, 79
  future of, discussion, 151–52
  history, 3–29
  military governments and occupation after World War II, 30–47, 56, 280
    American, 36–43, 45–47
    Russian, 43–45
  Nazism as a present-day force, question of, 241–58
  political developments after World War II, 49–67
  refugees in, 69–70
  religion, 215–16
  resistance movement under Hitler, 252–53, 280
  reunification proposals, 129, 145–50
    Berlin as a part of, 173–74
  zonal borders, 130, 131, 135, 153
  See also Democratic Republic, East Germany, Federal Republic, West Germany

Gerstenmeier, Eugen, 43, 102
  characterization of, 117
Gisevius, Hans Bernd, 43
Globke, Hans, 246–47
Grass, Günther, 210
Grewe, Wilhelm, 286–88
  quoted, 149
Gromyko, Andrei, 173
Grotewohl, Otto, 44, 134
Group 47, 211–12
Grundig, Max, 84–85
Güde, Max, quoted, 249
Guttenberg, Baron Karl von, 112,
  151–52

Hallstein doctrine, 150–51
Hamburg, 34, 77, 165
  description, 185–88
Harich, Wolfgang, 133–34
Hassel, Kai-Uwe von, 98, 232
  characterization of, 117–18
Haugen, Gen. Victor L., 232
Hayek, Friedrich A., 207
Henle, Günther, 87, 110
Herter, Christian, 174
Hesse, 57, 196–97
Heusinger, Gen. Adolf, 223
Heuss, Theodor, 102
Hilger, Gustav, quoted, 148
Hitler, Adolf, 22–28
  assassination attempt on, 252–53
  responsibility for World War II,
  255
  See also Nazism
Hoffman, Johannes, 65
Hoover, Herbert, 51
Housing and building construction,
  77–78, 88
  in East Germany, 138
Hrabak, Col. Dietrich, 228
Hull, Cordell, 32
Hungary, 1956 revolt, 224

IG Farben, 76, 86
Income:
  national, 76
  personal, 77
Industry and industries, 79–90
  dismantling program, postwar
  Germany, 70–71, 133

East Germany, 141
West Germany:
  factory management, 90
  rate of growth, 75, 79, 188
  See also names of individual industries
Israel, indemnity from Federal Republic, 64, 101, 244

Jews:
  reparations to, 64, 101, 244
  in West Germany, 244
Johnson, Uwe, 210–11
Joint Export and Import Agency, 49
Jugendweihe, 143–44

Kaiser, Jacob, 104
Karajan, Herbert von, 210
Katzer, trade unionist, 110
Kennedy, John F., 175, 290
  quoted, 274
Khrushchev, Nikita, 171–75
  See also Union of Soviet Socialist
  Republics
Kiesinger, Prime Minister, 192, 193
Kirkpatrick, Sir Ivone, 101, 246
Klausener, Mgr. Erich, 251
Knappstein, Hans Heinrich von, 288
Koblenz, 226
Korean War, 61, 74, 222
"Kraft durch Freude," 27, 81, 82
Krekeler, Heinz, 286
Krone, Heinrich, 103, 110, 113
  characterization of, 117
Krupp, Alfried, 42–43, 83–84
Kuby, Erich, 212, 213

Labor, 87–88
Leber, Mrs. Annadore, 253, 282
Leipzig, 139
Lemnitzer, Gen. Lyman, 238
Leonhard, Wolfgang, 183–84
  quoted, 132–33
Leopold, Kurt, quoted, 169
Leuschner, Bruno, 141
Lilje, Hanns, quoted, 216
Lochner, Robert, 170
Lübke, Heinrich, 99
Ludwigsburg Center, 192–93, 218,
  250

McCloy, John J., 56, 60, 284
McNamara, Robert, 235, 236
Malmédy case, 41–42, 43
Mann, Golo, 151–52
Mannesmann (steel and coal), 85
Mende, Erich, 97, 109, 123
Merchant, Livingston, 293
Metal Workers Union, 90
Mewis, Karl, 141
Mezière, Gen. Ulrich de, 226–27
Mikoyan, Anastas, 172
Monetary reform, post-World War II, 52
Morgenthau, Henry, Jr., 31
Morgenthau Plan, 31–32, 280
Muenemann, Rudolf, 85–86
Munich, 86
  description, 188–92
Münster, 230

National Socialist Party (Nazis), 22, 25
  postwar denazification, 38–43
Naumann, Werner, 101, 246
Nazism and Nazis:
  ex-Nazis in public office, 245–49
  punishment or escape of war criminals, 250–54
  question of, as a force in West Germany today, 241–58
  remnants, 241–45
Neumann, Alfred, 141
Neumayer, Fritz, 37
Nevermann, Mayor of Hamburg, 186
Nordhoff, Heinz, 80–83
Norstad, Gen. Lauris, 238
North Atlantic Treaty Organization (NATO), 128, 149, 173, 223, 230, 232, 236, 237, 239
  West German membership in, 65
Nuclear arms and power, 233–36, 289–90, 292–93
Nürnberg Trials, 42

Oberammergau, 191
Oberländer, Theodor, 246
Oder-Neisse Boundary, 212, 281, 284
Oelssner, Friedrich, 134
Ollenhauer, Erich, 58

Organization for European Economic Co-operation (OEEC), 60

People's Police (East Germany), 142, 159, 245
Pferdmenges, Robert, 104, 110
Pieck, Wilhelm, 43, 143
Pleven, René, 62
Plittersdorf, 181
Poland, 212, 264
  annexation of German territory, 152–53
Political parties:
  East Germany, 132–33
  West Germany, 57, 110, 124, 271
  See also names of individual parties
Potsdam Declaration, 32–33, 50
Preysing, Cardinal Konrad von, 247
Production, industrial:
  East Germany, 140
  West Germany, 73
    1962 statistics on, 91–92
Prussia, 11–14

Question 7 (film), 143, 209

Radio broadcasting:
  Free Europe Committee and American Committee for Liberation, 190
  West Berlin (RIAS), 170
Rearmament, West German, 64, 220–40
Refugees, 69–70
  Munich as center for, 89–90
  from Soviet East Germany, 130, 135, 136, 161–63
Religion in East Germany, 135, 143–44
Rheinhausen, 83–84
Röpke, Wilhelm, 72
Rosenberg, Ludwig, quoted, 89
Rostock, 141
Rothfels, Hans, 217–18
Rusk, Dean, 287
Russia, see Union of Soviet Socialist Republics

Saar, 50, 65–66, 264
Sauerbruch, Willy, 40
Schiller, Karl, 168–69
Schirdewan, Karl, 134
Schlieker, Willy, 86
Schmid, Carlo, 100
   characterization of, 122
Schmidt, Helmut, 186–87, 235
Schmölders, Günther, 183
Schöngau, 228–29
Schroeder, Gerhard, 113, 247
   characterization of, 114
Schumacher, Kurt, 58–59, 96, 222
Schuman, Robert, 60–61
Schuman Plan, 61, 63
Shipbuilding, 92
Social Democratic Party (SPD), 16,
      56, 57, 65, 90, 96, 97, 100,
      197, 222
   characterization of, 111–12
   in East Germany, 132
   platform, 100
Socialist Unity Party (SED), 132,
      142
Sohl, Hans Günther, 85
   quoted, 88
Soviet Union, *see* Union of Soviet
      Socialist Republics
Speidel, Gen. Hans, 223, 238
Spiegel, Der (periodical), 97–98,
      115–16, 188, 213
Stahl, Walter, 188
Stammberger, Wolfgang, 98
Steel industry, 61, 83–84, 85, 87
   in East Germany, 141
Stimson, Henry L., 32, 60
Strauss, Franz Josef, 98, 113, 212,
      232, 233
   characterization of, 115–16
Stuttgart, description, 192–94
Sudetenland, 53
Swabia, 192

Thielicke, Helmut, 215
Thyssen (steel firm), 85
Tin Drum, The (book), 210
Trade, export and import:
   between West and East Germany,
      170
   East Germany, 142

Soviet Union, 150
   West Berlin, 169–70
   West Germany, 73–76, 88
      1962 statistics, 91–92
Trade unions, 89–90
Tresckow, Gen. Henning von, 253

Ulbricht, Walter, 43, 129
   background of, 134
Union of Soviet Socialist Republics
      (USSR):
   annexation of German territory,
      152–53
   demands to demilitarize West Ber-
      lin, 171–72
   proposals for German reunifica-
      tion, 146–49
   relations with East Germany, 129,
      131, 133, 147
   relations with West Germany, 149–
      50
   war memorials in Berlin, 160
United States:
   as ally of West Germany, 274–96
   economic aid to postwar Germany,
      69
   occupation of postwar Germany,
      36–43, 45–47, 275
   Seventh Army in West Germany,
      230

Van Dam, Hendrik G., 243
Volkswagen Company, 75, 80–83

Wall, *see* Berlin wall
Wall, Michael, quoted, 139
War crimes, prosecution, 250–51, 257
War debts, payment of, 64
Wehner, Herbert, 122
Weichmann, Herbert, 244
Weimar Republic, 20–22
   comparison with Federal Republic,
      260–73
Welt, Die (newspaper), 188, 214,
      216, 217
West Berlin, 97, 165–66, 177–78
   aid from Federal Republic, 165,
      166

blockade (1948), 53–54
economic development, 168–69
effect of Wall on, 167–68
Marienfelde refugee center, 161–63
postwar reconstruction, 156–58
representation in Bundestag, 55
Social Democrats in, 120
Soviet demands for demilitarization of, 171–72
See also Berlin; Brandt, Willy; East Berlin
West Germany:
Adenauer and, 93–108
agriculture, 197–98
"Americanization" of, 205–6, 294–95
campaign against, 256–58
cities, 179–97
comparison with Nazi Germany, 244–45
cultural life, 208–11
drama and films, 209
economic development, 68–92
education, 203–4
Nazism in curriculum, 252–54
university, 206–8, 269
intellectuals' criticism of Federal Republic policies, 212–14
literature, 210–11
Group 47, 211–12
military development:
Air force, 225, 231
Army, 224–30
Defense Ministry, 232
Navy, 231

nuclear weapons, question of arming with, 233–36, 289–90, 292–93
occupation:
Allied commitments, 62
Statute, 1949, 56
Statute, 1951, 63, 66
public-opinion polls, 200–4
rearmament, 64, 220–40
Saar annexation, 65–66
spirit, 200–19
United States as ally of, 274–96
as Western ally, 288–89
youth today, 265–66, 269
See also Adenauer, Konrad; Federal Republic
Western European Union, 63, 64
Wheeler, George Shaw, 39
White, Harry Dexter, 31, 35, 39
Wilson, Harold, quoted, 289
Winkhaus, Hermann, 85
Wirsing, Giselher, 192, 193
Wolff, Jeannette, 244
Wolff, Theodor, 217
Wolfsburg, 80–81
Wollweber, Ernst, 134
World War I, German image in, 277–78
World War II, 27–28
occupation of Germany after, 30–47
Würzburg, 77

Zeit, Die (periodical), 188, 217
Zink, Harold, quoted, 36–37, 46
Zinn, Georg August, 196–97